IMPURE WORLDS

IMPURE WORLDS

The Institution of Literature in the Age of the Novel

Jonathan Arac

Fordham University Press

New York   2011

Fordham University Press has no responsibility for the persistence or accuracy of URLs for external or third-party Internet websites referred to in this publication and does not guarantee that any content on such websites is, or will remain, accurate or appropriate.

Fordham University Press also publishes its books in a variety of electronic formats. Some content that appears in print may not be available in electronic books.

Library of Congress Cataloging-in-Publication Data

Arac, Jonathan, 1945–
    Impure worlds : the institution of literature in the age of the novel / Jonathan Arac.—1st ed.
        p.   cm.
    Includes bibliographical references and index.
    ISBN 978-0-8232-3178-2 (cloth : alk. paper)
    ISBN 978-0-8232-3179-9 (pbk. : alk. paper)
    ISBN 978-0-8232-3180-5 (ebook)
        1. Fiction—19th century—History and criticism.   2. Politics and literature—History—19th century.   3. Literature and society—History—19th century.   I. Title.
PN3499.A68   2011
809.3'93581—dc22

                                                                    2010013605

Printed in the United States of America
13 12 11   5 4 3 2 1
First edition

Contents

Preface

The year 1968 dramatically conjoined culture and politics in Paris, Prague, Mexico City, and many other parts of the world. In my own life as a student, the year framed my first encounter with two great critics, one on the page, one in person, whose work continues to provoke and sustain my thinking about the connections between literature and the conditions of people's lives—that is, politics. Walter Benjamin's work entered English at this time, decades after he killed himself (1940) while attempting to flee Hitler, and I began my vocation as a teacher by assisting the course in modern British literature taught at Harvard Summer School by Edward W. Said.[1] The critical thinking of these two exiles, the Jew and the Arab, has fueled decades of my explorations.[2]

Impure Worlds names a zone of inquiry and resource that has shaped my thought for a long time. It stirred me years before I learned of Mikhail Bakhtin's work on heteroglossia, before talk arose in postcolonial studies concerning hybridity, and in borderlands theory about *mestizaje*. Back around 1970, I still had not read Robert Penn Warren's classic New Critical essay "Pure and Impure Poetry" (1942). Warren favors the impure, surprising most readers now, who imagine that as formalists, New Critics were purists. The power and the striking effects of impure forms animate my reading and set the problems that as a critic and scholar I try to define and explore.[3] What I do shares much with recent work in cultural and minority studies, but they tend to focus more exclusively on heterogeneity, while my work is distinguished by attending to heterogeneity in its relationships to form.

As I was launching my dissertation in 1970, I was stirred by two closely related books by Richard Sennett that appeared that year: *The Uses of Disorder: Personal Identity and City Life* is more theoretical and contemporary, *Families against the City: Middle Class Homes of Industrial Chicago, 1872–1890* more specific and historical. Against the streets of the city, Sennett argued, families strove to produce in their children a purified identity that would, they imagined, protect them against the contaminations of people who spoke other languages, looked other colors, and came from other national origins than the white Anglophone Protestants who made up his focus. As the grandchild of Yiddish-speaking immigrants, I took the side of impurity.

The nineteenth-century writers who compelled my imagination and formed the core of my dissertation, Charles Dickens and Herman Melville, both took pleasure in making big, complicated, messy worlds. So did major writers of my time. *Gravity's Rainbow* (1973) by Thomas Pynchon and *The Golden Notebook* (1962) and *The Four-Gated City* (1969) by Doris Lessing crucially shaped the perspective I took in composing my first book, *Commissioned Spirits: The Shaping of Social Motion in Dickens, Carlyle, Melville, and Hawthorne* (1979). I wanted to break barriers, not only to cross the Atlantic but also to connect preferences in artistic practice to meaningful choices in the realms of politics and society.

This preference for impurity, and the search to find means of analyzing and explaining it, runs through the essays gathered to compose this book. It also guides my work more distinctly as an Americanist: In *Against Americanistics* (2011) I mess with exceptionalism, toward goals that are international and comparative. Scholars now take this perspective beyond what I have done here in my chapters that explore Melville's German connections, or that discuss Dickens and Twain as seen by the Australian Christina Stead. I think, for example, of Dohra Ahmad's *Rotten English* (2007), a global reader of literary works written in varieties of English new to the printed page.

The chapters that follow pursue the complex entanglements of culture, politics, and society from which great literature arises. This mode of study is "worldly" in the sense that Edward Said developed. He adapted the notion from Arabic philologists and from Giambattista Vico, whose *New Science* (1744) fed the great historical imaginations of the nineteenth and twentieth centuries and directly inspired writers, including James Joyce. The literary and cultural critic Edmund Wilson responded to the breakthroughs of Joyce, Marcel Proust, Gertrude Stein, and others in *Axel's Castle* (1931), the earliest major book about what we now call modernism. Wilson's next big book, *To the Finland Station: A Study in the Acting and Writing of History* (1940), placed Jules Michelet's discovery of Vico in 1831 at the beginning of a story that led through Karl Marx to the hopes of socialism.

Right in the heart of the nineteenth century, where my own scholarly emphasis falls, even Gustave Flaubert grudgingly acknowledged the value of Hippolyte Taine's great *History of English Literature* (1863). Taine's emphasis on historical and social contexts ("*race, moment, et milieu*") overthrew the belief of "the old days," when "people thought literature was an entirely personal thing and that works fell from the sky like meteorites."[4] Flaubert recognized that his own aesthetic quest was neither purely personal nor heaven sent but very much of, even though against, his world.

What is impure about paying so much attention to top-drawer canonical writers? Shakespeare (Chapters 1, 2, and 3), Dickens (Chapters 3, 4, and 6), and Mark Twain (Chapters 4, 5, and 10) figure in three chapters each; overall the volume treats Johann Wolfgang Goethe, John Keats, and Herman Melville (Chapter 1); George Eliot (Chapter 7); Gustave Flaubert (Chapter 8); Charles Baudelaire (Chapter 9); and Ralph Ellison (Chapter 5). These writers figure as resources in politically charged arguments about value. Neither Shakespeare's plays nor the novels of the nineteenth century were valued as major in their own times. Both were judged popular, commercial, minor, even trash. The gothic mode of writing, which I argue derives from *Hamlet*, and which played a crucial role in Dickens's most ambitious and important works, even now most immediately raises thoughts of drugstore paperbacks and creepy movies. In 1857 not only Flaubert's *Madame Bovary* but also Baudelaire's *Les fleurs du mal* was prosecuted for indecency, and some of Baudelaire's poems were not freely circulated in France until 1949.

Only posterity has validated these authors' greatness, and many of these chapters examine processes of posterity at work, as does my book *"Huckleberry Finn" as Idol and Target* (1997). In the era of the Napoleonic Wars the British, Germans, and Russians combated the French culturally through Shakespeare (Chapter 1). More than a century later, Christina Stead, as a radical leftist woman from Australia, challenged the patriarchal weight of established English and American progressive culture through mocking the roles that Charles Dickens and Mark Twain had come to play as iconic figures (Chapter 4). This chapter registers the impact of the feminist movement in criticism. In the 1970s, Victorian studies, the area of my initial professional formation, reconfigured into feminist studies through powerful work by Elaine Showalter (*A Literature of Their Own*, 1977), Nina Auerbach (*Communities of Women*, 1978), Sandra Gilbert and Susan Gubar (*The Madwoman in the Attic*, 1979), and others. Carol Kay, my closest intellectual interlocutor during those years, in her own work thought as much about the political as the literary dimension of feminism (*Political Constructions*, 1988).

Against the purist view of great literature as an autonomous act of creation, I agree with my dissertation director, Harry Levin: Literature is a social institution.[5] In making their choices of style, subject, genre, and form, writers both draw from and differ from other writers of the past and of their own times. Thus, I argue in Chapter 6, Dickens in *Bleak House* advanced his art of fiction by drawing on techniques and ambitions from the nonfictional forms of essay and history. To achieve the realism of putting the present onto the page, writers not only reject but also adapt, even inaugurate, conventions.

Many great works construct their inventiveness through critical thinking about other literature. This is as true of Flaubert as of Cervantes and of Twain as of Flaubert. Criticism is not just a minor, secondary practice, segregated from the primary work of creativity. The reflections of Goethe and Keats and Melville about Shakespeare, as I argue in Chapter 1, crucially contributed to their most distinctive accomplishments as novelists and poets. The weight of my chapters falls historically from Balzac and Dickens to the deaths of Joyce and Woolf, a century in which the Western novel seems to dominate cultural accomplishment.[6] This cultural configuration arises in response to revolutions in economic and political life, but also to energies transferred from Shakespeare on the stage to a new practice of solitary devotion to the page, as I explore and elaborate in the first three chapters.

Great new literature does not arise from pure imagination, nor purely from within its authors' own time and place. Cultural accomplishments do not transcend history, but in the complex temporality of human action, works do extend history by reaching readers beyond their own times, and those readers include writers. I prefer Harold Bloom's concern with precursors to New Historicism's tendency to flatten history into synchronicity, seeing connections transdiscursively but not across time. Rather than the mid-twentieth-century New Critics' preferred figures of symbol, metaphor, and irony, each of which is understood to achieve a totality, I prefer to emphasize the shattering excess of the sublime in Shakespeare and Twain (Chapters 2 and 10, respectively), to read for figures that overgo or undershoot, such as hyperbole in George Eliot and ellipsis in Flaubert (Chapters 7 and 8, respectively), or that seem antiquated, such as allegory in Baudelaire (Chapter 9).

These guiding premises combine in a practice that makes this book unusual. These chapters pursue intensive close reading that does not demand unity as its goal. They reach out over a substantial span of time, too large to permit detailed narrative, and the result is a textured, contoured, discontinuous history. In *Critical Genealogies* (1987) I elaborated Walter Benjamin's insights to propose such a way of writing new literary history, and this volume tries to provide further substance to those hopes.

Chapter 1 originally appeared as "The Impact of Shakespeare" in *Cambridge History of Literary Criticism: The Romantic Era*, ed. Marshall Brown

(Cambridge: Cambridge University Press, 2000), 272–95. Copyright © 2000 Cambridge University Press, reprinted with permission. Many thanks to Marshall Brown, who invited me to contribute and encouraged me to pursue an unconventional frame of thinking. Since this chapter was written, Pascale Casanova in *The World Republic of Letters,* trans. M. B. DeBevoise (1999; Cambridge, Mass.: Harvard University Press, 2004) has done most to develop the topic, broached here, of J. G. Herder's impact in transforming Western literature.

Chapter 2 was first presented at an MLA session in 1985 sponsored by the Division on Philosophical Approaches to Literature and chaired by Marshall Brown. I am grateful once more for his critical dialogue, as well as that of fellow panelists Paul Fry, Raimonda Modiano, and David Simpson, plus my *boundary 2* colleague Michael Hays. It was originally published as part of a "Forum on the Sublime" in *Studies in Romanticism* 26 (1987): 209–20. It is reprinted by permission of the Trustees of Boston University. The chapter's emphasis on "media" shows the impact of cultural studies, for me especially of Raymond Williams, and it points toward work still in progress on the history of the novel.

Chapter 3 arose from my opportunities as an assistant professor at Princeton in the 1970s, where I had the luck to teach Shakespeare frequently. With my head full of *Hamlet,* I read *Little Dorrit* differently. I sketched the argument at an undergraduate comparative literature colloquium hosted by David Quint in 1979, and I elaborated it for professional colleagues in 1986 at one of the memorable summer sessions of the University of California Dickens Project, hosted by Murray Baumgarten and John Jordan at the Santa Cruz campus. Frank Lentricchia recruited it for a special issue of *South Atlantic Quarterly* 87 (1988): 311–28. It is reprinted by permission of the publisher, Duke University Press. This chapter's concern with the relationship between great literature and popular gothic modes has also fueled my work as an Americanist, especially concerning *Absalom, Absalom!* and *Beloved.*

Chapter 4 emerged from an internationally focused, year-long course, The Novel, 1880–1980, that I taught while visiting Columbia University in 1981–82. The Dickens Project again provided the chance to improve it through colleagues' responses at a 1984 gathering on Dickens and Twain. This was the occasion when I met Susan Gillman, whose colleagueship in Twain studies has been indispensable, and whose work in progress on adaptation in American studies shows "impure worlds" at work. The paper was further refined for the conference inaugurating the journal *Cultural Critique,* then edited by Donna Przybylowicz, at the University of Minnesota. It first appeared in *Cultural Critique* 2 (Winter 1985–86): 171–89. As an Americanist, my concern with the Popular Front continues in work on Kenneth Burke and Ralph Ellison.

Chapter 5 was developed for an international cross-disciplinary conference on "Cultural Property and the Negotiation of National and Ethnic Identity," organized by Ron Bush and Elazar Barkan, at St. John's College, Oxford University, April 19–21, 1999, sponsored by the Getty Research Institute and the Drue Heinz Trust of Oxford University. My essay appeared as "The Birth of Whose Nation? The Competing Claims of National and Ethnic Identity and the 'Banning' of *Huckleberry Finn*" in a volume edited by Elazar Barkan and Ronald Bush, *Claiming the Stones / Naming the Bones: Cultural Property and the Negotiation of National and Ethnic Identity in the American and British Experience* (Los Angeles: Getty Research Institute, 2002), 302–14.

Chapter 6 was sketched as a talk to the Harvard Victorians in the fall of 1972 and addressed a group of older colleagues who welcomed a beginner. After many changes it was published in *Nineteenth-Century Fiction* (now *Nineteenth-Century Literature*) 32 (1977): 54–72. This journal's openness to work treating both England and the United States was an important comfort to me during the years when transatlantic Anglophone comparatism seemed a grave professional risk. The large question this essay addresses continues to compel me: It considers the relations between fictional and nonfictional forms, but also between print and other media forms, in making it possible for a society to know its own reality. I recall from my youth the *New York Times Book Review* proclaiming, perhaps apropos of Oscar Lewis's anthropological study of a Mexican family, *The Children of Sánchez* (1961), that the ambition to grasp human life as fully and intimately as possible had passed from Tolstoy's fiction to the work of humane social science. More recently, *The Wire* on HBO has seemed to many of us to accomplish the task of realism better than any current novel.

Chapters 7 and 8 descend from a paper circulated for a conference on new approaches to literary study organized at Princeton University by Earl Miner in 1976. Knowing that Hayden White would be among its readers was an important inspiration. I am deeply grateful for Earl Miner's mentorship at a difficult time, and I commemorate his exemplary career as a major scholar of seventeenth-century British poetry and a leader in opening the still-emerging field of comparative poetics on a truly global scale. Chapter 7 was published in *ELH* 46 (1979): 673–92.

Chapter 8 was presented as one of the Ward-Phillips lectures at the University of Notre Dame in 1984. This occasion was organized by my longtime friend and *boundary 2* collaborator Joseph A. Buttigieg, the English-speaking world's leading scholar of Antonio Gramsci, and it was animated by exchanges with Paul A. Bové, Michael Hays, Daniel T. O'Hara, Donald Pease, and William V. Spanos, all colleagues from *boundary 2*. It was published, together with their essays, in *Criticism without Boundaries: Directions and Crosscurrents in Postmodern Critical Theory*, ed. Joseph A. Buttigieg (Notre Dame, Ind.: University of Notre Dame Press, 1987), 160–76.

Chapter 9 was commissioned for a reference series by George Stade, with his characteristic pleasure in giving a younger person a chance. It has been trimmed to emphasize its relation to this book's concerns. It originally appeared as "Charles Baudelaire" in *European Writers: The Romantic Century*, ed. Jacques Barzun and George Stade, 3 vols. (New York: Charles Scribner's Sons, 1985), 1323–48. The series protocol required writing accessibly, without footnotes, at as high a level of intellectual energy as could also sustain a crucially necessary body of fact. Much of the intellectual energy was generated in dialogue with the summer 1982 Institute for Culture and Society, held at Amherst College, sponsored by the Marxist Literary Group, and organized by Doris Sommer and Theodore Mills Norton. This intense week began conversations—with John Beverley, Fredric Jameson, and Laura Kipnis—that continue, diversely, to this day.

Chapter 10 was commissioned by Franco Moretti for his extraordinary five-volume collaborative project, *Il romanzo* (Turin: Einaudi, 2001–4), and appeared in English as "Adventures of *Huckleberry Finn*" in *The Novel*, ed. Franco Moretti (Princeton, N.J.: Princeton University Press, 2006), 1:841–54. Copyright © 2006 Princeton University Press. The challenging vigor of Moretti's own writing, plus the opportunity to reach a readership of cultivated nonspecialist European readers, tempted me to have one more go at Twain's masterpiece.

In concluding this preface, I offer thanks to the institutions that supported my work during the years these chapters were written: Harvard University, Princeton University, the University of Illinois at Chicago, Duke University, Columbia University, and the University of Pittsburgh. Much of this book was first written before Susan Andrade and I knew each other, but it would never have been completed without her love, and our many searching conversations, now for over a decade.

I. *Politics and the Canon*

I. *The Impact of Shakespeare: Goethe to Melville*

This chapter was composed for a standard reference work, so it fulfills obligations to facts and coverage, but it also enacts a generic impurity. It generates new thinking by developing an argument and the claims that undergird this book. I argue that literary history operates discontinuously, by what I call "impact" rather than what many have called "tradition." Literary history's discontinuity leaps across, rather than remaining confined within, the borders and barriers of nation or language or genre. Critical response to Shakespeare at the start of the nineteenth century was crucial in producing the modern conception of *literature*, and hardly had *literature* come to replace *poetry* as the key operative term than *literature* came to mean novels.[1]

The impact of Shakespeare on romantic literary criticism may be measured in at least three ways. First, by the canon: Starting in the later eighteenth century, a transformation in taste, led and articulated by critical writings, radically changed the value of Shakespeare. In the world of culture and learning, Shakespeare ceased to be a source of pleasure and of interest almost exclusive to England; he became by the 1830s a universal genius known and admired, throughout the West, for his deep insight into the human condition. This newly exemplary pedagogical value made Shakespeare the basis for England's educational mission in India.[2] Shakespeare's cultural destiny was thus linked to Britain's rise to world power in the decades from the Seven Years' War through the Napoleonic struggles. Britain's wars against France counterpointed and reinforced the challenge Shakespeare offered to the literary values of the French neoclassicism that dominated European thought for more than a century. Second, the place of romantic critics in the canon of Shakespeare studies: German works by August Wilhelm Schlegel and English works by Samuel Taylor Coleridge and William Hazlitt are landmarks that still serve as points of departure for fresh thinking nearly two centuries later. Third, Shakespeare was a crucial starting point for important romantic writers as they made innovative contributions in poetry and fiction, as well as in literary criticism and theory: Johann Wolfgang Goethe, Friedrich Schlegel, John Keats, and Herman Melville provide the major cases for this chapter.

In 1850 the American poet and essayist Ralph Waldo Emerson published *Representative Men*, choosing Shakespeare to represent "The Poet." Looking back over the period covered by this chapter, Emerson defined the change: "Now, literature, philosophy, and thought are Shakspearized." Emerson asserts that only in the nineteenth century could "the tragedy of Hamlet find such wondering readers," and the reason is because the "speculative genius" of the century is itself "a sort of living Hamlet." Emerson compares the place Shakespeare had assumed to that which religion was relinquishing: "[T]here is in all cultivated minds a silent appreciation of his superlative power and beauty, which like Christianity, qualifies the period."[3]

In the writings about Shakespeare by those in the first generation to feel his power as a tremendous, surprising discovery (not part of an already-known literary culture), there is indeed a feel of religious conversion. Through Johann Gottfried Herder, the young Goethe came to a new awareness of Shakespeare. Goethe's first public text on Shakespeare, composed to be read among friends at the celebration of Shakespeare's name day in 1771, testifies, "The first page I read of him made me his own for life, and when I had finished the first play I stood as a man born blind to whom a miraculous hand had returned sight in an instant."[4]

Such enthusiasm had not characterized the language of Samuel Johnson, even when Johnson judged Shakespeare unmatched except by Homer in the powers of invention and innovation. Scarcely had Johnson consolidated one point of view in the preface to his edition of Shakespeare (1765, two centuries after Shakespeare's birth in 1564), than quite a different way of writing about Shakespeare began to emerge in Germany, led by Herder's "Shakespeare" (1771). Herder at this time exercised an immense effect on Goethe, whose *Götz von Berlichingen* (1771) was a history play clearly inspired by Shakespeare, but Goethe's Shakespeare was most importantly enunciated in his novel *Wilhelm Meister's Apprenticeship* (1796). This novel, and its use of Shakespeare, formed a major nucleus for the thoughts of the younger generation in Germany, especially the brothers Friedrich and August Wilhelm Schlegel, whose writings in their journal *Athenaeum* (1798–1800) activated the term "romantic," which is now used for the whole movement leading up to them and extending well into the nineteenth century. August Wilhelm Schlegel contributed to German culture the verse translation of Shakespeare (seventeen plays from 1797 to 1810) that made Shakespeare an accepted masterpiece of German literature. As a critic his 1808 Vienna lectures on dramatic art and literature, published the next year as a book, made the conception of organic unity widely known.[5]

The most dynamic critical intelligence in England from the 1790s was Samuel Taylor Coleridge, and in 1798 he traveled to Germany to improve his knowledge of the tremendous intellectual work there being accomplished. In Coleridge's literary lectures, starting in 1808 and continuing until 1819, and in his *Biographia Literaria* (1817), Shakespeare formed the crux for his thinking, which made possible—slowly in a process extending into the twentieth century—a new mode of critical writing in English. Shakespeare was not new in English culture, but even so, a manuscript document testifies to the impact of Shakespeare on Coleridge as he made the decision around 1800 to focus his energies on criticism rather than on poetry (at this date, Coleridge had published considerable political prose and several volumes of poetry, including *Lyrical Ballads* with Wordsworth, but none of the critical writing by which he is known). Coleridge's "Memoranda for a History of English Poetry" lays out a rather bland agenda (e.g., "3. Spenser—with connecting introduction") until item 5, which is briefer and by far more emphatic than any of the preceding: "Shakespeare!!!"[6]

Coleridge helped to inspire—to emulation and at times to controversy—the essayists Charles Lamb and William Hazlitt, as well as the Scottish historian and social prophet Thomas Carlyle. Carlyle began his career as a highly active and significant bridge between Britain and Germany through his many essays and translations—notably the first, and long-standard, English version of Goethe's *Wilhelm Meister* (1824). Besides essays and a selection, with commentary, of *Specimens of English Dramatic Poets Who Lived about the Time of Shakespeare* (1808), Lamb wrote with his sister, Mary, *Tales from Shakespeare* ("designed for the use of young persons," 1807).[7] Criticism and retellings are two of the various ways by which romantics lovingly turned Shakespeare's poetry and drama into prose and narrative. Hazlitt's writing is saturated with Shakespeare in quotation and allusion; his direct critical address to Shakespeare includes "Shakespeare and Milton" in *Lectures on the English Poets* (1818) and a volume, also from lectures, *Characters of Shakespeare's Plays* (1817), which a knowledgeable judge has declared the founder of a genre, the "one-volume critical introduction which surveys the full range of the plays."[8] What now would be a university course was then open to the public by subscription. Carlyle's contemporary John Keats took his critical bearings to a large extent from Hazlitt, and Herman Melville, a novelist of America's belated romanticism, echoes both Keats and Carlyle on Shakespeare just as he is asserting his own most idiosyncratic self-orientation.

This is the cast of characters most important to this chapter, for the English- and German-speaking cultures felt Shakespeare's impact first and most powerfully. It soon spread more widely. As the question of romanticism became an issue for European cultural polemics, Shakespeare was a touchstone by which the romantics could distinguish themselves from their adversaries.[9] Before his career as a novelist, Stendhal began his pamphlet *Racine and Shakespeare* (1823, 1825) with a debate in dialogue between "The Academician" and "The Romantic" on the neo-Aristotelian unities of place and time that had dominated French critical thought and dramatic practice since the later seventeenth century. The upshot of Stendhal's argument was to value Shakespeare, and the romantic, as what was most vital in the present cultural moment. In the manifesto serving to preface his never-staged drama *Cromwell* (1827), Victor Hugo elaborated German metahistorical typologies to define the centrality of Shakespeare and launch a romantic movement in France. Hugo schematizes the history of poetry as the interrelation of ode, epic, and drama, identified with the Bible, Homer, and Shakespeare. Drama, which Shakespeare embodies, "combines in one breath the grotesque and the sublime, the terrible and the absurd, tragedy and comedy." This comprehensive mixture is the defining characteristic of "the third epoch of poetry, of the literature of to-day."[10]

In Italy Alessandro Manzoni published a letter in French explicating and defending the practice of *Othello* against that of Voltaire's *Zaïre* with regard to the unity of time.[11] In Russia, likewise, Aleksander Sergeyevich Pushkin demonstrated the key issue in the impact of Shakespeare: During the romantic period the most consequential writers of the various Western national cultures found Shakespeare an indispensable means of defining their own innovations.[12] Romanticism has been seen both as a revival of earlier literary modes and as a revolution that overturned existing modes and made literature new. Shakespeare's impact demonstrates the close connection of revival and revolution.

The impact of Shakespeare operated most importantly at a higher level than that of work-to-work influence. Romantics, through their engagement with Shakespeare, conceived a mode of writing that seemed quite different from the prevailing modes of the later eighteenth and earlier nineteenth centuries, and that seemed to offer opportunities for originality, the creation of new forms. In Friedrich Schlegel's review essay on Goethe's *Wilhelm Meister*, the most innovative critic of the age is discussing the major novel of the era's most influential writer. It is a crucial fact of this period that both these figures are German, but it is equally crucial that Goethe's Wilhelm breaks through toward his maturity by engaging with Shakespeare. This novel, as the founding exemplar of what later came to be called the bildungsroman, offers a model of development, and Shakespeare is an essential part of that development. Schlegel argues that "there is an immeasurably wide gulf between the first apprehensions and elements of poetry with which the first volume concerned Wilhelm and the reader" and the point later in the novel "where man becomes capable of grasping both the highest and the most profound." The "passage" across such a gulf, Schlegel thinks, always requires "a leap," and this leap is made possible by "the mediation of a great model." This formulation of Schlegel's catches the crucial dimension of Shakespeare's impact. For many of the most important romantic writers, the model is Shakespeare, because of all poets, he is "the one who deserves so eminently to be called unlimited."[13]

Because Shakespeare is unlimited, it is not possible simply to copy the externals of his practice. Rather, to make use of Shakespeare requires the modern writer to grasp the productive principles by which Shakespeare achieved his art. That is, an act of critical formulation necessarily precedes innovative creation. Such an argument is fundamental to the decades-long critical theorizations of Coleridge. As early as a notebook entry of 1804, he reflects on the structure of similarity and difference that makes possible linguistic symbolization, and he links it to "the *imitation* instead of *copy* which is illustrated in very nature *shakespearianized*."[14] And in the *Biographia Literaria*, he contrasts Shakespeare's representation of madness in *King Lear* with a mad passage in Thomas Otway's *Venice Preserved* (1682) in order to elucidate the dynamic at work in Shakespeare. He explains that such critical theorization is necessary for the future of great writing: "To admire on principle is the only way to imitate without loss of originality."[15] In the structure of the *Biographia*, Shakespeare is the hinge between German theory (chapters 5–13) and English poetry (specifically the discussion of Wordsworth that begins in chapter 4 and then occupies 17–22). The contrast of Otway to Shakespeare opens the topic of the imagination, provoked by Wordsworth's poetry and pursued theoretically by Coleridge. Then, after the definition of imagination (chapter 13) and the related characterization of "the poet, described in *ideal* perfection" (chapter 14),[16] chapter 15 prepares for the later analysis of Wordsworth's strengths and weaknesses by using Shakespeare's *Venus and Adonis* as the proof-text for the application of the theory. The term Coleridge introduces for his performance has had a great fortune in twentieth-century Anglophone literary criticism: "practical criticism."[17] Shelves of books have been written in this new form.

Schlegel's discussion of Shakespeare in Goethe's *Meister* made a point similar to Coleridge's: To understand Shakespeare is to understand a force like that of nature, which operates by the laws of its own nature. It is not simply "the greatness of [Shakespeare's] nature" that is the crux for Wilhelm and Goethe and Schlegel, but rather "his profound artistry and purposefulness."[18] In his notebooks from this period, Schlegel cited John Milton's characterization in "L'Allegro" of Shakespeare's "warbling his native woodnotes wild" as "the earliest wrong view" of Shakespeare.[19] Shakespeare's great nature is manifested only through his great art. Therefore, Schlegel argues, Goethe's novel engages Wilhelm with a specific work of Shakespeare's *Hamlet*, for "no other play . . . offers the occasion for such varied and interesting debate on what the secret intention of the artist might be."[20]

The impact of Shakespeare mediates the relations between criticism and new creative work. Some of this new creative work is by major poets who also wrote important criticism, such as Goethe and Coleridge. Some of the new creative work is itself criticism, as in essays by Lamb, Hazlitt, and Thomas De Quincey, and in the writing of Friedrich Schlegel himself, whose "fragments" helped to define a characteristic romantic literary practice. These interrelations between critical thinking about Shakespeare and the new creative work of the era helped to open larger theoretical perspectives and arguments about the category of literature itself. Coleridge's theory of the imagination begins from his intuition that what he felt to be the greatest work of his own time, the poetry of William Wordsworth, had some fundamental relation to what was valuable in Shakespeare, and in turn the combined work of Wordsworth and Coleridge allowed Thomas De Quincey to make his distinction between the "literature of knowledge" and the "literature of power," which codifies the understanding of imaginative belles lettres that still guides much critical and pedagogical debate.[21] These new understandings of literature, in turn, helped writers to orient their own work—as for instance Keats's letters reflecting on Shakespeare in dialogue with Hazlitt's critical views—and they also provided means by which readers, including a posterity still active in the twenty-first century, can understand that work.

The impact of Shakespeare in romantic criticism is a case study of the role of literary criticism in a larger literary history. This history proves to be international, and therefore its study must be comparative. There is a compelling story to be told that would work only with the British impact of Shakespeare, but an account is richer and more significant for including not only Germany and France but also the United States.[22] The crucial role of Goethe's *Meister*—both as a powerful new understanding of Shakespeare and as provocation to Schlegel's metacritical theorization—indicates that this larger literary history in which the impact of Shakespeare figures is inseparable from the emergent form of the Western nineteenth century—the novel.

Like the fictional Wilhelm Meister, the career of John Keats suggests the use that a culturally ambitious young man of high powers could make of the "mediation of a great model." As with Friedrich Schlegel, for whom thinking about the great past figure of Shakespeare went together with thinking about the great contemporary figure of Goethe, so for Keats Shakespeare signaled the possibility of a path to poetic accomplishment that might be different from that of William Wordsworth.[23] Keats's reflections in his letters show that his process of thought was enriched by the critical writings, lectures, and conversation of William Hazlitt.[24]

April 1817 was a crucial moment in Keats's career. Just after the publication of his first volume of poems, he determined to test his powers by writing the long narrative *Endymion* in six months. At the opening of this process, he bought himself a set of Shakespeare (preserved now in Harvard's Houghton Library) and also, by chance, came into possession of a picture of Shakespeare, which he set over his desk and kept with him through various moves until the end of his life. In the letter (May 11) in which he told his friend, the painter Benjamin Robert Haydon, about the acquisition of this image, Keats refers to Haydon's belief that there was "a good genius presiding over you" and applies the belief to himself: "Is it too daring to fancy Shakespeare this presider?"[25] The same letter, near its opening, draws from *King Lear* a phrase to characterize Keats's state of mind and near its end returns to link his state of mind to Shakespeare: "I never quite despair and I read Shakespeare—indeed I shall I think never read any other book much. . . . I am very near Agreeing with Hazlitt that Shakespeare is enough for us."[26]

Hazlitt's "depth of Taste" was for Keats one of the "three things to rejoice at in this Age,"[27] and Hazlitt's specific way of thinking seems to have

helped Keats to a formulation concerning Shakespeare that not only is crucial in understanding Keats's own trajectory as a writer but also has been
highly influential in the continuing conversations of criticism at large. In
December 1817, after finishing his self-appointed task of *Endymion*, Keats
reported suddenly being struck with an insight into "what quality went to
form a Man of Achievement especially in Literature & which Shakespeare
possessed so enormously." That quality Keats calls, somewhat mysteriously,
"*Negative Capability.*" He explains it thus: "when man is capable of being in
uncertainties, Mysteries, doubts, without any irritable reaching after fact &
reason."[28] He contrasts this condition with Coleridge's quest for systematiz-
ing his thought.

The contrast of Keats with Coleridge, the difference between "negative
capability" in Keats and the "balance or reconciliation of opposite or discor-
dant qualities" that is for Coleridge the mark of "the poet, described in *ideal*
perfection" in chapter 14 of the *Biographia Literaria*,[29] became a crucial concern for the rejection of Coleridge-inspired New Criticism by postmodern
criticism in the United States.[30] The key term in this postmodern discourse
is the highly romantic *openness*, and this is what, it may be argued, Keats
found in Hazlitt's critical response to Shakespeare.

Hazlitt's fundamental intellectual experience was his discovery of what
has since been called the sympathetic imagination. His aim was to rebut
the long tradition that explained morality by self-interest, and he did it by
unbinding the self. He argued that my connection to my future self can only
be made by an act of imagination not different in kind from the imaginative
leap by which I link myself to other persons,[31] and he thereby erased in
theory the difference between self and other, not by making everything me
(as German idealism often seems to) but by opening the possibility of oneself
as another. This was the theory. Shakespeare was the practice. Hazlitt asserted in his lectures on the English poets that Shakespeare "was the least of
an egotist that it was possible to be." He was "nothing in himself," but he
"had only to think of anything in order to become that thing."[32]

Keats, in a letter of October 1818, just preceding his year of great accomplishment, returned to Shakespeare as model, and it is clearly a Shakespeare
he shares with Hazlitt. Against the most powerful poet of his own time,
William Wordsworth, who strongly asserted his selfhood, Keats posed
Shakespeare. Wordsworth represented the "egotistical sublime," but the
true "poetical Character," of which Keats considered himself "a Member,"
can be defined only negatively: "[I]t is not itself—it has no self. . . . It has
no character . . . has no Identity." Positively, it may be defined by feelings

and actions: "[I]t enjoys light and shade; it lives in gusto." But by allusion, it has a name, for "It has as much delight in conceiving an Iago as an Imogen."[33] Tragic villain or romantic heroine, it is all the same to Shakespeare. And many readers have felt that Keats's poetic accomplishment, though in lyric rather than drama, was similarly an outgoing that found its fullest self-realization through the particulars of other lives and ways of being.

By the middle of the nineteenth century, the response to Keats by Matthew Arnold, for all he owed to Coleridge, marks an ossifying of the romantic Shakespeare. Arnold warned that neither Keats nor the Elizabethans were sufficiently "mature" to achieve the "very plain direct and severe" style required for "modern poetry." Their "exuberance of expression" and "richness of images" seemed to Arnold only "ornamental work" that ignored the "whole," while the crux for modern poetry must be "*its contents.*"[34] Arnold's critique shows that he has lost the substance of the empathetic form that Keats achieved through engagement with Hazlitt and Shakespeare.

In the romantic period, the impact of Shakespeare played a large role in the newly emerging definition of *literature*, and in turn this new conception of literature led to a theoretical remaking of Shakespeare. Difficulties, challenges to understanding, that had once been condemned as obscurity were newly praised as deep meaning. Four emphases seem most important: the shift from stage to page; the shift from judgment to interpretation; the changed character of mimesis, by which the work becomes a resource for learning; and the tendency to understand what is learned as involving "uniqueness," a particularity.

The shift from stage to page redefines Shakespeare as producing literature to be read rather than drama to be staged, watched, and heard. The larger shift in which this is implicated is the long-ongoing definition of a canon of high culture in the vernacular languages. As Greek and Latin became standard for an ever-smaller percentage of the total reading public, a select group of honored works in the modern literatures played an increasing role as alternatives to commercialized mass culture, what Wordsworth in his 1800 preface to *Lyrical Ballads* called "gross and violent stimulants."[35] This cultural struggle, in turn, was involved with what Lionel Trilling called, in an important retrospective essay, "The Fate of Pleasure."[36] Samuel Johnson had defined his high evaluation of Shakespeare in response to the question of what "can please many, and please long."[37] Shakespeare, it began to seem, offered a higher, deeper, overall more challenging and difficult experience than the term "pleasure" conveys. The discourse of the sublime was one influential way of conveying Shakespeare's value in a new affective idiom.

The best-known work in English that links Shakespeare's sublimity to his status as difficult text rather than pleasing spectacle is Charles Lamb's 1811 essay, "On the Tragedies of Shakespeare, with Reference to Their Fitness for Stage- Representation." Lamb finds actors inadequate to convey, and spectators inadequate to receive, Shakespeare's meaning. Instead, Lamb's model is individual and private, the reflective response of an elite, as against the vulgar theatergoer who lacks "the very idea of *what an author is.*"[38] The value of Shakespeare becomes a spiritual communion between readers' minds and the mind of the author. Lamb no longer finds the value of Shakespeare's works in the pleasure we gain from the representation of an action; instead the value comes through understanding the meaning of the play's expression of mind. As readers of Shakespeare, we become interpreters, in quest for something not evident on the stage, in the action. We become connoisseurs of a text, distinguished from, and elevated above, the masses who applaud the play.[39]

A comparable pattern prevails in Goethe's *Wilhelm Meister* (1796). Although Wilhelm's crucial engagement with *Hamlet* comes through his attempt to become an educator for Germany by bringing great works to popular performance, the overall effect of his encounter with Shakespeare is to turn him away from this public role and toward the self-development with which the German ideal of *Bildung* has become associated—and this use of Shakespeare occurs in a novel to be read.[40] A belated and parodic echo of *Wilhelm Meister* may be found in James Joyce's *Ulysses* (1922), in the ninth chapter ("Scylla and Charybdis"). Stephen Dedalus holds forth in the Dublin library his theory of how Shakespeare came to write *Hamlet*. Through Stephen, Joyce mocks the century of impassioned biographical speculation that had grown from romantic ideas about Shakespeare, but in the instance of Stephen he also reflects critically on the relation of the innovative artist to culture and nation. At the end of *A Portrait of the Artist as a Young Man* (1914), Stephen had hoped "to forge in the smithy of my soul the uncreated conscience of my race,"[41] but no such public function may be found in the character of Stephen in *Ulysses*. Like Wilhelm, the intended path of national artistic education proves instead individual and solitary— and for Stephen by no means successful.

In the generation before the romantics, whether phrased in the negative with Voltaire or more positively with Samuel Johnson, it had been understood as the critic's task to judge Shakespeare and his works. In *Wilhelm*

Meister, it is more important to understand, to interpret, than to judge. One of the newspaper reports from a lecture of Coleridge's strikes the keynote for this romantic tendency. It speaks of Coleridge's comments on the history plays as "deciphering the character of Falstaff."[42] Across the range of romantic critical writing, and more widely yet, there recurs the notion of the "hieroglyph," the riddle that needs unraveling. The play's action only inscribes the mystery of the productive mind, which becomes the true object of critical attention.

As Wilhelm Meister begins to study the role of Hamlet, he finds himself lost in a "strange labyrinth," where "the further I progressed . . . the more difficult did it become for me to perceive the structure of the whole."[43] Wilhelm defines his task as an actor in trying to make sense of the play as a whole and of its central character. It all seemed a mystery until he discovered a means of interpretation by which he "really entered the mind of the author."[44] Only in the romantic period did Hamlet become a mystery, and only then did it become necessary to solve the mystery through an act of psychological interpretation.

Wilhelm unraveled the mystery by searching for "any clues to Hamlet's character previous to the death of his father. I observed what this . . . young man had been like without reference to that sad event . . . and considered what he might have become without them."[45] In other words, Wilhelm treats Hamlet as a real person and performs a speculative psychological interpretation of his whole character and development. This form of "character criticism" became almost universal in Germany and English-speaking countries for well over a century.[46] Its spread was closely linked to changes in the human science of psychology. In the letter in which Freud first proposed the Oedipus complex, he immediately went on to suggest its applicability to Hamlet.[47] By this interpretive path backward into the character's past, Wilhelm finds a way to escape from the labyrinth into which he had wandered. Finally, he discovers "the key to Hamlet's whole behavior" in the exclamation:

> The time is out of joint: O cursed spite,
> That ever I was born to set it right![48]

This specific analysis of *Hamlet* became a point of reference for generations of subsequent criticism. Wilhelm argues that "Shakespeare set out to portray . . . a heavy deed placed on a soul which is not adequate to cope with it." This formulation explains how "the whole play [is] constructed." Wilhelm's interpretation is sealed by a metaphor: "An oak-tree planted in a precious pot which should only have held delicate flowers. The roots spread out, the vessel is shattered."[49]

Wilhelm's criterion of the "structure of the whole" is a crucial feature of the new romantic understanding. As Friedrich Schlegel put it, "there probably is no modern poet more correct than Shakespeare," when "correct," that term so dear to earlier generations, is understood "in the nobler and more original sense of the word—meaning a conscious main and subordinate development of the inmost and most minute aspects of a work in line with the spirit of the whole."[50] In the neo-Aristotelian discourse of the eighteenth century, the key term had been *unity*. Coleridge stands as strongly as Schlegel for a new criterion: "Instead of unity of action, I should great[ly] prefer the more appropriate, tho' scholastic and uncouth words— Homogeneity, proportionateness, and totality of interest." This shift in terminology, for Coleridge, brought out the difference between the "skill of mechanical Talent" and the "creative Life-power of inspired Genius."[51]

Shakespeare had been criticized in neoclassical criticism for his failure to observe the unities, but the question of the "whole" is not at all the same as the question of "unity." As Herder put it in the primal text for the German romantic response to Shakespeare, "whereas in Sophocles's drama the unity of a single action is dominant, Shakespeare aims at the entirety of an event." The distinction is that Sophocles "makes a *single* tone predominate," but in contrast Shakespeare "uses *all* the characters, estates, walks of life he needs to produce the concerted sound of his drama."[52] The "concerted sound" is what later critics will theorize as "polyphony" versus the "monologic" classical.

This criterion of wholeness was developed influentially by August Wilhelm Schlegel and Coleridge in the metaphor of the organism. Coleridge contrasts "mechanical regularity" to "organic form":

> The form is mechanic when on any given material we impress a pre-determined form, not necessarily arising out of the properties of the material—as when to a mass of wet clay we give whatever shape we wish it to retain when hardened—The organic form on the other hand is innate, it shapes, as it developes itself from within, and the fullness of its development is one & the same with the perfection of its outward Form. Such is the life, such is the form.[53]

Such organic power is the power of "Nature, the prime Genial Artist," and "our own Shakespear" is "himself a Nature humanized," whose "genial Understanding" wields "self-consciously a power and a[n] implicit wisdom deeper than Consciousness." Shakespeare, then, as a power like that of nature, has his own laws, which must be studied and learned even as are those of nature.[54] Contrary to the neoclassical critics who had condemned Shakespeare as wild and irregular, Coleridge asserted that "Genius" must not and cannot be "lawless," for every "work of true Genius" achieves "its appropriate Form"; the very definition of genius is "the power of acting creatively under laws of its own origination."[55] This power, which has often been called *autonomy*, was attributed by romantic theorists in various contexts to the work, the author, the culture or "spirit" of a nation, and to every person as an individual.

By this logic, we cannot know in advance what we will find in Shakespeare's work, or in the works of any other genius. We must learn from the work. The very sense of the key term *nature* is shifted. For Samuel Johnson it was Shakespeare's greatness that he was "above all writers, at least above all modern writers, the poet of nature," but this meant that Shakespeare better than any other "holds up to his readers a faithful mirrour of manners and of life."[56] Nature here is the way things already are, what we recognize in human passions and experience. For Coleridge, in contrast, nature is a shaping force actively in process:

> Whence the Harmony that strikes us in the wildest natural landscapes? In the relative shapes of rocks, the harmony of colours in the Heath, Ferns, and Lichens, the Leaves of the Beech and Oak, the stems and rich choc[ol]ate-brown Branches of the Birch, and other mountain Trees, varying from . . . Autumn to returning spring? . . . [They] are effected by a single energy, modified ab intra [from within] in each component part. Now . . . this is the particular excellence of the Shakespearean Dramas.[57]

By long tradition, nature might be understood as the book in which God had written his teachings,[58] and in the same spirit by which Shakespeare's power as nature was assimilated to divine power, so was Shakespeare's text assimilated to that of God's other book, the Bible, as the expression of an incomparable inner power requiring endless exegesis.[59]

Friedrich Schlegel defined a *classical text* (not in this usage to be distinguished from *romantic*) as one that "must never be entirely comprehensible." Such a text requires, solicits, and rewards an endless process of interpretation: "[T]hose who are cultivated and who cultivate themselves must always want to learn more from it."[60]

For Friedrich Schlegel, Goethe's choice of *Hamlet* for his definitive accomplishment in *Wilhelm Meister* demonstrated an affinity between Shakespearean drama and the novel. Both, in Schlegel's terms, were *romantic*, a connection made easier in German because an adjectival form derived from the word for novel (*Roman*) is *romantisch*, which is identical with the term for *romantic*.[61] One of Schlegel's fragments links drama and novel in ways that take us immediately to *Wilhelm Meister* on *Hamlet*:

> Many of the very best novels are compendia, encyclopedias of the whole spiritual life of a brilliant individual. Works which have this quality, even if they are cast in a completely different mold—like *Nathan* [referring to the play *Nathan the Wise* by Lessing]—thereby take on a novelistic hue. And every human being who is cultivated and cultivates himself contains a novel within himself.[62]

In *Wilhelm Meister*, consideration of *Hamlet* leads to larger debates over genre. Novels are contrasted to drama: In novels, "it is predominantly *sentiments* and *events* that are to be presented"; in the drama, "it is *characters* and *deeds*." As opposed to the active hero of drama, "the hero of a novel must be passive," or at least function as a "retarding" personage. From this insight, the application was made back to *Hamlet*: "[T]he hero . . . really only has sentiments, and it is only external events that work on him, so that this play has something of the breadth of a novel."[63]

In studying and endlessly interpreting Shakespeare as we do the Bible, what we learn is not universal truth but rather a uniqueness, something highly particular. To contrast Johnson in 1765 with Herder in 1771 again makes the point very starkly. Johnson finds that Shakespeare's characters are "not modified by the customs of particular places"; rather, they are "common humanity, such as the world will always supply." This means that Shakespeare's "persons act and speak by the influence of those general passions and principles by which all minds are agitated." For most writers, "a character is too often an individual," but in the plays of Shakespeare, a character is "commonly a species."[64] It is Shakespeare's praise that "his story requires Romans or kings, but he thinks only on men."[65]

For Herder, however, different circumstances of life not only mean that characters will be different, but that the whole aesthetic of one culture will differ from that of another culture. Sophocles is taken as representing not simply classical drama but a whole Greek way of life, and Shakespeare exemplifies the way of life of the "North." If, in contrast to the Greek world, the northern world did not offer such "simplicity in its history, traditions, domestic, political, and religious conditions," then correspondingly northern drama will not display any such simplicity. A different "world" will "create its drama out of its own history, the spirit of its age, customs, views, language, national attitudes, traditions, and pastimes, even if they are carnival farces or puppet-plays."[66] Since Shakespeare "found nothing like the simplicity of the Greek national character," his works build instead from "a multiplicity of estates, ways of life, attitudes, nations, and styles of speech."[67] Johnson found Shakespeare essentially human, but Herder understood him as quite local. The work itself builds out of these local details a "splendid poetic whole" that is its own particularity.[68] In this register we again confront the prestige of the "whole"—valued as rich—over the earlier criterion of "unity"—devalued as simplistic.

The impact of Shakespeare on romantic criticism was sometimes muffled. Romantic criticism was capable of finding in Shakespeare commonplace banalities. When Coleridge boasted that "Hamlet was the play, or rather Hamlet himself was the Character, in the intuition and exposition of which I first made my turn for Philosophical criticism, and especially for insight into the genius of Shakespeare, *noticed*,"[69] it is quite disappointing to learn from him that in *Hamlet*, Shakespeare seems to have "wished to exemplify the moral necessity of a due Balance between our attention to outward objectives, and our meditation on inward Thoughts—a due Balance between the real and the imaginary World."[70]

More characteristic was a crucial feature of much romantic criticism, the need for criticism itself to be(come) poetic. Friedrich Schlegel was the figure who most theorized this view, as well as being one of the many brilliant critical performers in prose of the period. Here is one of his slogans for this perspective: "Poetry can only be criticized by way of poetry. A critical judgment of an artistic production has no civil rights in the realm of art if it isn't itself a work of art."[71]

Schlegel in this spirit praises Goethe's discussion of *Hamlet* in *Wilhelm Meister* because it is "not so much criticism as high poetry."[72] He asks, "what else but a poem can come into being when a poet in full possession of his powers contemplates a work of art and represents it in his own?" This "poetic criticism" does not arise simply because a critic "makes suppositions and assertions which go beyond the visible work"; for Schlegel any criticism must do that much, "because every great work . . . knows more than it says," which the critic therefore must explicate. The key to poetic criticism for Schlegel is rather in its own formal relation to the work being criticized. The analytic procedure of poetic criticism will only divide the whole of the work under discussion into its "articulated parts and masses," but will "not break it down into its original constituents," because these raw materials "in respect of the work are dead things." Coleridge made a similar point in his description of the secondary imagination, which "dissolves, diffuses, dissipates, in order to re-create" and in doing so is *vital*, whereas "all objects (*as* objects) are essentially fixed and dead."[73] For Schlegel, the "living unity" of a work of art has transformed the elements it has taken in from "the universe," so that they should no longer be related back to that first source, but only to the newly organic role they play in the poetic composition. This is a theory of contextual rather than referential criticism, which has strong echoes in the arguments of American New Criticism in the middle twentieth century. But unlike the modest stance of New Critics, who presented themselves as servants to the poem, Schlegel was willing to acknowledge the competitive artistic ambitions of the critic, even as the critic honors the work from which the critic's new work is formed.

Friedrich Schlegel was the great activator of the term *romantic*, and Shakespeare was the great activator of Schlegel's thinking about the romantic. The term signaled the contrast of modern vernacular Germanic and Romance languages to the ancient classical languages of Greece and Rome, and of northern and Christian cultures to southern and pagan cultures, but an important further dimension of the romantic for Schlegel was its element of the prosaic, the "interesting," the "characteristic," in opposition to the universal purity associated with the classical.

As early as 1795, in the midst of Schlegel's essay "On the Study of Greek Poetry," the impact of Shakespeare erupts in a way that links it to Schlegel's understanding of the literature of his own time as represented by Goethe. The "aesthetic tragedy" accomplished by the Greeks finds its "complete antithesis" in the more recent "philosophical tragedy," which is the highest form of "characteristic" poetry. Although the outcome of philosophical tragedy is tragic, the work as a whole is not cast in this single mode; the "purity" of aesthetic tragedy contrasts to the "disharmony" that is the "truth" of this modern mode. To illustrate this idea of philosophical tragedy, Schlegel cites "one of the most important documents for the 'characteristic' qualities of modern poetry": *Hamlet*. Against those who praise this work for particular passages, Schlegel asserts its "coherence"; he emphasizes, however, that the "basis of this coherence" is not readily evident, but lies "deeply hidden." Schlegel locates the "center of the whole" in "the character of the hero." Hamlet's self-division exemplifies the "most perfect representation of irresolvable discord, which is the true subject of philosophical tragedy."[74]

Schlegel names Shakespeare as the figure who "most completely and most strikingly embodies the spirit of modern poetry," and who in crucial respects has "anticipated the developments of our own age." These are the features that Schlegel attributes to Shakespeare and to the most important writing of his own age: "the inexhaustible supply of what is interesting"; the "intensity of all passions"; the "inimitable truth of the 'characteristic'"; and finally, "unique originality." Then Schlegel brings into dialogue with *Hamlet* the fragment of *Faust* that Goethe had published in 1790; if it were completed, Schlegel thinks, it might even surpass Shakespeare. In the next year Goethe's new novel incorporates a discussion of *Hamlet* considerably in the spirit of Schlegel's own. Goethe's *Hamlet* interpretation had been in manuscript for at least a decade, showing the extent to which Shakespeare's impact was working across the culture in ways not simply calculable by measures of influence.[75]

In this discussion of Shakespeare, Schlegel conceives the notion of a whole composed by "dissonance." Leading twentieth-century theorists of the novel, schooled in the traditions of German philology and aesthetics that Schlegel did so much to form, include Mikhail Bakhtin and Georg Lukács, both of whom characterize the novel as a form that must deal with, and build itself from, dissonance.[76] Schlegel, as we have seen, places Shakespeare at the defining center of what for him was equally the "modern" and the "romantic." The "great triple chord of modern poetry," the core of any "critical anthology of the classics of modern poetry," for Schlegel, would be defined by Dante's "transcendental poetry," the "purely poetical poetry" of Goethe, and at the very "center of romantic art," he places "Shakespeare."[77] In his *Dialogue on Poetry*, Schlegel distinguishes between the work of his own time and that of "the older moderns," such as Shakespeare and Cervantes. These older moderns are above all romantic, and Shakespeare forms "the actual center, the core of the romantic imagination."[78] This romantic imagination includes both the goals of the highest synthesis and also the disruptions of deep irony—the technique corresponding to what Schlegel had earlier called "dissonance."

In his 1800 essay of self-reflection, "On Incomprehensibility," Schlegel comments on the modes of irony of his own recent essays and fragments and warns of the self-annihilating spiral of "the irony of irony." He asks, "what gods will rescue us from all these ironies?" but he abandons hope of finding "an irony that might be able to swallow up all these big and little ironies" and thereby get rid of them. For irony, Schlegel argues, is too serious and complex to be evaded: "Irony is something one simply cannot play games with," and "It can have incredibly long-lasting after effects." Even "hundreds of years after their deaths," the "most conscious artists" continue to exercise ironical power over their "followers and admirers." The only writer mentioned in this discussion of irony is Shakespeare, because he "has so infinitely many depths, subterfuges, and intentions" that the "insidious traps in his works" snare the "cleverest artists of posterity."[79] Yet the dissonances of irony are themselves part of a project that Schlegel understands as one of totalization: "The whole history of modern poetry is a running commentary on the following brief philosophical text: all art should become science and all science art; poetry and philosophy should be made one."[80] It is important to recognize that in German the term translated as "science" is *Wissenschaft*, which has the sense of "an organized body of thought and learning," rather than its usual current English sense of an empirical and mathematical discipline.

Schlegel's most quoted text, Fragment 116 from the *Athenaeum*, takes as its subject "romantic poetry" in its largest sense.[81] The classical is "perfected" and thus limited, but romantic poetry is "infinite" and therefore "free." It is the "only kind of poetry that is more than a kind"—that is, it is the genre that transcends genre because it is both "progressive" and "universal," thus going beyond fixity and limitation. In this fragment Schlegel sums up his thoughts from an intensely creative period of theorization, and its terms resonate with those from his discussion of Shakespeare: He emphasizes his desire "to reunite all the separate species of poetry and put poetry in touch with philosophy and rhetoric," and to "mix and fuse poetry and prose, inspiration and criticism, the poetry of art and the poetry of nature." This kind of work "can so lose itself in what it describes that one might believe that it exists only to characterize poetical individuals of all sorts; and yet there is still no form so fit for expressing the entire spirit of an author." "Like the epic," romantic poetry wields large mimetic power; it forms "a mirror of the whole circumambient world, and image of the age," but its armament of mirrors is multiple. Therefore, romantic poetry, "more than any other form," can "hover at the midpoint between the portrayed and the portrayer . . . on the wings of poetic reflection." This capacity to "raise that reflection again and again to a higher power," to "multiply it in an endless succession of mirrors" is, we have seen, the power of irony in which Shakespeare is preeminent.

Schlegel had in mind not only Shakespeare but also the crucial form of his own age, the novel. *Romantische Poesie*, "romantic poetry," is also "novelistic poesis." And so in the midst of Schlegel's *Dialogue on Poetry*, there is interposed a "Letter about the Novel." This disruption of the play of voices in conversation by a written text mimics the generic crux of the novel. For Schlegel, "A novel is a romantic book." The self-conscious "tautology" here ("Ein Roman ist ein romantisches Buch") allows the weight to fall on the material means and its implications. The "manner of presentation" of a novel will differ from that of drama because it is "for reading," not for viewing; in thinking of a book, one thinks of "a work, an existing whole."[82] Here Schlegel anticipates the "rhetorical" basis of Northrop Frye's theory of genre, in which prose "fiction" is the genre of the written word.[83]

This distinction—the special force of literature in its form as book—was crucial for Coleridge some decades later as he reflected on why so fine a critical mind as Ben Jonson had been unable to recognize Shakespeare's greatness so fully as Coleridge thinks he should have. The answer is that Jonson had only the plays, one after another "as acted," to respond to; only since 1623 have we had the book that allows us to think about the plays in relation to each other, and thereby "to form a just notion of the mighty mind that produced the whole."[84]

Schlegel argues against those who derive the novel only from epic. Because of its distinctive "mixture" of various forms, it is rather Shakespeare's drama "which is the true foundation of the novel."[85] For Schlegel a true theory of the novel "would have to be itself a novel," and in its pages "Shakespeare would converse intimately with Cervantes."[86]

No less than in Schlegel's exemplary case of *Wilhelm Meister*, or in Keats, the "mediation of [the] great model" of Shakespeare fostered Herman Melville's radically innovative *Moby-Dick*.[87] In the midst of writing *Moby-Dick*, Melville registered a double encounter with literary greatness which, scholars have argued, caused him to reconceive his work in progress at a higher level of ambition and complexity. He had been passionately reading in a recently acquired edition of Shakespeare (now in Harvard's Houghton Library), which had print large enough for his bad eyes.[88] The fruits of this reading mark his letters and found their first printed form in "Hawthorne and his Mosses" (1850), a review essay on Nathaniel Hawthorne, to whom *Moby-Dick* was dedicated when it appeared in 1851. Melville's praise of Hawthorne at its highest point is caught up in the web of romantic writing on Shakespeare. Melville pursues the contrast of stage and page, the need for appreciative interpretation, the sense that Shakespeare does not so much confirm our understanding of life as give us new, particular knowledge. Melville draws especially from his reading of "The Hero as Poet" in Thomas Carlyle's *On Heroes, Hero-Worship, and the Heroic in History* (1840),[89] a work that culminated some twenty years in which Carlyle had been translating and discussing German works in the hope of transforming his Anglophone audiences.

In the key passage, Melville begins by singling out for praise and attention a feature of Hawthorne now familiar but far less recognized by his early

readers, "that blackness in Hawthorne." This "infinite obscure" in Hawthorne recalls to Melville the example of Shakespeare, who, Melville believes, is admired by theatrical crowds for "Richard-the-Third humps and
Macbeth daggers," but who is valued by "philosophers" as the "profoun-
dest of thinkers." He explains, "It is those deep, far-away things in him;
those occasional flashings-forth of the intuitive Truth in him; those short,
quick probings at the very axis of reality:—these are the things that make
Shakespeare, Shakespeare." Melville invokes the theme of interpretation:
"[F]ew of his endless commentators and critics seem to have remembered,
or even perceived, that the immediate products of a great mind are not so
great, as that undeveloped (and sometimes undevelopable) yet dimly dis-
cernible greatness, to which these immediate products are but the infallible
indices. In Shakespeare's tomb lies more than Shakespeare ever wrote."[90]

Melville here closely resumes Carlyle's rhetoric in "The Hero as Poet."
Because Shakespeare is a force like that of nature, Carlyle writes, his works
"grow up withal *un*consciously from the unknown deeps in him;—as the
oak-tree grows from the Earth's bosom." This comparison allows Carlyle
to emphasize "How much in Shakespeare lies hid; his sorrows, his silent
struggles known to himself; much that was not known at all, not speakable
at all: like *roots*, like sap and forces working underground!" Carlyle concludes this passage with a sentence that became a commonplace, circulating
far more widely than in the criticism of Shakespeare: "Speech is great; but
Silence is greater."[91]

Through Shakespeare, Melville feels his own powers. To be original, and
thus like Shakespeare, is for Melville to be fully human, and thereby also to
be not abstractly universal but rather peculiarly national. For "to write like
a man" means that a writer "will be sure to write like an American."[92] For
Carlyle, too, in "The Hero as Poet," an original writer plays a national role:
"[I]t is a great thing for a Nation that it get an articulate voice."[93]

This topic of Shakespeare and national identity had been part of the romantic Shakespeare, from Herder on. For the Germans in the later eighteenth century, Shakespeare was a compelling alternative to the previously
dominant canons of French neoclassicism (in the aftermath of the English
triumph over France in the Seven Years' War), and then in the age of the
French Revolutionary wars for both Germany and for Britain, Shakespeare
played an even larger polemical role as an antithesis to French culture, as
one may see at various moments in Coleridge that are now rather embar-
rassing. He ended a lecture in 1813 by noting that "England, justly proud as
she had a right to be, of a Shakespeare, a Milton, a Bacon, and a Newton,

could also boast of a Nelson and a Wellington."[94] The same valence operated in Russia in the decades after the Napoleonic Wars in which German
cultural values—including Shakespeare—prevailed among many of the in-
telligentsia over the longstanding prestige of French as the culture and language of international politesse. In the United States, Melville made his use
of Shakespeare part of his democratic commitment to bring "republican
progressiveness into Literature."[95]

Shakespeare as a political issue is not at all absent from romantic criticism,
but also not generally integrated within it. Hazlitt was provoked by the
open politics of *Coriolanus* to argue that "the language of poetry naturally
falls in with the language of power," because the imagination is a "mono-
polising faculty" and therefore "aristocratic."[96] This is the "original sin in
poetry."[97] But he does not carry this extraordinarily challenging claim into
relation with his analysis of Shakespeare's selflessly outgoing imagination.

Carlyle, in contrast, is explicitly concerned in *Heroes and Hero-Worship*
with the varying modes in which power may be exercised; his heroes have
appeared "as" poet, prophet, priest, or king. The modes are not at all fully
exchangeable. Carlyle concludes "The Hero as Poet" with questions of
how poetry relates to global politics, to nations in the world. He contrasts
Italy to Russia: Italy is politically fragmented but nationally "bound together" through Dante, while Russia is a vast empire "which cannot yet
speak."[98] (Carlyle, like most Western intellectuals of his time, was evidently
unaware of the work of Pushkin, who had recently died.) Shakespeare, in
Carlyle's model, does even more than Dante, for Shakespeare has represented England not simply to itself but to the whole world. Carlyle asks his
contemporaries a question that sets cultural power against political power:
"[W]ill you give up your Indian Empire, or your Shakespeare?" He argues
that the empire in any case "will go . . . some day," but that Shakespeare
"lasts forever." (At least, Shakespeare is still very widely taught in Indian
schools.[99]) Even after the loss of British political sovereignty over
"America," Shakespeare is unparalleled for his continuing "*in*destructible"
power as the "noblest, gentlest, yet strongest of rallying-signs" that gives
him cultural "sovereignty" as "King Shakespeare."[100]

The impact of Shakespeare moved Carlyle to imagine culture as a category that may have more power than politics does to organize the way people live with one another. This insight illuminates the Shakespearean
inspiration for much of the work done in and since the nineteenth century
by novelists, in the "romantic" genre beyond genre.

2.   The Media of Sublimity: Johnson and Lamb on King Lear

In dismissing the nineteenth century's "semi-ethical criterion of 'sublimity,'" T. S. Eliot in 1919 banished the sublime from the canonical discourse of literary modernism. Starting in the early 1970s, however, following the work of Harold Bloom, Neil Hertz, and Thomas Weiskel, the sublime returned both as an indispensable concept and as a positive value. Jean-François Lyotard made the sublime fundamental to his definition of post-modernism, and Paul Fry reoriented literary theory by displacing Aristotle with Longinus.[1] We are now increasingly likely to agree that the disruptive force of the sublime works for the good both aesthetically and politically, exorcising the coercions of totalizing form and the totalitarianizing state.

I participated in this movement that advances into the future by returning to romanticism, but I also have some trouble with it. The study of the sublime requires not only theoretical but also historical differentiations,[2] and the complex subjectivity of the romantic sublime may be both a less obvious good and a less inevitable fate than it once seemed, requiring ongoing political debate. The history of the sublime in our cultural practices, our reading and our discourse of reading, is intimately bound up with what in *Discipline and Punish* and *The History of Sexuality* Michel Foucault explored as the genealogy of the "post-Christian soul," a process in which Foucault located a decisive step around 1800. I have chosen two treatments of *King Lear*—the exemplary sublime drama—neatly spread around 1789, each a little over twenty years away: Charles Lamb's "On the Tragedies of Shakespeare Considered with Reference to Their Fitness for Stage-Representation" (1811) and the remarks on *King Lear* and on Shakespeare more broadly by Samuel Johnson (1765).

Lamb's essay, one of the rare romantic works that actually much used the term "sublime," clearly displays the transfer of religious terms of value into a new psychological space.[3] A second connection to present concerns in the history of our culture makes Lamb especially interesting, as I have signaled in my title: his detailed comparison of Shakespeare's effects in two media, print and stage. For in recent years, our sense of what "literature" is and its place among other cultural forms has been complicated, and shaken, by the tremendous growth of cultural production and transmission in film, video, radio, television, recorded sound media, and all the other nonprint media that nonetheless wield the power of the word. What kinds of power and what kinds of value do we attribute to these media? Such questions link British Marxist work, most notably exemplified in Raymond Williams and Stuart Hall, with French poststructuralist work on representation, the archive, the simulacrum, grammatology, and many other modes of the non-original.[4] This is the matrix from which American cultural studies emerged.

Looking back from these current questions to Lamb, whose essay marks an important moment in the history of the comparative valuation of media, I take my inspiration from "The Work of Art in the Age of Mechanical Reproduction" by Walter Benjamin, an earlier German cousin of the current British and French work just mentioned.[5] Tightly bound in its method and concerns with his great essays "On Some Motifs in Baudelaire" and "The Storyteller," Benjamin's essay is exemplary for relating a comparative analysis of media and their effects to the historical conditions of experience that constrain, but also enable, the production and reception of cultural works. It seeks both a relatively precise periodization and an analysis that focuses on the relations of aesthetics to politics. Benjamin argued that their mechanical reproducibility has caused artworks to lose the "aura" that characterized them in traditional culture. That aura derived from the works' function in religious ritual, which distanced them from ordinary use and observation. But since printing, and most crucially since photography, mass availability has erased distance, and what was arcane has become familiar. One effect of this transformation has been first to bring into existence the category of the "aesthetic," which did not apply when what we call "art" was wholly religious, and then to supersede that category just at the point it had become established, since the mass-reproduced work is no longer "art" as defined by aesthetics.

As sketched here, Benjamin's argument retains its intended polemical edge, but it cannot appear wholly convincing. Part of the value of reading Lamb while thinking of Benjamin is the chance to test Benjamin's theses rather more directly than is often possible. For Benjamin and Lamb chose to focus on closely comparable elements of culture. As part of his argument over changes in media, Benjamin contrasted stage acting with film acting; Lamb centrally contrasted stage acting with reading. Benjamin contrasted the "concentration" of the audience in aesthetic theory with the "distraction" of mass reception; Lamb claimed for reading the power of "abstraction" over theatrical viewing. Benjamin emphasized that the new mass audience for the mechanically reproduced work, despite its distraction, could judge what it saw, unlike the passive absorption of other modes of reception; Lamb sought a response, through reading, that would be sympathetic rather than "critical" like the response of a theatrical audience. By taking account of such historically specified claims, I aim to help establish a differential history of the sublime, which has been studied only typologically by the theoretically powerful critics who have renewed its currency, while the standard historical studies have sunk the subject so deep into the perspectives of another age as to make the connection to present concerns extremely hard to reach.[6]

Lamb's historical importance may be further focused by comparison with Johnson. Both Lamb and Johnson distinguished between media by contrasting the reading and the staging of *King Lear*. In line with Edmund Burke's arguments, in part 5 of his *Enquiry into the Origin of Our Ideas of the Sublime and the Beautiful*, that the power of words over the passions is independent of specific visual images, both gave reading much more power than viewing. As readers, however, they evaluated this power quite differently. Reading seemed for Lamb a thoroughly safe activity, while for Johnson it proved shocking. Both the French Revolution itself and the economic and social changes in England associated with the emerging democratic possibilities of this period bear on another sharp difference between the two. Johnson was pleased to turn away from the intense idiosyncrasy of his own reading response and instead accept the "suffrage" of "the publick" on the "case" of *King Lear*.[7] Lamb, on the contrary, attacked the public and relied instead on an elite of individual readers, a gesture much like that of Wordsworth in the 1800 preface to *Lyrical Ballads*. Michael Hays has incisively illuminated the shift in the social structure of theatergoing that might account for this difference. A more popular, and socially heterogeneous, audience acted as what Coleridge called "explosive material," to be understood only through comparison with "the history of Paris," from "the commencement of the latter half of the reign of Lewis XIV, to the time of Napoleon."[8] Johnson's more democratic rhetoric enjoyed the security of a more effectively circumscribed public sphere, for theater and politics alike.

To make this comparison of Lamb with Johnson fully work, however, I must establish that the sublime entered into Johnson's response to *King Lear*, for he differs from Lamb in not invoking the term.[9] The fascination for our

time in reading Johnson on *King Lear* is trying to understand how so powerful a critical intelligence could have preferred to Shakespeare's play the revision by Nahum Tate (1681), which omitted the Fool, tidied up a great deal
and above all altered the plot so that Cordelia "retired with victory and
felicity." For Johnson, Tate's version satisfied "the natural ideas of justice"
by which "all reasonable beings naturally love justice," but Shakespeare denied us this pleasure.[10] Johnson's explicit premises lacked any criterion of
greatness beyond that of enduring pleasure, which depends on mimesis:
"Nothing can please many, and please long, but just representations of general nature,"[11] and he confessed that Shakespeare's *King Lear* was a "just representation."[12] Yet it did not please.

Johnson's own laudatory account of the play, however, drew upon a vocabulary quite different from that of representation and pleasure:

> The tragedy of Lear is deservedly celebrated among the dramas of Shake-
> speare. There is perhaps no play which keeps the attention so strongly fixed;
> which so much agitates our passions and interests our curiosity. The artful
> involution of distinct interests, the striking opposition of contrary characters,
> the sudden changes of fortune, and the quick succession of events, fill the
> mind with a perpetual tumult of indignation, pity, and hope. . . . So powerful
> is the current of the poet's imagination, that the mind, which once ventures
> within it, is hurried irresistibly along.[13]

Johnson's vocabulary here echoes that of the sublime; compare Burke's
analysis "Of the passion caused by the SUBLIME": "The mind is so entirely
filled with its object, that it cannot entertain any other," and "hence arises
the great power of the sublime. . . . [I]t anticipates our reasonings and hur-
ries us on by an irresistible force."[14] The intensity of this experience is at
once valuable and dangerous, for its power can overcome "our consciousness of fiction,"[15] which allows the "auditor" to enjoy tragedy. In supreme
contrast to this safe social pleasure, Johnson's own first reading of the play
traumatized him: "I was many years ago so shocked by Cordelia's death,
that I know not whether I ever endured again to read the last scenes of the
play till I undertook to revise them as an editor." He rejected his solitary
pain and turned to the communal pleasure that "the publick has decided"
to prefer, in choosing Tate over Shakespeare.

Although Lamb did not significantly invoke the Christian morality so
important to Johnson, his essay runs from its beginning through its end in a
religious idiom. It begins with his criticism of the memorial for the eighteenth-century actor David Garrick in Westminster Abbey: "I was not a

little scandalised at the introduction of theatrical airs and gestures into a place set aside to remind us of the saddest realities."[16] It goes on later to evoke the mind of King Lear as moving like the Holy Spirit, which "blows where it listeth."[17] And near the end, it criticizes the staging of *Macbeth* for being like the way a "Romish priest" celebrates mass.[18] As opposed to the constant tension Johnson found between the artistic requirements of pleasure and (moral) instruction, Lamb assimilated great art to the idiom of English Protestantism, as did Keats's sonnet on *King Lear*, Matthew Arnold, and many others. Lamb made no direct attempt to claim theological sanction for the greatness of art (which Coleridge did claim through his theory of the symbol), but he relied upon firm categories delimiting the kinds of religious activity or perspective appropriate to Englishmen. Lamb was a scripturalist, not a ritualist: For him the letter alone gave life, not the attempts to give it body or voice.[19] He was metaphysically a dualist, but on the opposite side from where either Benjamin or Derrida would lead us to expect to find him.

The defining feature of Lamb's aesthetic sect was the category of the author. Only this idea could forestall two false judgments concerning stage actors: identifying them with the power that gave existence to the drama in which they are acting, and identifying them with the characters they are embodying (for as Benjamin observed, "The aura which, on the stage, emanates from Macbeth, cannot be separated for the spectators from that of the actor").[20] Lamb insisted that to "unlettered persons," the "very idea of what an author is cannot be made comprehensible without some pain and perplexity of mind," but even some "persons otherwise not meanly lettered" are liable to these confusions.[21] As the author par excellence, who plays the role in this argument that the deity does in theology, Shakespeare has the "power of originating" and thus "absolute mastery over the heart and soul of man."[22] His plays are *"in themselves essentially . . . different from all others"*[23] and he therefore "positively creates in us . . . powers" that we exercise in responding to his plays alone, although we mistake them for "indigenous faculties of our own,"[24] which "echo" his in kind, as if we possessed "a mind congenial with the poet's."[25]

Lamb's first hierarchical division separated Shakespeare from all humankind; a second separated from everyone else those few who could properly respond to Shakespeare. If Shakespeare's plays are "natural," they are "grounded deep in nature, so deep that the depth of them lies out of the reach of most of us." So "ninety-nine out of a hundred" cannot distinguish the nature of *George Barnwell* (in a once-popular eighteenth-century play) from that of *Othello*.[26] For in the "motives and grounds" for their "passion," Shakespeare's characters differ from "low and vulgar natures,"[27] whether those of other dramatists' characters, of the actors who play them, or of the audiences that admire them. This notion of the author, then, radically distinguished Lamb's critical position from Johnson's. Johnson could invoke "the authority of Shakespeare" against critical rules,[28] but even Shakespeare's authority could not stand against the public's long-standing decision to prefer Tate's ending. For Lamb, however, that authority underwrote his turn from the theater and its audience. If Johnson, in admiring Thomas Gray's "Elegy Written in a Country Churchyard," could "rejoice to concur with the common reader," Lamb scorned the "common auditors."[29]

Lamb's case thus provides further evidence for the arguments of Foucault in "What Is an Author?" for the historically determinate position of our concern with the category of authorship, an important enlargement of context for the arguments of M. H. Abrams in *The Mirror and the Lamp* for the romantic shift from audience-centered to author-centered poetics. Specifically, Foucault argued that "modern criticism, in its desire to 'recover' the author from a work, employs devices strongly reminiscent of Christian exegesis when it wished to prove the value of a text by asserting the holiness of its author."[30] This process emerges clearly in a moment from Coleridge that echoes the issues we have been investigating in Lamb. Coleridge was concerned that so generally estimable a critic as Ben Jonson should so frequently have been severe against Shakespeare. "The best excuse that can be made," he decided, was that Shakespeare's "plays were present to men's minds chiefly as acted." Coleridge understood the publication history well enough to recognize that "they had not a neat edition of them, as we have." Therefore, unlike us, they could not "by comparing the one with the other . . . form a just notion of the mighty mind that produced the whole."[31]

Against the whole constellation of "acting," Lamb placed the authorial constellation, organized around "reading." In the light of our ongoing theoretical concerns with both the concept and the practices of "reading," Lamb's distinctions take on significance. They bring us to the core of the paradox implicit in my title, for the sublime proves never unmediated, immediate, but always responsive, yet it arises from a failure of mediation: Our usual modes of conveyance have broken down, and something new breaks out. No less than Wordsworth's turn to imagination in the Alps in Book 6 of his *Prelude*, Lamb's emphasis on reading is an idealizing reaction: His reader's sublime supervenes to supplement the failure of dramatic representation. Lamb's reading is "slow," as opposed to the "instantaneous nature of the impressions which we take in at the eye and ear at a play house."[32] It requires that we "earn" for ourselves "thought and feeling," as opposed to the "vast quantity" provided at no cost by the "conveying" of actors.[33] It awakens in us "meditation" about Shakespeare's characters, as opposed to "interest or curiosity as to their actions."[34] Specifically, even in Shakespeare's great criminals, "the inner mind in all its perverted greatness, solely seems real and is exclusively attended to, the crime is comparatively nothing."[35] We are "elevated" into "sublime emotion" precisely through the "vantage ground of abstraction which reading possesses over seeing."[36]

Reading is conceptual, seeing merely sensual. As opposed to "the painful sense of presence" in "the deed doing" when acting an action, the "delight which the words in the book convey" arises only from "sublime images" like those of "history": "something past and inevitable." But this history perhaps does not have "anything to do with time at all." In contrast, then, to the painful seeing of the theater, "we see not Lear, but we are Lear." An identification operates through reading that does not—as in the deluded response of the theatergoer—join the actor to the character or author; rather, this identification joins us, as readers, not to the actor but to the author, and the result is that against the "corporal infirmities and weakness" and "impotence" in Lear as spectacle, "we are sustained by a grandeur," borne up by a "mighty irregular power" that "blows where it listeth," to achieve a "sublime identification" with the "heavens themselves," and their suggestion of transcendence and eternity. The pettiness that "we see upon a stage is body and bodily action"; the greatness that "we are conscious of in reading is almost exclusively the mind."[37]

After this extravagance, it is extraordinary that Lamb descends to a modest summarizing phrase for his chosen activity, the "beautiful compromise which we make in reading." What possible compromises could there be after such delights? To begin with, the irregularity of sublime energies is restricted; that is, their connection with death and pain, so crucial both in Burke and in Longinus but so repressed in the long first moment of Lamb's argument, is once again acknowledged. For Lamb maintained that Lear must die, against the Tate version that Johnson defended and that still held the stage in Lamb's day: "A happy ending!—as if the living martyrdom that Lear had gone through,—the flaying of his feelings alive, did not make a fair dismissal from the stage of life the only decorous thing for him. . . . As if the childish pleasure of getting his gilt robes and sceptre again could tempt him to act over again his misused station—as if, at his years and with his experience, anything was left but to die."[38]

Lamb showed no sense of contradiction between his rhetoric of the sublime and his recourse to the "decorous," even at the cost of death. Some might prefer life and its excesses, but Lamb's rhetoric makes clear that over against reading he has set the stage and all of life with it, acting and action alike. In invoking the metaphor of the "stage of life," he condemned Lear by his very greatness to forgo it, along with the external garments of his role, lest he "act over again" his part. Lamb thus chose the bargain that Foucault defined as "humanism," "the totality of discourse through which Western man is told: 'Even though you don't exercise power, you can still be a ruler,' a discourse exercised through a system of 'subjected sovereignties.'"[39] The sublime has been domesticated within a beautiful compromise.

Lamb shared this compromise with Wordsworth and Coleridge in their responses to the political events of their times. By carrying the rejection of "acting" to the rejection of "action" and of life itself, Lamb repeated Coleridge's reading of Hamlet and joined in a new anti-Aristotelian aesthetic of character. For all these writers, that new aesthetic was deeply correlated with the loss, or abandonment, of a decent public world of politics. In preferring to emphasize the "inner mind" rather than the "crime," Lamb chose solitude against society; he joined the reaction against the democratic hopes of the French Revolution that Wordsworth wrote into his early play *The Borderers*. That play Wordsworth prefaced with the first major work of romantic character criticism, and a few sublime lines from it became famous long before the play was ever published[40]—quoted, among other places, in Coleridge's lecture on *Hamlet*. The lines are spoken by the tempter Oswald (Rivers):

> Action is transitory—a step, a blow,
> The motion of a muscle—this way or that—
> 'Tis done, and in the after-vacancy
> We wonder at ourselves like men betrayed:
> Suffering is permanent, obscure and dark,
> And shares the nature of infinity.[41]

This context helps to place the melancholy resignation that encompasses the sublimity Lamb allows, for the sublime is available only as unrealized. Every attempt at fulfillment proves that instead of "realizing" an idea, we have only "materialised" it.[42] Thus the racial democracy of the love between Othello and Desdemona is "soothing" and "flattering" to "the nobler parts of our natures," so long as only read about, but even acted, let alone lived, "the actual sight of the thing" is "extremely revolting" (here

Lamb felt free to go beyond his own discriminations and "appeal to every one that has seen *Othello* played").[43] The privilege of literature is such that it stands as far above the other arts as it does above life. In the Eden of reading *Paradise Lost,* we enjoy "Paradisaical senses," but try to paint it, and we have only "a man and his wife without clothes in the picture."[44] Only the "mind" is "free," against a "strait-lacing actuality."[45] Benjamin, in his essay on mechanical reproduction, emphasized a utopian dimension to art quite different from the one Lamb defined, because Benjamin invoked the possibility—the necessity—of historical change: "One of the foremost tasks of art has always been the creation of a demand which could be fully satisfied only later."[46] Lamb read art as an alternative, not a directive.

Contrary to the almost unanimous belief in our current critical speculation, the sublime does not always function for liberation; it has served as an agency of consolidation, and it may again. As well as depriving us of something, Eliot also knew what he was rejecting in the romantic heritage of the sublime. Against Lamb's decorous giving up of life and happiness, and society, for the visionary power of death in imagination (a strange Faustian bargain), Johnson seems immensely attractive, as utopian as Northrop Frye in his claim that life does enough to us; can't we at least find "victory and felicity" in our art? Yet Johnson's trust in his fellow human beings ("the public," "the common reader"), his acceptance of both pleasure and knowledge as goods, his recognition and distrust of the overwhelmingly painful are not simply available for us to repossess by an act of will, however inspiring they may be precisely through their difference from any position that we can actually attain to. Although my students do not at once accept Lamb's critique of the theater, they do at once recognize that he, much more than Johnson, is our contemporary still. The terms through which our educational system teaches us to value literature are overwhelmingly more those of Lamb than those of Johnson, for the emergence of democratic politics and mass culture makes our world more like Lamb's, and Wordsworth's and Coleridge's, than Johnson's. Authorial genius remains the high cultural protection of English studies against a public that prefers what Wordsworth stigmatized as "gross and violent stimulants."

Johnson lives in our cultural memory for his powers as a critic who made judgments; he stood up to Shakespeare and Milton, and everyone else, in ways that scarcely even make sense to us any longer. Lamb concluded his observations with a comparison that made the difference between reading and theatergoing analogous to that between reading and reviewing. In theatergoing or reviewing, as opposed simply to reading, one looks to test the effects, which "call upon us to judge"; one is cast in the position of "being called upon to judge."[47] Lamb's rejection of judging in favor of reading makes sense as a reaction against the rise in the previous decade of the great quarterly reviews and the consequent popularization of cultural debate along the lines of partisan politics. The "literary" as we know it was formed in the renunciation of judgment through its inevitable association with politics at that moment, and in the turn instead to positive appreciation of the highest genius. Benjamin's essay on reproduction tried to bring an end to the notion of "art" that underlies the "literary." To do this, Benjamin invoked viewers' powers to act, even in their "distraction," the role of "examiner" putting to the test the cultural goods offered them in a context at once that of capitalist commodification and that of political choice.[48] In the internalization that M. H. Abrams charted in *Natural Supernaturalism*, the romantics aestheticized politics lost; Benjamin called instead for a regained politicization of art.

3. Hamlet, Little Dorrit, *and the History of Character*

The upshot of the theory movement, contrary to what many have understood, pointed toward finding what it will take to forge a new literary history. From Fredric Jameson's slogan, "always historicize," to Michel Foucault's genealogies, to the critiques of traditional (teleological, periodizing, objectifying) historiography by Jacques Derrida, Paul de Man, and Hayden White, to British historical materialism and American New Historicism, this is the message.[1] The conjunction of Shakespeare and Dickens is propitious for taking another step into this project, for Shakespeare has been the object of intense attention by theorists concerned with history.[2] In the United States, the Berkeley journal *Representations*, widely acknowledged as most brilliantly instantiating New Historicism, counted among its founding editorial group two powerfully learned and innovative Shakespeareans, Stephen Jay Greenblatt and the late Joel Fineman.

In order to reach my topic, I will emphasize one respect in which the work of Fineman and Greenblatt still follows an old historicism. Both continue a massive nineteenth-century line of belief, broadly epitomized by Jakob Burckhardt on Renaissance individualism, in holding that Shakespeare inaugurated what Fineman calls "a recognizably modern literature of individuated, motivated character"; or as Greenblatt puts it, "Shakespearean theater virtually defines in our literary tradition the representation of individuals."[3] This is true enough in one sense, but my claim (not uniquely mine) is that the sense of character, and of literature, that they find in Shakespeare became available only in the nineteenth century. Recall that Samuel Johnson in the 1765 preface to his edition differed from us: Johnson praised Shakespeare for providing the typical and general, not the individual or particular. This nineteenth-century sense of individuality is still considerably ours, but it is also no longer ours, at least enough that it becomes possible to put that sense of character and literature to historical examination, and to find that it is part of our romantic and Victorian rather than Elizabethan heritage.

Dickens provides a focus for thinking about the process by which the modern sense of character was brought into existence through—not by— Shakespeare. If Shakespeare is our contemporary—as Jan Kott memorably titled his book in the 1960s—it is only because of a continual process of reworking that has continued to produce him in successive cultural formations since his own. My exploration thus furthers the project of new literary history by paying attention to the reception history of works after their time of initial production, by concern with their cultural afterlives.[4] It also involves two other areas crucial for recent work: the historical study of the production of the subject and the process of intertextuality.[5] My procedure involves some characterization of *Little Dorrit* that moves to establish a precise philological connection between *Hamlet* and *Little Dorrit*, with a focus on Arthur Clennam. This connection sustains the larger set of intertextual claims and connections that I then wish to develop. With the leading string of Hamlet, I relate the construction of Arthur Clennam as a character—in the larger sense of one who is conceived of as a character, not just characterization but also metacharacterization—to three distinct discursive strands that come together: one line from the inward-turned practices of *Bildung* fiction, one line from the highly externalized theatrical practices that feed into the projective and expressionistic atmospheric effects of gothic fiction, and an intellectual line from the new literary criticism of Shakespeare that began in the romantic period, as discussed in the previous two chapters.

The project that brings me to this conjunction is the attempt to elaborate a full historical poetics of the novel in the nineteenth century. Although obviously crucial in any such attempt, character has not been an effective concern of current criticism.[6] Indeed, "character" in our times may be a critical concept useful only for thinking about popular fiction and biography. It thus marks the historical specificity of a particular period within high culture. In reading the nineteenth-century novel (as for some other purposes), the notion of character has two major valences, predictive and interpretive. These correspond roughly to what E. M. Forster designated flat and round (a better word might be *deep*) characters.[7] Of flat characters, one feels safe in predicting what they will do in a situation; round characters are more appropriately subject to interpretation after the fact: Of them we say, "That is just what they would do." The sense of individual complexity and development associated with the round character is my present concern.

To locate the emergence of the *individual* in life, or in literature, is impossible. Persuasive arguments have been made for "the discovery of the individual" in the twelfth century, at the time of the Reformation, by

Shakespeare, by Descartes, at the time of the Seven Years' War, by Fichte—and so on.[8] Only to the extent, however, that they are all the retrospective artifacts of historical interpretation as practiced in a given time and place (or culture) does it make sense to say of these that they are all the "same" individual. The sense of character I am studying here can be delimited politically between the French Revolution and World War I, and economically between the full beginning of the Industrial Revolution and the height of imperialism. Culturally, this character is correlated with the rise of the science of psychology and its transformation by psychoanalysis, and it closely coincides with the emergence of the institution of "literature" in the sense that we still lingeringly know it:[9] a moment that might begin with Goethe's *Wilhelm Meister* and end with Joyce's *Ulysses*. That concept of "literature" is now obsolescent, "residual"—just as Kantian aesthetics survives despite Heidegger.

In the nineteenth century, there was a close correlation between literary characterization and the scientific study of human personality. For psychology and literature alike in this period, *Hamlet* is crucial. This confluence may be signaled by Coleridge's dual role: He helped to found the criticism of character as an effective, gradually dominant critical mode, and he was one of the first to use such terms as "psychological" and "psychologist." Melville's *Pierre* and Dickens's *Little Dorrit* come in the middle of this period, and each, in returning to the model of Hamlet that had been crucial to Goethe and Coleridge and would be again for Freud and Joyce, significantly inflects both the literary genre of the novel of development and the larger cultural sense of how to understand a character. The culmination of character criticism in English comes in A. C. Bradley's lectures on Shakespeare, which are contemporary with the earlier work of Freud—who himself formulated the interpretation of Hamlet's character that would much later be elaborated in Ernest Jones's *Hamlet and Oedipus*.[10] By the 1930s, the New Critics had turned against character criticism, teaching us no longer to care how many children had Lady Macbeth, but to attend instead to patterns of language. (This affected criticism of the novel as well.) The renewed understanding of Freud begun in France through Lacan's work highlighted in Freud a more fundamental linguistic emphasis—and genius—than had previously been recognized. In this context, the study of character becomes newly possible, bearing in mind that character may be understood as one possible effect of language under certain historical and social conditions. Derrida began his essay on "Freud and the Scene of Writing" by asking, "[W]hat must a psyche be if it can be represented by a text?"[11]

Little Dorrit has won strong admiration since the 1950s for its comprehensively critical sense of society and for its richness of character analysis, deepened by autobiographical reflections to which Dickens was impelled at a crucial turn in his life and career. The literary means by which this psychological deepening was mediated have been less remarked. Dickens overlaid the 1850s onto the 1820s and thus narratively combined the genesis of the Victorian age with its fully developed problematic complexity, including financial and administrative scandals contemporary with his time of writing. Thus the plot takes several years while feeling as if it stretches several decades: Arthur Clennam's difficulties enact the problem of the Hamlet-like self-consciousness that for Thomas Carlyle vitiated England around 1830, while the cure of his will that Arthur finds by the novel's end marks a fully Victorian rectification of that problem. At the same time, the discovery of Arthur's parentage offers a wishful new genealogy for the Victorian age, from the love and art of Arthur's true mother rather than from the iron will of Mrs. Clennam's Protestant ethic.[12] Yet through the disastrous failure of the fraudulent financier Merdle and the governmental bureaucracy of the Circumlocution Office, Dickens keeps always in sight the pathology of the high Victorian moment, not allowing the imaginary new foundation to obscure continuing urgencies. Moreover, the new lineage and new birth do not wholly work, for Clennam differs from his prototype in Goethe's founding novel of development. Wilhelm Meister passed through a phase of involvement with Hamlet before discovering his true vocation. Clennam remains enveloped by Hamlet, rather than like Wilhelm Meister producing both the play and an interpretation of it, for Dickens produces Arthur through Hamlet.

Arthur's situation is clarified by a reflection from Georg Lukács (citing Marx): "In imagination the individuals under the rule of the bourgeoisie are freer than before, because their conditions of life are more accidental for them; in reality, they are naturally more unfree, because much more subsumed under material power."[13] I am not persuaded that "the" individual under substantially different social orders is the "same" individual. Extending the work of Michel Foucault through study of nineteenth-century statistical inquiry, Ian Hacking concluded that through the new power of a "particular medico-forensic-political language of individual and social control," the "sheer proliferation of labels" may have "engendered vastly more kinds of people than the world had ever known before."[14] That is to say, the increased "material power"—and cultural powers—of the fully developed bourgeois age made possible the specific type of individuality characterized in the quotation from Lukács, an individuality possessing an interior space of problematic freedom that cannot be separated from a strictly limited set of exterior, worldly probabilities. Arthur Clennam is set firmly within the social world Dickens represents: the Protestant ethic of his "mother"; the imperial power of British trade that placed him with his father in China for twenty years; the new bureaucracy satirized for its incompetence while acknowledged in its crucial omnipresence; the entrepreneurial and engineering values of Daniel Doyce's industrial activity; and the "allonging" and "marshonging" of the Democratic Revolution (in terms that give the language of the French revolutionary anthem a distinctly British pronunciation). In the 1820s, the Napoleonic Wars were still a vividly recent memory; in the 1850s, the example of France's return to revolution in 1848 was constantly present to politically concerned Britons.

I want to argue in addition, however, that Arthur has been textually produced by a web of interpretive reading and writing that, despite vigorous effort, escapes him, while he by no means escapes it. *Little Dorrit* is a mystery novel, and what Roland Barthes in *S/Z* called the "hermeneutic code" of the novel is crucially triggered by the repeated appearances of the watch that Arthur sent back from his father's deathbed to Mrs. Clennam.[15] The watch contains a watch-paper on which are cunningly "worked" in beads the letters "D. N. F."[16] They are woman's "work," but they are caught up in the play of a man's testamentary supplement, for the secret to which they point is the codicil to Arthur's great-uncle's will. Arthur sees the watch-paper, suspects that it signals some "wrong to set right,"[17] but he never succeeds in learning the facts. He never even learns of the codicil's existence as such, although as a "folded paper" it is placed into his hands by Little Dorrit with the request that he burn it, which he does.[18] Yet it was the codicil that established the connection between the Clennams and the Dorrits, thus allowing Arthur to meet Little Dorrit, and the watch-paper has provoked the state of anxiety that makes him especially susceptible to interest in her.

As read by Blandois in the middle of the book, the watch-paper contains "cyphers," which "might be almost anything." He deciphers them as "D. N. F.," and proposes that they might be the initials of "some tender, lovely, fascinating fair-creature," but Mrs. Clennam corrects him: They are the initials "of a sentence." That sentence is, "Do Not Forget."[19] We are already tangled in ambiguity, for the three words form a *sentence* of at least three types: grammatically they specify a complete relationship of subject and predicate; they also compose a wise saying, a sententious observation; they have seemed as well to many readers the judgment passed upon Mrs.

Clennam that sentences her to a paralytic preservation of the past. Blandois is, moreover, partially correct in his initial suggestion, for while the signified of these letters is no person (but a sentence), their initial referent was the love relation between Arthur's father and (real) mother, which Mrs. Clennam has hidden from Arthur while pretending to be his mother.

After Arthur's great-uncle tried by the codicil to make amends for this initial suppression, however, the letters took on a different meaning for Arthur's father, who intended by them to remind Mrs. Clennam to put into effect the long-hidden document. Or at least Jeremiah Flintwinch believes that they "could only mean" this.[20] Mrs. Clennam, however, insists that she is right, and she declares, "I do not read it as he did."[21] By this time, for the reader, too, meanings have changed. When we first learned of the watch, Arthur explained to Mrs. Clennam that "it was not until the last, that [his father] expressed the wish; when he could only put his hand upon it, and very indistinctly say to me 'your mother.' A moment before, I thought him wandering in his mind, as he had been for many hours."[22] This could just as well mean that Mr. Clennam wanted Arthur to have this only token of his mother, to whose love and fate his mind has wandered, as that he wished Arthur to bring it to Mrs. Clennam: It may have been intended to mean only love and inadvertently brought Justice, too—but not knowledge.

Wholly unknown to Arthur, despite his suspicions, this network of conflicting interpretations has crucially, although not totally, determined his life. This model of textual efficacy complicates our understanding of what Northrop Frye calls the "archetype" of Hamlet—that is, an element of literary experience that recurs often enough to be recognized—and brings it closer to what Nietzsche called a "sign-chain," the point of which is the differing interpretations to which it has been subjected over a history defined through those reinterpretations.[23] It took some two hundred years for the romantic reading of *Hamlet* to occur, and that reading has now largely passed, but it is crucial to understanding *Little Dorrit* and its place in the shaping of what is still our culturally unreflective sense of the self: that is, what we think of as the self when we don't think about it too hard.

For the "sentence" of the watch-paper alludes to the play that, by the time Dickens wrote, had come to signify within English and German culture the mystery of character, with equal emphasis on both terms. In the closet scene, the ghost of Hamlet's father says to him:

Do not forget. This visitation
Is but to whet thy almost blunted purpose.

But look, amazement on thy mother sits.
O step between her and her fighting soul.[24]

Thus the situation from which the "sentence" is drawn bears immediately upon Arthur's own situation, that of a man caught between his dead father and his morally compromised mother. More fully interpreted, the ghost's words continue to be relevant to Arthur, for the ghost is urging Hamlet to get on with things: Paradoxically, by using his memory, he should whet his purpose for future action, rather than remaining tied to the past.

This problem strikes the keynote of the romantic interpretation of Hamlet, which finds him inhibited, overscrupulous, lacking will. In *Little Dorrit*, within ten lines after Arthur Clennam is named for the first time, he declares, "I have no will," or at least, "next to none that I can put in action now."[25] For he has been "always grinding in a mill I always hated" as a result of his upbringing. The notion of "will" is Janus-faced, pointing back to inheritance and forward to volition.[26] *Little Dorrit* sets both these dimensions to work in Arthur's backward-looking explanation of his problem in facing forward. Not only psychologically, however, as he recognizes, but also legally (and, as we have observed, without his knowledge) Arthur is enmeshed in a problem of inheritance that is resolved only when the codicil is burned—that is, he has a problem about a will in quite another sense. Driven by guilt over a wrong of which he is unconscious, Arthur seeks to find a secret wrong to rectify. At the same time, however, he falls prey to an impotent self-denial, figured in the trope of "nobody" that the book develops around him.[27] Hamlet's romantic problem in Arthur exemplifies Lukács's formula of imaginative freedom ("king of infinite space") cripplingly subsumed under material power ("bounded in a nutshell").[28]

This double problem of Arthur's inheritance that mars his volition may be posed this way: He inherits both secrets and dreams ("It had been the uniform tendency of this man's life . . . to make him a dreamer, after all");[29] his volition is marred both by a drivenness, related to the secrets, and a paralysis, related to the dreams. The paralysis paradoxically carries a positive value to the extent that it preserves Arthur from the fate of Pancks, who is always busy at work for Casby "like a little labouring steam-engine."[30] Yet Arthur's inhibitions and Pancks's compulsions are equally removed from the normative definition of character that John Stuart Mill offered in *On Liberty*: "A person whose desires and impulses are his own—are the expression of his own nature, as it has been developed and modified by his own culture—is said to have character. One whose desires and impulses are not his own, has no character, no more than a steam-engine has character."[31] For in the problematic of the book, Arthur's desires and impulses are not his own but "nobody's."

In the literary development of character in the nineteenth century, the depths, recesses, and intricacies made possible by such self-alienation, rather than Mill's integrity, became the model for what it was to *be* a character (whereas Mill was concerned with the ethical sense of *having* character). And Hamlet offered the model for a character whose identity, emblematized in the problem of his "madness," was marked precisely by his deviation from the ethical norm, as in his apology to Laertes. Like Arthur, he was at once an impotent "John-a-dreams" and compulsively driven into activity by his sense that "the time is out of joint." Hamlet as the exemplary character of romantic criticism exemplifies Foucault's claim in *Discipline and Punish* that a "post-Christian soul" was produced by the new social technologies of the nineteenth century, defined as an individual exactly by means of a pattern of deviations from the norm. Foucault's analysis illuminates why so special a case as Hamlet could also be understood to have such representative significance.

But the production of Arthur Clennam as a character owes more to the aftermath of *Hamlet* than can be accounted for by this inward-turned psychological line I have been pursuing. *Little Dorrit* is not only a novel in the realistic mode; it also draws heavily on gothic elements. *Hamlet*, as well as serving Goethe for the bildungsroman, was the primary earlier literary point of reference (along with *Paradise Lost*) for Horace Walpole and Ann Radcliffe as they founded the mode of gothic prose fiction, paralleled by a line of similar dramas, from Walpole's Oedipal The Mysterious Mother (1768).

In contrast to romantic, bookish inwardness, what I call a projective tradition is associated with the popular stage history of Hamlet and helps to determine the gothic fictional mode so important in *Little Dorrit*. The key figure is the ghost in armor walking the battlements of the castle his brother has usurped from him.[32] In the remarkable unity of place in Shakespeare's play, the castle of Elsinore offered the model for later gothic materializations of the tragic "houses" of legend into the concrete architectural spaces that so concern the novelistic genre. We could speak of a shared claustral imagination. Such charged spaces helped the novel develop its means of concentration, working against the earlier fictional model of picaresque wanderings.

Hamlet is the great model in earlier English literature for the haunting ancestral presences, the ghosts, that define the ambience of the gothic, even when displaced from a fully spectral figure into the discomforting vivacity of a portrait. In *Hamlet*, the ghost's appearance in the closet scene comes directly after Hamlet's comparison between the portraits of his father and Claudius; the portrait of the ancestor standard in gothic fiction becomes in *Little Dorrit* the portrait of Mr. Clennam, associated with Arthur's sense of his mother's hidden wrong: "His picture, dark and gloomy, earnestly speechless on the wall, with the eyes intently looking at his son, as they had looked when life departed from them, seemed to urge him awfully to the task he had attempted."[33] Later, Blandois tauntingly suggests that the portrait seems to utter the ghostly admonition, "Do Not Forget."[34]

Along with the castle, the ghost, and the portrait, the other crucial element *Hamlet* offered to gothic fiction that finds its way emphatically into *Little Dorrit* is the motif of usurpation. Recall the false "patriarch" Casby, who is father to Arthur Clennam's first love; the paternal inadequacies of old Dorrit, "father of the Marshalsea"; or the false motherhood of Mrs. Clennam. *Little Dorrit* is full of false father figures through whom are questioned the privileges of patriarchy, patronage, and gentility, but part of its importance springs from its shift to the false mother, Mrs. Clennam, as the hidden key. Dickens is one of the first to reorient the situation of *Hamlet* toward the mother, as T. S. Eliot and Ernest Jones did in their interpretations of Hamlet, and as Joyce did in *Ulysses*, where Stephen is haunted by his mother.

The gothic in *Little Dorrit* emerges powerfully as Arthur approaches the "grim home of his youth":

> It always affected his imagination as wrathful, mysterious, and sad; and his imagination was sufficiently impressible to see the whole neighbourhood under some tinge of its dark shadow. As he went along, upon a dreary night, the dim streets by which he went, seemed all depositories of oppressive secrets. . . . The shadow still darkening as he drew near the house, the melancholy room which his father once had occupied, haunted by the appealing face he had himself seen fade away with him when there was no other watcher beside the bed, arose before his mind. Its close air was secret. The gloom, and must, and dust of the whole tenement, were secret. At the heart of it, his mother presided . . . firmly holding all the secrets of her own and his father's life, and austerely opposing herself, front to front, to the great final secret of all life.[35]

This passage demonstrates one of the generic transformations that Georg Lukács specified in the shift from historical drama to historical novel around this period. Citing Hegel, he noted that drama has as its unity a totality of action, but epic (which in this case includes novel) a totality of objects.[36] The London world of counting houses, books, papers, chests, safes, keys, church vaults, iron coffers—all of which I passed over in abridging the passage—provides the world of "things" that etymologically is what "realism" is about.[37]

Lukács notes too that from *King Lear* to Balzac's *Père Goriot*, interest shifts to Rastignac, the figure corresponding to Edgar.[38] That is, the novel differs from both epic and tragedy in focusing on the unheroic, the younger generation. Even at its most serious, the novel carries traces of comic plot form.

Goethe's interpretation through Wilhelm Meister of the contrast between novel and drama as that between retardation and rapidity already begins to find *Hamlet* novelistic in its "expansiveness," and Wilhelm's distinction between the activity of the dramatic hero and the passivity of the unheroic novelistic protagonist also aligns *Hamlet* with the novel.[39] But *Hamlet* differs from all of Shakespeare's other major tragedies because the identity of its protagonist remains to be forged. Unlike Othello, Antony, King Lear, Coriolanus, or Macbeth, Hamlet has no heroic preexistence. It was his father who "smote the sledded Polacks on the ice."[40] If in this sense he is more oriented to the future than they are, he is at the same time more bound to the past. He lives in the aftermath of someone else's dreadful action, the crime of his mother and stepfather—with which he must come to terms that are not his own to set.

Through the gothic, we have returned to ground more familiar to modern readers for thinking about Hamlet. This "inner" tradition of understanding Hamlet is intimately related to the romantic project of self-production. For the castle of Hamlet becomes not only the gothic house of the Clennams but also the prison so crucial for the plot and decor of *Little Dorrit*. Recall that Hamlet's imagination is not just claustral but carceral: "Denmark's a prison."[41] Yet contained within that enclosure is the possibility of an inner richness. Hamlet could be "bounded in a nutshell" yet still consider himself "king of infinite space." We return to Foucault's argument in *Discipline and Punish* for the role of prisons and comparable institutions in producing what he called the "post-Christian soul"—what we may take as character. *Hamlet* stands on both sides of a cultural debate crucial for the formation of English romanticism: *Hamlet* fostered the "gross and violent stimulants" that Wordsworth rejected in gothicism in his 1800 preface to *Lyrical Ballads*, but another Hamlet was involved in the delicacy by which the romantics constructed their alternatives to the gothic.

I am calling the romantic production of the self the cultural work shared by Wordsworth's poetry and Coleridge's criticism and metaphysics, and then by their interpreters through the nineteenth century. The distinctions I have drawn from Lukács seem to me especially valuable not because I believe in the genre categories of German idealism, but because Lukács is one of the few to have reflected in any terms on the tremendous change in medium that Shakespeare underwent in this period. The romantic Hamlet leaves drama and the stage to enter narrative and critical writing.

These were the decades that Shakespeare's "own" text was restored to its full authority on the stage, denying the opportunity to make Shakespeare "our contemporary" that the Restoration and eighteenth century had exercised. In the same vein of responsibility to Shakespeare—however different and mistaken it seems to us now—the "authenticity" of settings was insisted on, making for stifling antiquarian baggage and a radically reified mise-en-scène.[42] Just at the time of this double monumentalization, verbal and visual, the energies of Shakespeare seemed to pass over from the stage into prose narrative. I mean above all the novel, but it is worth recalling how much else there was. Charles and Mary Lamb in their *Tales from Shakespeare* (1806–7) turned the plays into popular narratives for children. Anna Jameson (1832) and Mary Cowden Clarke (1852), wife of Keats's friend Charles Cowden Clarke, published books on Shakespeare's heroines that explored their lives offstage.[43]

Charles Lamb's essay on the suitability of Shakespeare's plays for "stage-representation" (1811) enunciates the fullest version of a position that he shares with Coleridge and Hazlitt.[44] He shows that you cannot interpret Shakespeare merely by repeating his words, which is what actors do; he must be interpreted by more, different words. Shakespearean exegesis can only be critical, textual, rather than dramatic—soulwork, not bodily gesture. This antitheatrical understanding of Shakespeare also strongly determines such Victorian works as Carlyle's treatment of Shakespeare in "The Hero as Poet" and Melville's interpretation of Shakespeare in "Hawthorne and His Mosses," in which he lays out the premises that were being put into practice in *Moby-Dick* (which narrativizes a certain understanding of *King Lear*).

A beginning for this romantic shift from the expressively theatricalized to the meditatively interiorized may be registered in Wordsworth's early drama *The Borderers*, which was never staged and remained unpublished from its completion in 1797 until 1842. It is notable that Wordsworth prefaced the play with the earliest piece I know of romantic character criticism, analyzing the villain Oswald (Rivers). The lines I am about to quote became famous long before they were published. However much recent critics might argue that they are unrepresentative of the play's overall message, spoken as they are by the villain, and as part of a temptation, they were quoted by Hazlitt, by Evert Duyckinck in his review of Hawthorne's *Mosses from an Old Manse*, and most notably by Coleridge in his lecture on *Hamlet*:

> Action is transitory—a step, a blow,
> The motion of a muscle—this way or that—
> 'Tis done, and in the after-vacancy
> We wonder at ourselves like men betrayed:
> Suffering is permanent, obscure and dark,
> And shares the nature of infinity.[45]

Trapped in the sublime recesses of interiority, the richness of character is formed at the expense of action.

My argument holds that between *Hamlet* and *Little Dorrit* there intervened a series of cultural shifts mediated by the romantic critics of Shakespeare, who staged him in their writings. The corpus of this criticism provides a third intertextual strand for Dickens's work. Dickens was saturated in the Shakespearean milieu of the 1830s and 1840s. By 1824, Carlyle, whom Dickens admired beyond all other contemporaries, had translated *Wilhelm Meister*, but in fact Goethe's discussion of *Hamlet* had been separately translated almost immediately. August Wilhelm Schlegel's *Lectures on Dramatic Literature* was translated (1815) by John Black, with whom Dickens was associated in the 1830s on the *Morning Chronicle*.[46] Also around that paper was Dickens's friend Thomas Noon Talfourd, who put together an edition of Lamb in 1840. No idiosyncratic "influences" are required to account for the traces of *Hamlet* in *Little Dorrit*, however much interest may follow from close comparative reading of the two.

My emphasis now is not on Dickens but on the broader cultural process. In seeing himself in Hamlet, Coleridge helped renew the figure for its further cultural life in the nineteenth century, but Coleridge was hardly a less special character than Hamlet himself. William Hazlitt performed the necessary generalization by which Hamlet was turned from a Renaissance prince to a petty bourgeois of the nineteenth century, which allowed Hazlitt to proclaim, "It is *we* who are Hamlet." Hazlitt transforms the figure of the play—both verbal and theatrical—into his own typification, elements of which are reprocessed in Dickens's narrative reindividualization:

Whoever has become thoughtful and melancholy through his own mishaps or those of others; whoever has borne about with him the clouded brow of reflection, and thought himself "too much i' th' sun"; . . . whoever has known "the pangs of despised love, the insolence of office, or the spurns which patient merit oft of the unworthy takes"; he who has felt his mind sink within him, and sadness cling to his heart like a malady, who has had his hopes blighted and his youth staggered by the apparitions of strange things; who cannot be well at ease, while he sees evil hovering near him like a spectre; whose powers of action have been eaten up by thought. . . . This is the true Hamlet.[47]

The "grave dark" face of Clennam—literally "clouded" and like Hamlet too much the "son" in other senses also—his alienated love for Pet, the insolence of the Circumlocution Office to a man who "wants to know," the gothic apparitions, all these combine to give us an Arthur Clennam–Hamlet. Hamlet's mysteriousness, his unheroism, his alienation as what Goethe called a "stranger in the scene which from his youth he had looked upon as his inheritance," all these for the romantics had become his universality—no longer an individual so much as the paradigm for all individuality.

From what he considered Hamlet's universal popularity, Coleridge surmised that "this character must have some common connection with the laws of our nature."[48] Here the path lies open to Freud's analysis of Hamlet along with Oedipus in discovering what he came to call the "Oedipus complex." Freud's theoretical matrix finally provided a justification for the interpretive method to which Wilhelm Meister had felt driven. Wilhelm was unable to make any sense of *Hamlet* as a whole until after "investigating every trace of Hamlet's character, as it had shown itself before his father's death." This genetic method was the key to the romantic Hamlet, as well as to the novelistic procedure that combined with the new techniques of social discipline to produce the kind of character that Freud could then analyze. In this history, *Little Dorrit*, I have argued, stands at a triple intersection: *Hamlet* as theatricalized, as novelized by Goethe, and as theorized by Coleridge.

4. *The Struggle for the Cultural Heritage: Christina Stead Refunctions Charles Dickens and Mark Twain*

The received cultural values with which we academic literary intellectuals most closely involve ourselves are the values of the "cultural treasures," the canonized masterpieces, for which we serve our students as intermediaries.[1] In the years between the first and the second world wars, the established canon and its transmission faced strenuous challenge and probing discussion, not just, as our training leads us to expect, because of modernism, but also through the revolutionary and reactionary political struggles of those years. The debates over proletarian culture and socialist realism in the Soviet Union counted heavily for the production and mediation of literature through the Western world. The French political strategy of the Popular Front first became visible as a cultural force the year before the Blum government was elected when in 1935 the League of Writers for the Defense of Culture sponsored a huge international conference.[2]

Prominent on the agenda for that conference stood the topic "The Cultural Heritage," and at the second League conference, held in 1936, André Malraux addressed this topic with remarkable vigor. Amplifying observations from 1935, he defined the "cultural heritage" as created by each civilization "out of everything in the past that helps it to surpass itself." This is no passive reception but an active struggle: "A heritage is not transmitted; it must be conquered."[3] The antithesis of this position emerged a few years later in Walter Benjamin's "Theses on the Philosophy of History," written at a moment when the Popular Front (which Benjamin had never supported) could be judged a dreadful mistake. Benjamin emphasized that "cultural treasures" form part of "the triumphal procession in which the present rulers step over those who are lying prostrate," for "there is no document of civilization which is not at the same time a document of barbarism."[4]

I want to explore the dialectic between these positions through the case of Christina Stead's novel of 1940, *The Man Who Loved Children*, which takes two cultural treasures of Popular Front leftist humanism, Charles

Dickens and Mark Twain, and shatters them as false idols, even while finding within their works resources that make Stead's own work possible. This
critical redeployment of cultural power I analyze as what Brecht and Benjamin called "refunctioning" (*Umfunktionierung*).[5] This exploration touches
on issues still relevant to our current cultural and political debates, ranging
from the values of "totality" and the strategies of feminism to the methods
by which literary studies may be put in touch with the study of mass media
and popular culture, a contemporary intellectual refunctioning.

I

Little direct connection can be positively established between Charles Dickens and Mark Twain. Sam Clemens was seen carrying volumes of Dickens
in Keokuk in the 1850s, but he was ashamed to admit that he never really
read them.[6] He attended a performance of Dickens's reading tour in
America in 1867, but he doubtless paid more attention to Olivia Langdon,
his future wife, with whom he was on his first date.[7] From such incidents I
take the moral that Dickens was for Twain, as Twain himself later became
for many Americans, a cultural presence that extended far beyond the
merely literary act of really reading.

Typically, Dickens and Twain have been brought together for contrast.
From the beginning, Twain's originality was set against the Dickensian imi-
tativeness of Bret Harte,[8] and if the project that led to *Tom Sawyer* bore some
relation to *David Copperfield*, that relation was burlesque. James Cox has
strikingly remarked on the disappearance of Dickens's early pseudonym,
"Boz," while "Mark Twain" wholly displaced Samuel Clemens.[9] In *The
Ordeal of Mark Twain*, the study that formed twentieth-century critical debate on Twain, Van Wyck Brooks some half-dozen times set Dickens
against Twain: Dickens succeeded in using "experience" as the basis for socially independent satire, in contrast to Twain's socially disarming and dis-
armed humor.[10]

The most telling connection was made by William Dean Howells, who
linked the two as preeminent among the world's great comic writers for
their "humanity."[11] More recently this has been elaborated by students of
popular culture: Dickens, and then Twain, became a "celebrity" by representing "the common sense and basic goodness of the mass of the people."[12]
In the 1930s, however, such insights were only formulated about each of the
writers separately. George Orwell singled out in Dickens a "good tempered
antinomianism," an opposition to laws and codes that Orwell considered

characteristic of "western popular culture."[13] Newton Arvin, in a centennial evaluation of 1935, judged that Twain would survive as a "grand half-legendary personality," loved for his "largeness and sweetness."[14]

Yet it was also in the 1930s that Christina Stead's major novel achieved what I still find the most powerful specific conjunction of Dickens and Twain. Stead was born in 1902 and died in 1983. From her native Australia, she came in 1928 to London, where she met and loved a Marxist journalist and financier named William Blake, with whom she lived until his death in 1968. They were in Paris from 1929 through 1935, and then in the United States from 1937 through 1946.[15] *The Man Who Loved Children* was written in the United States, has an American setting, and offers an intimate yet distanced interpretation of America.

Stead's link to Dickens is already well established by Joan Lidoff in her standard introductory study. Stead observed in an interview that "Dickens was in the family" as she grew up.[16] She was pleased to speculate that her grandfather had left England for Australia inspired by Magwitch's success as a sheep farmer in Dickens's *Great Expectations*. In *The Man Who Loved Children*, the father of the "man" puts on a Dickensian family entertainment:

> Come on, granddaughter! The Old One's about to present "Mr. Wemmick and the Aged Parent." Come along, come along, roll up, roll up, come right in, the show's just about to begin! All star performance: manager, Charles Pollit; business manager, Charlie Pollit; stage manager, Chas. Pollit, and the Aged, played by Charles Pollit. You must excuse, not stare at, the redundancy of that beautiful name Pollit, in the cast, ladies and gentlemen, if there be any of that name here, for it's all in the family. And the play written by Charles—Dickens, the greatest Charlie![17]

Sam Pollit, the "man" of the title and son of Charles Pollit, shares with his father the manic verbal inventiveness that is here attributed to Dickens as source. In such details as the ringing of changes on the name (Charles, Charlie, Chas.), Stead has caught and transmitted precise Dickensian characteristics, but also more largely in the whole parental mode of Sam Pollit's "love," enchanting in its constant flow of names, games, and rhymes.

Dickens and Stead form a familiar topic, but Twain's significance for her has not been discussed. Yet we read on the very first page that the title character, Sam Pollit, has as his full name "Samuel Clemens Pollit" (as if there were a genealogy from Charles the father to Sam the son, from the English comic genius to the American). Perhaps only an Australian, and a woman at that, could have sufficient distance to allow the images of Dickens and

Twain thus to superimpose, and from the perspective of "down under" they come out topsy-turvy.

Stead's constellation of Dickens and Twain may suggest something like what Harold Bloom called the creation of a "composite precursor," or else the kind of process Sandra Gilbert and Susan Gubar followed Virginia Woolf in analyzing for women writers, who must conjure away the "Milton's bogey" of male literary authority.[18] As opposed to the theories of the unconscious and repression that undergird both these positions, however, the debate in the 1930s over the cultural heritage makes it possible to understand Stead's novel in terms of a conscious revisionary polemic, that is, refunctioning. To understand this precisely requires some immersion in the book's specifics.

The Man Who Loved Children presents the life of a family from 1936 to 1938: Sam Pollit, in his late thirties; his second wife, Henrietta ("Henny"); his daughter Louisa ("Louie"), whose mother died in her infancy; and the five, later six, children of Sam and Henny. From the Baltimore fish market to world conferences on fisheries, Sam has risen from poverty to become a federal conservation bureaucrat, self-made with the help of connections from Henny's wealthy family. From the first page, man and wife rarely sleep, or even speak, together, and things get much worse, both financially and emotionally, yet Louie achieves a precocious adolescent independence, which carries the book's positive weight.

Sam and Henny, father and mother, are both terrible and wonderful, and above all *different* from each other: "He called a spade the predecessor of modern agriculture, she called it a muck dig: they had no words between them intelligible."[19] Different languages mean different ways of seeing the world:

> What a dreary stodgy world of adults the children saw when they went out! And what a moral, high minded world their father saw! But for Henny there was a wonderful particular world, and when they went with her they saw it: they saw the fish eyes, the crocodile grins, the hair like a birch broom, the mean men crawling with maggots, and the children restless as an eel that she saw . . . all these wonderful creatures, who swarmed in the streets, stores, and restaurants of Washington, ogling, leering, pulling, pushing, stinking, overscented, screaming and boasting.[20]

The grotesque energy of Henny's language is inseparable from her vision—saying and seeing cohere—and these different ways of seeing the world further ramify into differing ways of being in the world: "There were excitement, fun, joy, and even enchantment with both mother and father, and it was just a question of whether one wanted to sing, gallop about, and put on a performance ('showing off like all Pollitry,' said Henny), or look for mysteries ('Henny's room is a chaos,' said Sam)."[21] The surface clarity of "performance" in Dickens and Twain, Stead has isolated in Sam, while Henny shares their literary, textual "mysteries."

Stead explains these differences less by sheer human idiosyncrasy or by any biological distinctions between the sexes than by a socially produced dynamic of inequalities. Henny is aware of sinking from a higher economic position and of being oppressed because she is a woman, and her dark poetry springs from this consciousness. Despite setbacks, Sam is rising from a lower economic origin, and as a man he is master in the family. Louie will become an artist and thus (in the book's logic) declassed, yet also member of a rising sex.

Henny's angry claims for the "rights of woman," not just the American rights of man always on Sam's lips, her siding with "all women against all men" in the "outlawry of womankind," come only through painful recognition, across class lines, of women's fellowship as "cheap servants," an equality in degradation: "I hate her but I hate myself."[22] Even the power available to women through marriage can only be grasped in self-torment, as Henny meditates on her wedding band:

> If this plain ugly link meant an eyeless eternity of work and poverty and an early old age, it also meant that to her alone this potent breadwinner owed his money, name, and fidelity, to her, his kitchen-maid and body servant.
> For a moment, after years of scamping, she felt the dread power of wifehood; they were locked in each other's grasp till the end—the end, a mouthful of sunless muck-worms and grass roots stifling his blare of trumpets and her blasphemies against love.[23]

Sam's position blends classic patriarchy with modern social progressivism. The book powerfully suggests that while patriarchal family relations persist, there is little good to be hoped for from many otherwise promising developments. Here Stead tellingly challenges the limitations of "humanity" as Howells found it in Dickens and Twain, but also as it was found in the Popular Front rhetoric of Franklin Roosevelt's second term, a blissfully strange moment when "Marxists were not revolutionaries and liberals were not pessimists."[24]

Sam's paternalism is unembarrassed in his explanation to Louie that "a woman must not leave her father's home until she goes to her husband: that is what I am here for, to look after you." Later he more menacingly insists, "You are coming home to me, and I am going to watch every book you read, every thought you have." Over the whole globe he wishes for the same knowledge he desires to have of his daughter: "to know my fellow man to the utmost . . . to penetrate into the hearts of dark, yellow, red, tawny, and tattooed man. For I believe that they are all the same man at heart and that a good one; and they can be brought together sooner or later by their more advanced brothers into a world fellowship, in which all differences of nationality, creed, or education will be respected and gradually smoothed out, and eventually the religion of all men will be one and the same."[25]

The next paragraph displays this fantasy of penetration and homogenization, omniscience and omnipotence, as inseparable from Sam's masculinity and misogyny:

> Louisa was propping herself up against the railing. She was staring at her father absently. The morning was hot, and Sam had nothing on beneath his painting overalls. When he waved his golden-white muscular hairless arms, large damp tufts of yellow-red hair appeared. He kept on talking. The pores on his well-stretched skin were very large, his leathery skin was quite unlike the dull silk of the children's cheeks. He was not ashamed of his effluvia, thought it a gift that he sweated so freely; it was "natural." The scent that women used, he often remarked, was to cover lack of washing![26]

As the passage goes on, the political ugliness of Sam's vision becomes manifest:

> "My system," Sam continued, "which I invented myself, might be called *Monoman* or *Manunity*!"
>
> . . . Louisa said, "You mean Monomania." . . .
>
> Sam said coolly, "You look like a gutter rat, Looloo, with that expression. Monoman would only be the condition of the world after we had weeded out the misfits and degenerates." There was a threat in the way he said it.[27]

Stead makes us imagine an etymology in which "*weed*ing" means to form by exclusion a purified "we."

After Sam returns from the expedition to Malaya that had in prospect stimulated the fantasy of Monoman, his plans elaborate in a panoptic hope reminiscent of Michel Foucault's *Discipline and Punish*:

> Sam, a great partisan of the Roosevelt Works plans . . . and seeing with pleasure new works being acquired from several states and placed under the surveillance or control of federal bureaus, saw in President Roosevelt the first

great socialist ruler. . . . He favored a bureaucratic state socialism with the widest possible powers and a permanent staff, a bureaucracy intricately engineered, which would gradually engulf all the powers of [government]. . . . In his mind's eye he saw internations within internations; and overnations over nations, all separate functions of Federal Government rising to one crest of supreme judgment, sitting in a room; all glass, no doubt, with windows on the world.[28]

This "modern" American imperial administration, spurred by "public necessity's eminent domain," will replace the outmoded British Empire (as "Sam" follows "Charles").

The continuity that extends from the familial to the global in Sam's vision does not overlook—rather it intends to oversee—the local as well: "If I had my way—if I were Stalin or Hitler . . .—I would abolish schools altogether for children . . . and would form them into communities with a leader, something like I am myself, a natural leader, for only man learns in communities, he is a social animal."[29] Here the rhetoric of "community," so prevalent in the American thirties, is inseparable from a powerfully individualizing desire.[30]

Sam's vision returns to the domestic on a Sunday when he is "to superintend the housework and show them all how easily it could be managed by 'system' and 'scientific management'"; in other words, the household is to enjoy what Sam calls a "new deal." So, "commanding from his honorable position behind the coffee cup," he "made Little Womey [for "Little Woman," the Dickensian sobriquet Sam accords to Henny's daughter] and Looloo scrape and stack the dishes in the washbasin."[31] In America of the 1930s, it was widely understood that the phrase "New Deal" for Roosevelt's programs to combat the Depression derived from what Hank Morgan promised to Arthurian England in Twain's *Connecticut Yankee*.[32]

Even after the debacle of his family life and loss of his government career, Sam is eager to rebound with a radio show, in which he will be known as "Uncle Sam" and will teach the lore of America.[33] In the last decade of Mark Twain's life he was identified with the American national icon of Uncle Sam.[34]

II

Samuel Clemens Pollit—Stead's composite figure of Charles Dickens and Mark Twain as petit-bourgeois paterfamilias and socialist booster of the

1930s—allows her to explore, at once critically and imaginatively, the cultural meanings that Dickens and Twain took on in their historical afterlives. She forces upon us the question, "What are they good for now?" Such revisionary inquiry was provoked, not only for Stead but also for many others, by the social and economic crises of the 1930s, in which a whole way of life across the Western world was felt to be changing, and further to *need* changing. The Popular Front relied upon the belief that change could happen without a painful struggle against existing values. Stead came to think otherwise. Her criticism of the Popular Front is inscribed not only in her critique of humanism through Dickens and Twain but also, very precisely, in the family name of Samuel Clemens Pollit. For Harry Pollitt (1890–1960), a founding member of the Communist Party of Great Britain and its secretary from 1929, became a nationally visible political figure after 1936, when the Popular Front allowed his gifts as a "warm-hearted personality" to flourish (according to the *Dictionary of National Biography*).[35]

Revisionary undertakings by some of Stead's contemporaries are better known to history. Our current institutional forms of literary study owe much to F. R. Leavis's journal *Scrutiny* (begun 1932) and to the overall project summarized in the title of his book *Revaluation* (1936). In the United States, F. O. Matthiessen's *American Renaissance* (1941) established a canon of great American authors with such authority that we often forget its recent creation. In Europe during these same years, to meditate on the relations between form and life in the classic novel, especially that of the nineteenth century, seemed of crucial moment to Georg Lukács, the Hungarian Communist activist seeking refuge in Moscow; to Erich Auerbach, the German Jewish civil servant fled to Istanbul; to Mikhail Bakhtin, the Russian Christian polymath exiled to Kazakhstan.[36]

These great European critics of the novel stimulate insight into *The Man Who Loved Children*. Following Auerbach, it is at once more "everyday" than work by Dickens and Twain in its attention to sheer domestic routine, and more "serious" because its existential problematic is not discounted by the conventions of comedy, funny as the book often is. Following Bakhtin, its play of voices comes closer to Dostoevsky than to Dickens or Twain, in presenting alternative ways of life, embodied ideologies, among which the choice is not obvious. In contrast, Twain's scrupulous verisimilitude in rendering dialect variations does nothing to challenge the priority of Huck's values. Above all, Stead's work, like Solzhenitsyn's later, vindicates Lukács's claim, against both naturalism and modernism, that the power of critical realism remained available to a writer who was not afraid to face history. I think there is no doubt that the apparent anachronism of Stead's technique helps account for the neglect of her novel when first published, no less than what seemed the anachronism of feminist concerns.[37]

Yet such textually oriented reading as these great critics point to is somewhat beside the point for Stead's work with Dickens and Twain. She operates on the *images* of Dickens and Twain that the various media of culture had elaborated from their books, and at least equally from their lives. Once worked up and set loose, these images could circulate as signs for cultural values. Stead here approaches certain concerns of postmodern fiction such as E. L. Doctorow's *Ragtime* and Robert Coover's *Public Burning*. How could she acquire such a perspective so precociously? In the first place, even more than Pound, Joyce, and Eliot, she came from an imperial margin that knew the heart of Western culture only at a painfully felt distance of symbolic mediation (see her Australian revision of Hardy's Tess in *For Love Alone*, 1944). And then she went on to discover, through Blake's emphasis on economic theory and through her own immersion in international finance and commodity trade, that what drove that heart was itself another circulation of signs (see Stead's novel *House of All Nations*, 1938).

By cultural "images," I mean what Newton Arvin referred to as Twain's "grand, half-legendary personality," his immortality "less as a writer . . . than as a figure."[38] A decade earlier, Edmund Wilson had observed of Twain that "the man is more impressive than his work," and later he would insist of Dickens that "it is necessary to see him as a man."[39] Orwell concludes his essay on Dickens with the sense that what remains is "the face of a man who is generously angry."[40] This strikingly, and independently, echoes Walter Benjamin's "The Storyteller," which ends by defining the storyteller as "the figure [*Gestalt*] in which the righteous man encounters himself."[41]

Criticism had at this time the half-avowed task of humanist mythmaking, the production through reading of culturally potent images by which to sustain and orient ourselves in a time of historical crisis. Orwell, Wilson, Arvin, and Benjamin were all politically on the left, and at least in Wilson and Orwell, writing after the disillusions resulting from the Moscow Trials, the Spanish civil war, and the Molotov-Ribbentrop Pact, the image of human comprehensibility, a face that could be reliably known, compensated for political duplicity. The prestige of the *Gestalt* ("figure," "shape," "totality") appears also in radical social theory. Drawing upon not only his Resistance work but also upon his attendance at Alexandre Kojève's lectures on Hegel during the thirties, Maurice Merleau-Ponty wrote, "To be a Marxist is to believe that economic problems and cultural or human problems are a single problem and that the proletariat as history has shaped it holds the solution to that problem. In modern language, it is to believe that history has a *Gestalt*."[42] This context renders even more telling the force with which Jacques Lacan analyzed the role in ego development played by the "imaginary" production of an ideal figure (he uses the German *Gestalt*) of human wholeness.[43] His theory of the "mirror-stage," first proposed in 1936, turns away from such humanism.

Stead for her part draws little cheer from the human face of history. Her figure of Sam Pollit as Dickens and Twain appropriates human images that had been displaced from the relatively autonomous realm of literature into the culture at large then combines those images and sets them to work again within a new piece of literature, which allows for a fresh exploration of their possible effects, thus giving them a different force when they again are shifted from her literary work into the larger culture, and her readers' lives. This is refunctioning.

If her view of Dickens and Twain, and their meaning for America, is less positive than Wilson's or Orwell's or Arvin's, it is not because she is reactionary (like T. S. Eliot, who opposed "apeneck" Sweeney to Emersonian humanist historical optimism), but because she is writing as a woman. The worst trouble with Sam, her book shows, is patriarchy, his position within a socially established structure of sex and gender domination that even the organized left of the 1930s neglected.

Only a few years earlier, Stead had not criticized but had herself enacted such neglect. When in 1935 the first great cultural event of the Popular Front, the Congress of the League of Writers for the Defense of Culture, was held in Paris, Stead reported on it for the English journal *Left Review*. Her language in this report routinely casts writers in the masculine (e. g., "He rises to defend what has come to him from his father").[44] More than that, however, she writes with a normative, positivist biologism that in *The Man Who Loved Children* only Sam approaches: Writers who "enter the political arena" and "take lessons from workmen" will then "use their pen as a scalpel for lifting up the living tissues, cutting through the morbid tissues, of the social anatomy." And as their art is hygienic, so are their bodies: "The hall was not full of half-feminine masculine revolutionaries and half-masculine feminine rebels. They were neat, had no postures and poses."[45] Many years later, interviewed in 1973, Stead denied any identification with the contemporary women's liberation movement: "It's eccentric. It's not a genuine movement. It's totally, purely middle class."[46] Nonetheless, I think any reader now will find *The Man Who Loved Children* a serious feminist critique of domestic patriarchy and its larger ramifications.

The composite figure of Dickens and Twain adds something special. It emphasizes how marvelously, almost irresistibly fascinating and attractive that patriarchal power can be. Michel Foucault made a fundamental observation: "If power was never anything but repressive, if it never did anything but say no, do you really believe that we should manage to obey it? What gives power its hold . . . [is that] it does not simply weigh like a force that says no, but that it runs through and produces things; it induces pleasure."[47] Not only for men, but also for women, escaping patriarchy requires abandoning pleasures that we know as cultural treasures, and as forms of daily life; it requires learning to resist the "love" that "the man" offers, which keeps us "children" by producing and reproducing a system of domination.

All biographies make clear the magnetic personal power that Dickens and Twain enjoyed over those who knew and loved them, but what were their family lives like? Already by the 1930s, serious questions had begun to arise. Bechofer Roberts's novel *This Side Idolatry* imagined Dickens's cruelty to his wife,[48] and Gladys Storey's *Dickens and Daughter* (1939) offers filial testimony that "nothing could surpass the misery and unhappiness of our home."[49] So Stead's Louie never tells outsiders about home life because "no one would believe me," but she can no longer bear the "daily misery," the "horror of everyday life."[50] More recently, Hamlin Hill in *God's Fool* exposed the last years of Twain's life, but sensitized by Stead, we may reinterpret even material that Albert Bigelow Paine had considered appropriate for his adulatory biography. At the same early adolescent age as Stead's Louie, Twain's daughter Susy began to keep a diary, above all to capture her father's performances, which he made sure to put on for her: "He told us the other day that he couldn't bear to hear anyone talk but himself, but that he could listen to himself talk for hours without getting tired, of course he said this in joke, but I've no doubt it was founded on truth."[51] As Sam launches one of his enraptured monologues, he notices Louie writing. Flattered by the expectation that she is recording his wisdom, he looks over to see, "Shut up, shut up, shut up, shut up, shut up, I can't stand your gassing, oh, what a windbag . . ."[52]

In *The Ordeal of Mark Twain*, Van Wyck Brooks presented his case for attention to Twain's domestic life: Since what writers think and feel is "largely determined by personal circumstances and affections," and since "no one will deny that Mark Twain's influence upon our society has been, either in a positive or in a negative way, profound," we must therefore reckon with such matters. Brooks's debunking has certain affinities with Stead's, but they are separated by a fundamental gap, that of Brooks's virulent misogyny. For he argues that New England was "literally emasculated," and that cultural power consequently passed to "old maids" who worked their wills through Twain's wife Olivia, ensuring that his subservience to her dulled any serious critical edge his work might have had.[53] In Stead's book, by contrast, Sam carries on Victorian sentimental petit-bourgeois prudery, while Henny practices nihilistic critique. Stead has reversed the gender values and thus suggests, as against Brooks, that our culture needs but suppresses the criticism women could offer.

Edmund Wilson found in Brooks's Twain a model for repressed duality that gave Wilson the basis for his revaluation of Dickens as a covert rebel. In appropriating Brooks's model, Wilson enacted a transvaluation with large consequences for academic literary study. For in Brooks the structure of psychological duality explained the divided forces in Twain's work and thus accounted for his failure to achieve the highest literary greatness. Wilson, however, adopts the structure of Brooks's Twain to analyze Dickens, while carrying on from Brooks the positive judgment that Dickens's laughter was socially subversive (as Twain's had not been). By Wilson's dialectic of "the wound and the bow" (like Yeats's insistence on choice between perfection of life or work), the misery of the life explains the great energies of the work. Even though Wilson has been understood as differing from New Critics by his emphasis upon history and biography, the principle of paradox works as crucially for him as for them, the wish to find in division not damaging fracture but strengthening tension.

George Orwell judged otherwise the effect of Dickens's duality: "Dickens seems to have succeeded in attacking everybody and antagonizing nobody. Naturally this makes one wonder whether after all there was something unreal in his attack upon society."[54] Compare Paine's description of *Innocents Abroad* as "the most daring book of its day," yet received with overwhelming acclaim.[55] I think too how hard it proves to persuade students that the slavery denounced by *Huckleberry Finn* already had been abolished when Twain wrote. I do not mean that popularity automatically makes it impossible for a work to exert socially critical effects; *Uncle Tom's Cabin* powerfully demonstrates the contrary.[56] However, some forms of liberal self-criticism are almost impossible to separate from complacency, and therefore radical refunctioning may be needed to set loose the work's potential power.

Both Dickens and Twain were phenomenal successes, parvenus who married up from declining, marginally respectable families and then sky-rocketed far beyond. So in their own lives they were always at once the progressive opposition and the status quo itself. Indeed, Marx and Baudelaire could agree that it was the nature of the bourgeoisie to be progressive.[57] And Foucault's work underlined the support individualists like Dickens and Twain gave to the growth of the repressive state apparatus. So Sam Pollit is a self-made man devoted to the growth of agencies of social control, both one who is already a master (as a male) and one whose day is yet to come (because of his economic deprivation).[58]

III

My argument, then, holds that neither Dickens nor Twain is absolutely, objectively, critical, complacent, subversive, or anything else. If we accept Benjamin's claim that "there is no document of civilization which is not at the same time a document of barbarism," then it will depend upon circumstances which aspect we emphasize. There are different ways of using cultural objects. To take this seriously requires that we reconceptualize the books and authors we study. It requires abandoning "literature" as an autonomous sphere of aesthetic contemplation and it requires instead thinking about "media" as potentialities for mediation between the parties in particular cultural transactions. Dickens and Twain, of course, never distanced themselves from either journalism or the speaker's platform, and Sam Pollit's move onto radio charts the next step.

At the 1936 Congress of the League of Writers for the Defense of Culture, held in London, André Malraux defined the "cultural heritage" as created by each civilization "out of everything in the past that helps it to surpass itself," for "A heritage is not transmitted, it must be conquered." With less grandiloquence, but to the same effect, Orwell began his essay on Dickens, "Dickens is one of those writers who are well worth stealing." That is, he begins as another's and must be made one's own. This dialectic of alienation and appropriation motivates Orwell's pioneering exploration of mass-culture "Boys' Weeklies" no less than his study of Dickens: He wants to figure out how to write such things with a left-wing slant, to reach an otherwise inaccessible audience. For to Orwell, "All art is propaganda."[59]

This process of redeploying cultural powers, I have been describing (after Brecht and Benjamin) as refunctioning. So we could say of Stead that her technique refunctions the modernist use of myth. She takes not hallowed myths (as Joyce did in using the *Odyssey,* or Eliot the grail quest) but cultural images just beginning to acquire the apparently independent power of myth. Her content refunctions the critical *Gestalt* of Dickens and Twain. Refusing to validate them either by showing their continuing relevance (Ulysses in Dublin) or by decrying their contemporary degradation (the waste land in London), instead she criticizes them. Her tone refunctions the very "irreverence" that characterized the masculine comic philistine humanist genius of Dickens and Twain and makes it into a woman's weapon against them. In adapting the novel of adolescent development so vividly revitalized in English by Charlotte Brontë in *Jane Eyre,* Stead does not return directly to the passionate intensity of her female predecessor; she works with and against the literary history by which men had remade Brontë's form, as in *David Copperfield* and *Huckleberry Finn,* and she obliquely refunctions it.

Finally, Stead's book itself contains a model of such refunctioning; it not only enacts but also represents the process. A remarkable sequence begins with Sam's trying to educate Louie about sex. He gives her three books: "Shelley's *Poems* (to help her poetry, said he), Frazer's *Golden Bough* (for the anthropological side of the question, said he), and James Bryce's book on Belgian atrocities (to explain our entry into war and the need for America's policing the world, said he). . . . From the latter two books Louie was able to fill her daydreams and night thoughts with the mysteries of men's violence." Not Frazer and Bryce but Shelley most captivates her. At one point she declaims some startling verses from *The Cenci*, Shelley's tragedy of rape and murder, the conspiracy of fathers against a daughter, which disturb Sam until he is "reassured by the book in her hand, the very one he had given her." She writes her own "Tragedy of the Snakeman," made up of one terrible scene between father and daughter, clearly derived from her excited response to *The Cenci*. She casts it into a language she has invented, which baffles Sam completely.[60] It begins with the father: "Ia deven fecen sigur de ib. A men ocs ib esse crimened de innomen tach. Sid ia lass ib solen por solno or ib grantach." The daughter replies, "Men grantach es solentum. . . . Men juc aun. . . . Ben es bizar den ibid asoc solno is pathen crimenid."[61] (This soon is translated, for Stead deranges the process of signification only as a moment in something larger.)

This fascinating performance bears manifold significance for our concern with refunctioning. First, *The Cenci* itself is a revisionary drama. Just as Shelley's *Prometheus Unbound* reverses gender stereotypes by making the female Asia an active quester and the male Prometheus her still, suffering goal, so

The Cenci presents a Lucrece figure who kills her victimizer rather than herself, though she finally is condemned to death. Second, Shelley was under severe attack at the time Stead wrote. After his Victorian prestige as the exemplary lyricist, New-Critical modernism dismissed him as technically unsound, illogical, emotionally adolescent, indeed effeminate, compared to the cool, witty logic of the Metaphysical poets. This attack was partly political: Shelley's personal and social radicalism was unwelcome to Eliot and the Agrarians.[62] Stead, then, polemically renews Shelley's cultural dignity by endorsing the use an amateurish, adolescent girl makes of him. Third, Stead shows how what has been handed down as part of patriarchal oppression ("the very [book] he had given her") may be refunctioned. Through her "Tragedy of the Snakeman," which in itself echoes the deaths of Lucrece and Beatrice Cenci, Louie finds the strength to survive in her own life, and Stead lets her live. To see this process of use, revision, and transformation worked through within the book helps us to understand Stead's right not only to attack the humanist images of Dickens and Twain that had been transmitted as cultural treasures but also and in the same work to exploit the literary resources that Dickens and Twain left.

This much clarity about its procedures still does not make *The Man Who Loved Children* wholly lucid. In presenting Louie as the young artist breaking free of bourgeois origins, the novel seems too little aware that this model of free artistic development depends upon the bourgeois society it appears to transcend. Yet a version of this issue remains with us today as a crucial topic for debate within feminism. It might be phrased, "Should women's goal be an 'autonomy' comparable to that which men have individually enjoyed?" Or, put another way, "Must the agenda of feminism include a bourgeois revolution for women?" These questions endure, unfinished matters from the thirties and before.

5. The Birth of Huck's Nation

My book *"Huckleberry Finn" as Idol and Target* was written to challenge dominant commonplaces of American literary study and education.[1] This chapter arose from an invitation to develop the book's perspectives for an international interdisciplinary discussion concerning the relationships between "cultural property" and "national and ethnic identity."

According to the sociologist Paul Gilroy in *Against Race*, his challenging attempt at "imagining a political culture beyond the color line," a defining anxiety of our time is "the emphasis on culture as a form of property to be owned rather than lived."[2] As the historian Elazar Barkan has demonstrated, in the burgeoning discussion and debate around problems of cultural property, a key term has been cultural "appropriation."[3] Yet the negative connotation with which this term has been weighted somewhat puzzles me, given my own different use of it in the previous chapter. It doesn't sound half so bad to me as "expropriation." Appropriation focuses on the beneficiary of the process, expropriation on the loser, and I have far warmer fellow feeling for someone who likes something (and so appropriates it) than for someone who takes it away from someone else (expropriates it).

These issues of appropriation and expropriation bear on the history of debates concerning a great American novel, for *The Adventures of Huckleberry Finn* is implicated in a process of cross-cultural transactions that may not be so benign as give-and-take. For nearly a century in the United States, beginning in the 1830s, blackface minstrelsy was a widely popular form of entertainment. It allowed many white people to make a living by rendering their impressions of art forms and cultural practices that had originated with African Americans, who were denied access to the financial rewards a white audience could provide. Eric Lott's study of blackface minstrelsy transforms the terms "appropriation" and "expropriation," with straightforward power, into *Love and Theft*. In the 1970s, Ralph Ellison wrote with relief that in the United States the age of cultural expropriation was over:

"[W]e've reached a stage of general freedom in which it is no longer possible to take the products of a slave or an illiterate artist without legal consequence."[4] But the love and theft that produced minstrelsy also made possible the art of *Huckleberry Finn*, as Ellison pointed out in "Change the Joke and Slip the Yoke" (1958), in which he identified Twain's figure of the fugitive slave Jim as "fitted into the outlines of the minstrel tradition."[5]

It causes trouble to this day that Mark Twain's novel, first published in 1885, this product of radically unequal relations of power, has been widely taken as an icon of American identity, as the book that "we have embraced as most expressive of who we really are."[6] Who is "we" here, and what is real? Some Americans gain a desired identity by this process, but at a cost to other Americans.

Writing for an interdisciplinary and global audience makes me want to be certain that we hold in common a few fundamental facts about *Huckleberry Finn* as a cultural object in the United States. To this end, I begin with a moment of controversy in my home state of Pennsylvania, and after rather rapidly working through this incident, I then reprise the issues, both on a larger scale and in more detail.

Huckleberry Finn is the most widely known work of American literature, both the most admired and the most loved. In the United States, there is no nationally mandated curriculum, yet this book is taught in most schools across the nation. Since the 1950s it has been widely claimed by teachers and scholars as a weapon against racism in the classroom. For them it has become an idol of interracial goodwill. This educational role is the focus of my inquiry. Most of what is imagined to be the defense of *Huckleberry Finn* against banning is in fact argument over its place in the schools. It is not a first-amendment, free-speech issue, but a question of educational policy.

In February 1998, as part of what in the United States is Black History Month, the Pennsylvania state chapter of the National Association for the Advancement of Colored People (NAACP) put forward a resolution requesting schools not to require *Huckleberry Finn*.[7] The NAACP targeted it as racially offensive. How can this be? The answer lies in the explosive powers of the term "nigger."

Twain's novel is a bold experiment because it is told in the voice of Huck, a poorly educated preteen boy of the 1840s. He has grown up in Missouri amid a system of slavery in which some white people owned black people as property. It was part of his world, and he uses the offensive term hundreds of times.[8] So you can scarcely read a page without encountering it. Huck uses this word, which is associated with the domination of whites over blacks. Yet he helps Jim, who is fleeing from slavery. Huck's deeds are better than his words. His words are the book's strength, but they are also the obstacle it poses to many readers. This is the difficulty of irony. And as literary scholars have long recognized, irony cannot be reliably controlled, for it always depends on differences in position.[9] The NAACP did not want to ban the book. They want to change the way educators and parents think about it. The NAACP does not say the book, or Mark Twain, is racist. They say that the book makes for bad classroom experiences.

Why did *Huckleberry Finn* become the most widely taught American book, in schools at all levels? It is a tremendously funny book, but that has never been enough to win a place in the classroom canon. School boards demand higher values than pleasure. It has long been loved by millions of readers, but only after World War II did large numbers of critics, scholars, and teachers call it the greatest American novel and claim that it has high moral meaning. For many readers in authority, *Huckleberry Finn* seemed morally great because it showed a white person overcoming the prejudices of his background. This seemed a very important model for the schoolroom, because in the years after World War II, the Allied triumph over Nazi racism fueled the wish to bring about racial equality in the United States.

For many liberal teachers and writers, *Huckleberry Finn* symbolized the ideals of the civil rights movement. But for many African Americans it has seemed wrong that the classroom model for racial equality should be a white person who uses racially offensive language. So once *Huckleberry Finn* became an idol of interracial goodwill, it also became a target for criticism and protest by African Americans. This happened many times in the later twentieth century and was widely discussed in newspapers and broadcast media.

The cultural and educational establishment has accorded great value to Twain's novel. Against this, the Pennsylvania NAACP initiative argued that *Huckleberry Finn* should not hold the place it does in many curricula as the highest example of American excellence. Attempts like the NAACP's have regularly met fierce opposition, as witnessed once again in a controversy in 2009.[10] If the book symbolizes America's moral excellence, then it hurts to have it questioned. Because *Huckleberry Finn* has become an idol, its defenders, inadvertently but regularly, make inaccurate and misleading statements. They have lost contact with the book itself and recall only an idealized memory.

When the Associated Press learned of the NAACP initiative, they contacted the American Library Association, which has an Office for Intellectual Freedom. The director of the Office for Intellectual Freedom made a statement in defense of the book. Her defense included the claim, which I quote, "Jim's name is Nigger Jim in the book because that's exactly what he would have been called at the time."[11] But she is completely wrong about Jim's name. In *Huckleberry Finn*, Jim is called Jim. It is only innumerable cultural authorities—such as the *New York Times*, Harvard professors, Pulitzer Prize–winning historians, and Twain scholars in the *TLS*, as recently as 1996—who call him "Nigger Jim."[12] Idolatry of the book has successfully taught one lesson: that it's OK to use the word—after all, America's greatest novel does.

The way *Huckleberry Finn* has been taught, written about, and discussed since the 1950s has allowed many teachers, writers, and directors of Intellectual Freedom—though not all—to believe, wrongly, that there once was a time in the United States when "nigger" was not a term meant to wound and humiliate. The historian Edward Ayers, in his Pulitzer Prize–winning study of Southern life after Reconstruction, recounts this etiquette lesson from a memoir. A white youngster referred to a respected black man as "Mr. Jones." His aunt corrected him: "Robert Jones is a nigger. You don't say 'mister' when you speak of a nigger. You don't say 'Mr. Jones,' you say 'nigger Jones.' "[13] The term was clearly understood as a weapon to keep whites on top. Mark Twain showed sensitivity to this issue in keeping Jim "Jim," and yet humiliation is still felt when African American students are made to swallow the term hundreds of times in order to pass an English course.

Nonetheless, *Huckleberry Finn* is in almost every curriculum. A scholarly survey in the early 1990s indicated that *Huckleberry Finn* was required in over 70 percent of American high schools.[14] This means, among other things, that taxpayers are every year paying for scores of thousands of copies of *Huckleberry Finn*. Only Shakespeare was more required, but by a measure that added together all his plays. *Huckleberry Finn* was required far more than any particular play of Shakespeare, more than any other work of American literature, more than any other work of fiction, or any other long work in any genre. In my book, I coined a term to denote this extraordinary standing: "hypercanonization."

Huckleberry Finn was widely bought, read, and loved from its first publication in 1885, but it was slow to make its way into schools. It's not obvious that it sets a good example. Its title character, hero, and narrator, Huck, is shy of schooling, and his language is not that of the grammar lesson, either in its syntax or its vocabulary. Nathaniel Hawthorne's *The Scarlet Letter*, because its prose was decorous and its morality repressive, soon after its 1850 publication became the first still-canonical work of American literature to be taught in high schools. Only far more slowly, not until after the Second World War, did *Huckleberry Finn* became a national cultural property in this sense.

Almost as soon as it entered the classroom, *Huckleberry Finn* became an object of controversy. Ever since the 1954 Supreme Court decision in *Brown v. Board of Education* struck down racial segregation in the schools and gave the legitimacy of national policy to the presence of African Americans in classrooms with whites, there have been protests by African Americans against requiring a book whose language is saturated in the single most symbolically offensive term in the American vocabulary: *nigger*. The title of my book tries to capture this situation: *Huckleberry Finn* has become both an idol and a target.

Mark Twain died in 1910, and in 1920 the new-model intellectual Van Wyck Brooks, a Harvard contemporary of T. S. Eliot's, authored a psychobiographical cultural critique, *The Ordeal of Mark Twain*, that suggested Twain should be left behind as America grew up. Measured on the scale of Jonathan Swift, Voltaire, or even Charles Dickens, Brooks argued, Twain did not achieve a major body of satiric art. In Brooks's analysis, Twain had failed to keep his outsider's radical perspective and was too eager to be accepted by the dominant, genteel, corporate culture. For Brooks, because Twain was so widely read and loved, he provided an apt symptom for diagnosis of the national malady.

To answer Brooks involved a judgment of American culture as well as of Twain. Bernard DeVoto provided this in his 1932 *Mark Twain's America*, which concludes with an admonitory memento. As opposed to the optative mood motivating Brooks, whose America is still to be wished into being, DeVoto asserts a perfect indicative: "There is, remember, such an entity. It seems necessary to explain that America has existed, has had a past."[15] DeVoto was a figure in American letters and scholarship who is still not reckoned at his full consequence. He was from 1935 until his death in 1955 the "Editor's Easy Chair" columnist for *Harper's*; before being denied tenure at Harvard, he had contributed to the 1937 founding of its doctoral program in American Civilization; and in the 1940s he was a Pulitzer Prize–winning and best-selling historian of the American frontier. He was the first real scholar of Twain, and he contributed crucially to the process by which Mark Twain was converted from private intellectual property to national cultural property.

Samuel Clemens was the first to recognize Mark Twain as a matter of property: "Mark Twain" is not simply Clemens's pen name; it is a registered trademark. During the years that he was writing *Huckleberry Finn*, Mark Twain was also actively involved in arguing for international copyright agreements that would protect authors from what was called "piracy," the unauthorized but legal reproduction and mass sale of their works in cheap editions by publishers who paid no royalties to the author. The gaps in international copyright allowed British works to be appropriated by American publishers and allowed Canadian publishers to export pirated editions of Twain into the United States.[16]

In December 1881, Mark Twain traveled to Canada to establish a Canadian copyright for *The Prince and the Pauper*, and he spoke bitingly about the oddities in regulation of verbal property. He looked forward to the time when, "in the eye of the law," literary property "will be as sacred as whiskey, or any other of the necessaries of life." He explained that the identity of whiskey was guarded by the law, but that the identity of literature was not: "If you steal another man's label to advertise your own brand of whiskey with, you will be heavily fined . . . for violating that trademark." Moreover, "if you steal the whiskey without the trademark, you go to jail." However, in the existing state of law, you would be free to steal them both "if you could prove that the whiskey was literature." And by the same token, Twain speculated, literature might be treated with greater respect by the law if only "a body could . . . get drunk on it."[17]

As recently as a few years ago, when this chapter was first written, scholars of Twain were obligated to include a remarkable credit line in their archivally based publications (and note in the first line of what follows that the key term is indeed "words," not a misprint for "works"):

> Mark Twain's previously unpublished words quoted here are copyright [date] by Edward J. Willi and Manufacturers Hanover Trust Company as Trustees of the Mark Twain Foundation, which reserves all reproduction or dramatization rights in every medium. Quotation is made with the permission of the University of California Press and Dr. Robert H. Hirst, General Editor of the Mark Twain Project. Each quotation is identified by an asterisk (★).[18]

The little stars spattered in a scholar's text are the merit badges for having found good words of Twain's never before published, and in turn they mark the growth of the Foundation's legally certified property. Even as I wrote, however, the situation changed, and there are now no new words left: "Everything Mark Twain wrote for which the Mark Twain Project had even a partial text, as of the end of 2001, has now been published."[19]

A key moment in transforming Twain from private to state property occurred in the middle of the twentieth century, when the University of California undertook the guardianship of the Mark Twain Papers. The materials of the literary estate were deposited at Berkeley in 1949, and when Clemens's last survivor died in 1962, they were bequeathed to the University of California.[20] Shortly thereafter, the University of California and its press began the prodigious editorial and publication project that is, for instance, bringing out Twain's correspondence at a rate of about a volume per year of his adulthood. As a mark of the national cultural stakes, this editorial project has been "supported, without interruption, since 1967" by grants from the National Endowment for the Humanities, an agency itself established only in 1965.[21]

Before this current national public system began, and after the death, in 1937, of Albert Bigelow Paine, who had been Twain's Boswell—interviewer and authorized biographer—the Papers became for nearly a decade the care of DeVoto as literary executor for Samuel Clemens's estate. DeVoto's edited selection from manuscript autobiographical papers, *Mark Twain in Eruption* (1940), and his documentary critical study of fictional manuscripts, *Mark Twain at Work* (1942), books that still have currency, both arose from his labors in the archives.[22]

The trustees of the Twain estate, however, wanted to cash in their property more directly, and they kept instructing DeVoto to appraise the value of the materials. In January 1944, he wrote the Estate's lawyer a letter that laid the foundations for current academic scholarship on Twain. You will immediately see two things about the letter. First, it argues strongly, I think persuasively, for the value of the archive, the collection, as capital rather than as commodity, as a resource from which money may be made not by its being sold, but by the productive use it may be put to. Second, he argues that this capitalization of the archive will bring in greater income than would its sale. In the long run, he may have been wrong about this for two reasons: the immense growth in price for celebrity memorabilia, and the fact that the Twain Foundation does not necessarily receive the payoff from the kind of work DeVoto envisioned and that has in fact come to pass.[23]

Here is what he wrote:

> Over the years, it seems to me, by far the greatest asset is the sale of Mark Twain's books and of such subsidiary rights in them as movie, radio, etc.

Compared with this, the value of our collection is slight, even if you realize $100,000 from it (as you wouldn't). Our main job is what may be called institutional advertising—the spread of discussion of Mark Twain in order to maintain and increase the sale of his books. Thus, if I were to go on and complete the edition of letters and make the edition of notebooks as our original plan called for, both books would sell well and go on selling. Both would make 10 to 20 thousand dollars in themselves. But far more important would be the fact that they would lead old readers to buy Mark's books and create new readers who would also buy them. You have made $8,000 in royalties from *Mark Twain in Eruption*, which I edited, and in the end will make twice that. But in the end also you will make four times $8,000 from the sale of Mark Twain's books which would not have been sold except for the stimulation of old readers and the creation of new readers by *Mark Twain in Eruption*.

Similarly with the books I have written and may yet write—and the books which other qualified students may write about Mark Twain, the institutional advertising which such books will create will be of great and in fact indispensable value. In fact, if Mark Twain is to go on selling, he must go on being discussed, and if he is to be discussed books about him, especially controversial books, must continue to be written.

That is the one prime reason for keeping our collection together as a unit—so that I and other qualified students can use it for the writing of books about Mark Twain.[24]

DeVoto's logic still proves powerful. The most successfully controversial scholarly work about Mark Twain in my lifetime—Shelley Fisher Fishkin's 1993 *Was Huck Black?*—led immediately to an immense bookselling project. To attract new readers and rereaders alike, this project offers at modest price a set of twenty-nine nicely made cloth volumes reprinting facsimiles of the (now out-of-copyright) American first editions of Twain's books published in his lifetime, with introductions by notable literary figures and scholarly afterwords by an honor-roll of Twainians, all under the general editorship of Professor Fishkin and under the imprint of the world's greatest brand name for scholarship: Oxford University Press.

DeVoto had won the standing that brought him the Twain papers by his massive cultural history *Mark Twain's America*, published in 1932 and still in print. The title plays with the double sense of the genitive case. DeVoto provides the American context, which, he argues, explains Twain, but he also makes the case for Twain's possession of America. For DeVoto, Twain,

"more completely than any other writer, took part in the American experience."[25] As the scholar Louis J. Budd has detailed, by the later years of
Twain's life, he was widely known to American journalists as "our" Mark
Twain, and caricaturists imaged him in the iconography of the national fig-
uration his birth name echoed—Uncle Sam.[26] DeVoto contributed the
scholarly goods to make the connection of the man and nation endure beyond Samuel Clemens's death. Since DeVoto, scholars and journalists have
unhesitatingly, repetitiously, praised *Huckleberry Finn* by characterizing it as
"quintessentially American."[27]

For DeVoto it was an important feature of the Americanness of Twain
and of *Huckleberry Finn* that his book's America included the cultural contributions of its enslaved population. In the sixty years between DeVoto's *Mark
Twain's America* and Fishkin's *Was Huck Black?* no scholarly book did more
than his to emphasize the theme of her book—that the character of Twain's
accomplishment depended on what he took from African Americans.

Here are some of DeVoto's formulations on this matter: "Slavery as an
institution and Negroes as sharers of the scene are organic in the community
to which [Twain's] novels are devoted. It is a whole community; the effect
is totality." "Sam Clemens grew up among Negroes; the fact is important
for Mark Twain . . . [for] much that is fruitful in his art springs from the
slaves." The "two facets of democracy" were not only the "idyll" of river,
forest, and prairie, and the "rush and clamor" of America's development,
but also "the melancholy, the music, the laughter, the terror, and the magic
of the slaves." DeVoto saw Twain's art as what we now call "hybrid," drawing from established British culture, from marginal religious sectarians, and
from black culture. As he put it, "engraftments from Africa, England, and
the Apocalypse . . . are part of the American experience here, as nowhere
else, given existence in literature."[28]

Fishkin orients her argument in relation to Ralph Ellison, the most
widely admired African American novelist and cultural critic of his generation, who believed in the ideal of integration, not separatist Black Power,
and who drew theoretical and historical emphases similar to DeVoto's from
Constance Rourke's pathbreaking study of popular culture, *American
Humor: A Study of the National Character* (1931), which had appeared the year
before *Mark Twain's America*.[29] This use of Ellison not only allows Fishkin
an effective rhetorical stance in answering African Americans who object to
Twain; it also allows her to claim *Huckleberry Finn* for American patriotism
without confronting the language of empire that is so important for De-
Voto. For DeVoto, the America that emerged from the Civil War had been

deeply changed from the entity that entered the war; using the terms of Roman and French history, he saw it as a shift from republic to empire, and a shift carrying cultural consequence. As he put it, "Emerson is the classic literary man of the First Republic," and "Mark Twain was the classic writer of the Empire that succeeded it."[30]

Even though DeVoto considered *Huckleberry Finn* Twain's greatest work, the most fully expressive of his America, he has very little to say of the work itself. In this respect, however erudite, his work remains a kind of middle-brow appreciation. Something more was needed to make *Huckleberry Finn* the work it has become, not simply beloved to readers, not just "quintessentially American," but also a work amenable to the resources of the most advanced modes of criticism, which already by the rise of New Criticism in the 1930s had begun to mean the close analysis of specific passages.

Lionel Trilling, the most influential American literary intellectual of the cold war, began the final stage of work that made *Huckleberry Finn* the hypercanonical object it has become. In 1948 appeared the first college textbook edition of Twain's novel, with Trilling's introduction. For ten years Trilling had been teaching a general education course on great books of the Western tradition, from Homer to Goethe, and his hyperbolic praise of *Huckleberry Finn* is undergirded by comparisons to Homer, to Sophocles, and to Molière. But Trilling's key move was to endow the work with a moral authority it had never before been understood to possess, a moral authority that made it appropriate for the schoolroom by the test of Trilling's model, Matthew Arnold: It could be shown to offer a "criticism of life."[31]

In chapter 31, Huck is nagged by his conscience, which urges him to write to Miss Watson, who held legal title to Jim as property, telling her how to recover her chattel. His conscience warns him of the infernal punishments awaiting disobedience. Huck drafts the letter but finds he can't bring himself to send it. He tears it up, saying, "All right, then, I'll *go* to hell." Trilling was the first to name this scene as the book's "great moral crisis." He claims of this sequence that "No one who reads thoughtfully the dialectic of Huck's great moral crisis will ever again be wholly able to accept without some question and some irony the assumptions of the respectable morality by which he lives."[32] For this reason, Trilling asserts, the book is indeed "subversive," just as had been feared by the libraries that initially refused to carry it. So *Huckleberry Finn* was now both quintessentially American and a work of what Trilling would later call "the adversary culture,"[33] suitable simultaneously for patriotic reassurance and for highbrow strenuosity.

Fishkin combines DeVoto's sense of the essential Americanness of *Huckleberry Finn*, as amplified by Ellison, together with Trilling's praise for the book as being "subversive."[34] For she believes that in demonstrating the role of "African-American voices" in the book's language, she has given scholarly grounding to the white liberal belief that has been crucial to Huck's role in the schools: namely, that it presents an importantly progressive model for American race relations. As she put it in a 1995 newspaper interview, "It's a weapon in the battle against racism that we can't afford to take out of our classrooms."[35] This belief that the mere presence of *Huckleberry Finn* will have a specific, predictable, beneficial effect is part of the structure that I call "idolatry."

Not all cultural authorities participate in hypercanonization or idolatry. Wayne Booth, who was not an Americanist, reading with the rigor of someone pursuing a theoretical argument, judged of *Huckleberry Finn* that "few readers if any have ever learned from [it] that slavery is bad." He emphasized, in contrast to Trilling's claim for subversion, that *Huckleberry Finn* does not "teach . . . us a truth we did not know before," nor is it "an effective attack on slavery." Whatever " 'messages' " there may be, he argued, "are in fact brought by most readers to the passage, not derived from it." The achievement of the book, in his analysis, is made possible by what reader, implied author, and author already hold in common: "the convictions shared by Samuel L. Clemens, Mark Twain, and every successful reader." In Booth's reading, when Huck decides, "All right, then, I'll *go* to hell," the result is "wonderfully warm moral comedy."[36]

But Booth's argumentative scrupulousness prepared for even a further lowering in the pitch of what he was willing to claim for *Huckleberry Finn*. His generalizations concerned *few* readers, *most* readers, and *successful* readers. But clearly, by his analysis, in cases where there are not well-shared "convictions," then the interaction of text and reader will not be successful. When *Huckleberry Finn* is required in schools, the hope for warmth and intimacy sometimes dissolves not into laughter but into anger, because the cultural stakes are so much higher. For years Booth remembered with nagging puzzlement the African American colleague who had refused to continue teaching *Huckleberry Finn* in the required first-year humanities course at the University of Chicago. Booth's seriousness finally made this refusal the starting point for a book exploring "the ethics of fiction." Booth summarized the gist of his colleague Paul Moses's case: "The way Mark Twain portrays Jim is so offensive to me that I get angry in class, and I can't get all those liberal white kids to understand why I'm angry."[37] More than twenty years later, Booth got the point.

Booth's colleague Paul Moses had raised his protest in 1963; Booth's acknowledgment that there was a strong ethical case for Moses's critique appeared in 1988; yet authorities still repeat their claims for the obligatory classroom value of *Huckleberry Finn*. To this day, a significant number of African Americans feel compelled to resist the structure of idolatry, to protest the book's role, and thereby to dissociate themselves from the national consensus that it is supposed to represent. The actual character and terms of the protests do not indicate a strong assertion of ethnic identity in the sense of calling for a distinctive alternative culture. Rather, they seem to be calling the wishfulness of white liberal beliefs back to reality by insisting, "This book does not do the work you claim; it is not making an America where we can happily live together."

Let me cite a letter to the *New York Times* in response to their editorial asserting the merits of *Huckleberry Finn* against a protest in 1982:

> I still recall the anger and pain I felt as my white classmates read aloud the word "nigger." . . . I wanted to sink into my seat. Some of the whites snickered, others giggled. I can recall nothing of the literary merits of this work that you term the "greatest of all American novels." I only recall the sense of relief I felt when I would flip ahead a few pages and see that the word "nigger" would not be read that hour.[38]

Does the established public response to such concerns take them seriously? Not, it seems, the major newspaper of the Pennsylvania state capital. In response to the 1998 NAACP recommendation that *Huckleberry Finn* not be required, the front-page headline was offensively dismissive: "Group tries to sell 'Huck Finn' up the river."[39] In this headline, the NAACP is deprived of its character and history and reduced to the anonymity of any group, and the history of slavery in the United States, as well as the meaning of Twain's book, is mocked by the reversal of a key metaphor. For an enslaved human being to be sold southward *down* the river—as Jim, in *Huckleberry Finn*, is threatened with—was a terrible thing because it meant separation from friends and family and also meant exposure to even more severe conditions of forced labor. To forget this meaning, to think the bad direction was "up" the river, is a contemptuous, and contemptible, amnesia. Perhaps it also inadvertently reveals what has often been remarked—nowadays in the United States the worst problems of race relations may be northward. Certainly the 2008 presidential primary campaign in Pennsylvania bore this out, in Hillary

Rodham Clinton's evocation of "working Americans, hardworking Americans, white Americans."

To the extent that challenges to *Huckleberry Finn*'s obligatory primacy are taken seriously, they seem to be taken only as threats, not as opportunities for serious dialogue. To judge from the newspaper headlines that mark these incidents, you would think that what in Black Power days was called "mau-mauing" was going on. In the summer of 1995, the museum housed in the mansion that Mark Twain built in Hartford, Connecticut, held a workshop for schoolteachers. Look at the headlines: in the *Pittsburgh Post-Gazette*, "Mark Twain Museum Mounts 'Huckleberry Finn' Defense"; in the *New York Times*, "Huck Finn 101, Or How to Teach Twain without Fear." The *Post-Gazette* cast the workshop as "coming to the rescue" of beleaguered teachers, and the *Times* explained that "for the lovers of Mark Twain, the event is a pre-emptive effort to bolster the nerve of teachers."[40]

I do not support this logic, which insists that the book must be rescued from African American parents and students for their own good, and which therefore targets them for preemptive cultural strikes. If we take seriously Trilling's foundational claim that *Huckleberry Finn* teaches us to challenge the moral certainties of the culture that formed us, then we should be willing to meditate the possibility that *Huckleberry Finn* itself may not be entitled to so central a role in our culture as it has been asked to play. It may be as limited in its way as was Huck's conscience when it defended slavery. In his own time, Mark Twain was far more committed to human equality than were most of his contemporaries, and he was vastly better informed about and admiring of African American contributions to culture in the United States. *Huckleberry Finn* has made millions laugh and is a brilliant experiment in style. There are good ways to teach it, but too many schools require it because they think it is good for race relations. Instead of authorities telling students and parents who disagree that they are bad readers, I think it would be preferable to mount a genuine debate over what works against racism in the classroom.

Ralph Ellison greatly admired *Huckleberry Finn*, but he did not accept the principle that a black audience had no right to pass judgment on works produced by whites, especially when those works had the tendency to make whites feel complacent about participating in progressive race relations. In a 1949 review essay discussing four liberal films addressing racial issues, he warned against "the temptation toward self-congratulation which comes from seeing these films and sharing in their emotional release." Ellison urged, "as an antidote to the sentimentality of these films," that they be seen "in predominantly Negro audiences, for here, when the action goes phony, one will hear derisive laughter, not sobs."[41] *Huckleberry Finn* is a stronger work than *Pinky*, but it is being asked to serve many of the same purposes, and cultural authorities would be well advised to subject *Huckleberry Finn*, in earnest, to a version of Ellison's touchstone.[42]

II.   *Language and Reality in the Age of the Novel*

6. Narrative Form and Social Sense in Bleak House and The French Revolution

Juxtaposing *The French Revolution* (1837) and *Bleak House* (1852–53) allows us to define why Charles Dickens at his best can feel like Thomas Carlyle, and to describe the literary mode that history and the novel share in Victorian writing. Although Dickens wanted to have "Carlyle above all" present when he read *The Chimes* (1844),[1] dedicated *Hard Times* (1854) to Carlyle, and praised the "philosophy" of Carlyle's "wonderful" *French Revolution* in the preface to *A Tale of Two Cities* (1859), my subject is not Carlyle's influence on Dickens.[2] I will instead consider Carlyle's work in its public role in the institution of literature, as the first book to embody and articulate a mode of writing, a fusion of techniques and attitudes, that became dominant in early Victorian England.

The reception of *The French Revolution* marks it as the work that defined Carlyle for his audience. Its success gained an English publisher for *Sartor Resartus* (1838), spurred the publication of Carlyle's *Essays* (1839), and created the lecturing opportunities from which *Heroes and Hero-Worship* (1841) resulted. Praise for *The French Revolution* resounds, from the first reviews by Thackeray and J. S. Mill, who proclaimed it an "epic" and a work of "genius," to obituary notices (1881) by Andrew Lang and R. H. Hutton, who considered it "by far the greatest" of Carlyle's works, "the book of the century."[3] Dickens is said to have "carried a copy of it with him wherever he went" on its first appearance, and while beginning *Bleak House* he mentions reading "that wonderful book *The French Revolution* again, for the 500th time."[4] Carlyle's biographer and disciple, James Anthony Froude, called *The French Revolution* "the most powerful" of Carlyle's works, and "the only one which has the character of a work of art."[5]

The French Revolution achieved its exemplary status as a "work of art" in the Victorian mode by breaking with the literary procedures of the romantic visionary mode. In response to the French Revolution, writers of the 1790s transformed earlier views of historical progress into violently apocalyptic plots, organized around a visionary speaker, the "Bard," who presented a "panoramic view of history in a cosmic setting, in which the agents are in part historical and in part allegorical or mythological."[6] By the early nineteenth century, however, both political repression and political disillusionment drove writers inward to a private vision, in which refreshed perception rather than revolution created a "new heaven and new earth." The language of politics and redemption shifted into metaphors for states of consciousness. As symbols grew more opaque, the Bard became a Solitary.

These changes within romanticism demonstrate that a mode of writing is "an act of historical solidarity," through which the individual will to form connects itself to great shared crises.[7] At any historical moment those writers undertaking moral responsibility for their time will share techniques of presentation, patterns of plot, and structures of language that together define a mode of writing. In the new political situation that had emerged in England by around 1830, as Catholic Emancipation and reform agitation marked the unfreezing of counterrevolutionary repression, a new mode was necessary, a renewed relation between the writer and the public.

The French Revolution, therefore, transforms the romantic constellation of elements. Carlyle rescues the public voices and concerns of the 1790s while keeping also the private message that had come to later dominance. Like the Bard, *The French Revolution* ranges over history, attending to all levels of action, addressing to its age the words of most concern, but its story tells of no imminent apocalypse. There is no final ending. The irony created by this gap between a disillusioning plot and a visionary means of representation produces one of the work's most striking virtues. Through it Carlyle and his readers can safely reexperience revolutionary hopes and master the trauma of their disillusionment. Such irony yields both the meaning of a clearly told story and the vividness of immediate presence.

To find such a method of representing human lives in action, to join the "soundness and depth" of "Reason" and the "vividness" of "Imagination," to combine the virtues of "theory" and "fiction," was the task Macaulay had set his age in his essay on "History,"[8] and it was the problem that Carlyle too had perceived as the legacy of Walter Scott. Scott's fiction had made clear, as Enlightenment historiography did not, that history had been made by "living men . . . with colour in their cheeks, with passions in their stomach," and before projecting any "philosophy," the modern historian must succeed as well as Scott had in capturing the "idioms, features and vitalities" of concrete human "experience."[9] Macaulay defined the "Novel" as one extreme, the "Essay" as the other, and allotted to history the disputed but fertile ground in between. This centrality of history, based for both Macaulay and Carlyle on their belief that history taught while fiction merely amused, persisted in the Victorian novelists. In their attempt to prove that they too could be true teachers of the age, novelists drew upon the resources of the essay and thereby made their work more like history.

This focus upon the essay points to one of the major institutional facts of literature in the years around 1830, what Bulwer defined as the "revolution that has been effected by Periodical Literature."[10] As outsiders allowed by periodical writing to come to prominence and earn their livings before any major book cemented their positions, Carlyle and Macaulay both exemplify the new careers that this revolution permitted. The review journalist was above all a judge, weighing for his readers what was under consideration and defining the meaning of its thought in the broad terms of general human nature. Narrative could exist only as panorama and had constantly to be interrupted for its significance to be unfolded. There was no place for everyday experience.

Dickens also began his literary career as a periodical writer. Not Macaulay, however, but Lamb, not Edinburgh but the *London Magazine,* suggests his situation. The collected pieces of *Sketches by Boz* (1836), Dickens's analogue to the "Critical and Miscellaneous" collections of the review writers, are written not by a judge but by an observer close to the level of both his subject and his audience. Specific incidents, not general considerations, formed the basis of these sketches; not the outline of a panorama, but the nuance of an atmosphere, not meaning, but mood or incident, was their goal. Thus, as they turned to book-length writing, Carlyle and Dickens faced opposite problems of continuity and coherence.

Therefore, similar principles of organization in *Bleak House* and *The French Revolution* have different meanings in the contexts of their authors' whole careers yet define a middle ground on which opposed literary practices could meet. *The French Revolution* and *Bleak House* are about the same length, and Carlyle's subdivision into twenty books parallels the nineteen monthly parts of *Bleak House.* But neither work is merely an agglomeration. Despite the constant shifts in actors, *The French Revolution* holds together through the generalizing narrative voice that describes, both analytically and symbolically, the continuity of the process carried on by different people at different times. To engage the reader's activity in synthesizing these parts into a whole, each chapter bears a pointed, often enigmatic, title: not a listing of events, but a puzzle to provoke thought in advance and a catch phrase, laden with significance, to carry away after reading. The process of reading is a series of challenges and initiations.

From his first novel Dickens realized that sketches could be built into installments, and installments into a book, by stringing episodes along the movement of a central character, and in his early novels the chapter titles strive to maintain a clear narrative continuity. They are usually of the "in which . . ." type, which describes what will be going on in the chapter to follow. However, the use of a historical episode to join a variety of lives in *Barnaby Rudge* (1841), the growing role of London as a center of coherence in *Martin Chuzzlewit* (1843–44) and *Dombey and Son* (1846–48), and Dickens's attempts to organize these two novels by moral themes (selfishness in *Chuzzlewit* and pride in *Dombey*) all indicate a wish to discover methods of bestowing abstract intellectual significance on narrative. Just as Carlyle used novelistic "vividness" to go beyond earlier historians such as Hume and Gibbon, so Dickens drew on the essay for "theory" to surpass earlier novelists such as Lesage and Smollett.

In *Dombey and Son* the linear rush of the railroad, like a narrative of events, reveals only a senseless sequence of fragments (chap. 20), and the book's narrator pleads for "a good spirit" to "take the house-tops off" and in synoptic perspective reveal the realities of modern life. The comprehensive knowledge from such vision would lead human beings, no longer blinded "by stumbling-blocks of their own making," "to make the world a better place."[11] *Bleak House* presents a narrator who plays the part of this "good spirit," and the book's chapter titles (e.g., "Telescopic Philanthropy," "The Appointed Time," "Enlightened") are Carlylean (cf. "Questionable," "As in the Age of Gold," "Sansculottism Accoutred"). Like Carlyle's titles, they interrupt the flow of reading and emphasize relations that are paradigmatic rather than syntagmatic. No less than Carlyle in *The French Revolution*, this narrator by both analogy and analysis draws together the social classes and the individual lives that make up the multiple plots of *Bleak House*. The irony of Carlyle's abrupt references to Napoleon, present at some action as an obscure youth, or of his remarks on the strange conjunction of Marat and Charlotte Corday, also appears in *Bleak House* as the narrator poses arch questions and speaks knowingly about strange social interconnections. By these means *Bleak House* becomes more "spatialized" than Dickens's earlier works.[12] In this mode both Dickens and Carlyle combined the linearity of narrative with the solidity of completed significance.

The panoramic unity in these works absorbs many narrative perspectives and comprehends them in one whole. Carlyle quotes from contemporary sources, narrates in his own voice actions he has pieced together from such sources, jumps into action with a participatory "we," and rises to the visionary heights of summary and interpretation, like Dickens taking the reader on "an Asmodeus' Flight."[13] Dickens divides *Bleak House* between two narrators, a floating visionary eye like Carlyle's "eye of History,"[14] and Esther Summerson's retrospective "I." In both books the past tense is used in narration by the actors—Esther or Carlyle's contemporary sources—but the impersonal narrator speaks in the present tense. A letter of Dickens's, contemporary with his reading *The French Revolution* for the "500th time," shows the potency he attributed to such narration. He described a series of "Shadows," sketches of historical moments recounted in the present tense: "I understand each phase of the thing to be always . . . present before the mind's eye. . . . Whatever is done, must be doing."[15]

The mode of writing in *Bleak House* and *The French Revolution* combines shared techniques of narrative unity and variety with a similar plot of social action. The major action of *The French Revolution* is the phoenixlike "death-birth" of a society, and *Bleak House* portrays the transition from an old to a new order of society. Dickens shows this change in terms close to the events of England in his lifetime. *Bleak House* charts not a change of heart, no Scrooges or Dombeys, but a change in the structure of social and economic power.

This historical consciousness of old and new marks the story of Chesney Wold. In the course of the book, the Dedlock family, "as old as the hills, and infinitely more respectable," slips toward extinction.[16] To characterize Chesney Wold, Dickens uses the Burkean language of value, terms far from the vitriolic picture of "the good old days" in *Barnaby Rudge* or the exposure of sentimental medievalists in *The Chimes* or *Dombey and Son*. This house, however, has passed its great days and become a seat of deathly immobility. Yet it has also brought forth new life. The housekeeper's son Rouncewell has left home and gone north, to become not an anonymous chartist, as Sir Leicester Dedlock imagines, but an important ironmaster who has been asked to stand for a seat in Parliament. Sir Leicester finds in this no proof of the flexibility of British institutions but rather speaks of it "as if there were a general rising in the North of England."[17] He laughably misses the point, for Rouncewell has named his son Watt not after Sir Leicester's bogey Wat Tyler, the medieval insurrectionary, but after the inventor of the steam engine, the source of what the Victorians came to recognize as the Industrial Revolution: the bourgeois phoenix, born from the ashes of aristocratic decay.

The Victorian mode of writing shared by *Bleak House* and *The French Revolution* goes beyond techniques of narration and overarching movements of plot to include also the articulation and interweaving of specific "cultural codes."[18] In particular, three lexical systems—gothic, scientific, and apocalyptic—are organized by synecdoche, the rhetorical figure that connects part and whole. Thus by the end of *Bleak House*, Chesney Wold as an outward whole echoes the condition of Sir Leicester, its dominant inward part, and has itself become a "body without life," full only of "ghostly likenesses."[19] But this haunted house repeats the condition of Tom-all-Alone's, the ruinous slum held in Chancery and debated over in Parliament, the representation in small of the whole political system that Sir Leicester supports.

In literary history this play of similarity between dweller and dwelling, between the House of Dedlock and the edifice of state, the decay of institutions and the decay of what is "in" them, derives from the gothic fiction popular in the years following the fall of the Bastille, years that also saw political writings filled with images of the tottering house of state.[20] A gothic code thus links several spheres of discourse. To recall the pervasive power in the nineteenth century of gothicism as an idiom of historical representation, think of the "spectre" that haunts Europe in *The Communist Manifesto*, the echo of Hamlet's ghost in the "old mole" of revolution in *The Eighteenth Brumaire*, and the atmosphere of misty spirits that marks the "fetishism of commodities" in *Capital*.

Such gothic language in Marx and Engels suggests its availability for serious purposes and its compatibility with scientific intentions, a commitment to the truth, as best one understands it, about the historical depth of a given social situation. The mysterious correspondences that link character and architecture in gothic fiction blended with the holistic scientific language of the later eighteenth and early nineteenth centuries to create striking descriptions of the coherence of social process. Just as Herder's historicism tried to grasp as one whole the unique process of a given culture, so *Naturphilosophie* in Diderot, Goethe, Schelling, and others sought to define the cosmos as a dynamic continuum of becoming in which physical processes and human, moral significances were unavoidably linked.[21] Thus, when Carlyle considers the "swell of the public mind" before the Revolution, he notes that "there are swells that come of subterranean pent wind . . . even of inward decomposition, of decay that has become self-combustion:—as when, according to Neptuno-Plutonic Geology, the World is all decayed down into due attritus of this sort; and shall now be *exploded*, and new-made."[22] Similar processes change both the earth and society. In humankind these processes are both physical and mental: "One reverend thing after another ceases to meet reverence: in visible material combustion, château after château mounts up; in spiritual invisible combustion, one authority after another."[23]

This synecdochic sense of shared essence combated a mechanical sense of isolated cause and effect. For many areas of scientific discourse had not yet been converted into Newtonian comparisons of quantity. Diderot, for instance, understood chemistry as the science of quality and metamorphosis. He argued that central for the physicist should be not the attraction of discrete particles but the phenomena of blending and continuity, such as resonance, fire, electricity, and sulfurous exhalation. Concrete and historical, geology replaced the mathematical sciences in popular attention.[24] In their biological speculations, Buffon, Goethe, and Geoffroy Saint-Hilaire propounded metamorphic holism.[25] The transfer to social theory of language from such scientific writing yields the characteristic nineteenth-century terms of historical perception that relate parts and wholes: "milieu," "circumstance(s)," "influence," "air," "element," "atmosphere," "medium," "conjuncture," "mentality," and "background."[26]

Carlyle, who learned German to study Werner's "geognosy,"[27] found the whole linguistic complex that we have been charting, and he joined the holistic tradition of sociology, contributing to English the word "environment." As the sense of society in Dickens's novels grows more complex, his writing becomes simultaneously more gothic and more scientific. In *Martin Chuzzlewit* he mentions the biological theories of Monboddo and Blumenbach only to dismiss them (chap. 1), but in *Dombey and Son* the "good spirit" must reveal the "moral pestilence" that in the "laws of outraged Nature" is "inseparable" from the "vitiated air" found in the slums by "those who study the physical sciences, and bring them to bear upon the health of Man" (chap. 47).

Bleak House is full of both disease and mysterious spirits. Yet, like Marx, Dickens does not allow his pleasure in thick rhetoric to override an aim of clarification. Ghosts arise from human actions and may be dispelled by them. They are not supernatural; their explanation is social. As dirt is "matter in the wrong place,"[28] so the ghosts of *Bleak House* arise from displacements in social relations: undervaluing close relationships or overvaluing distant ones. Thus the case in Chancery of Jarndyce and Jarndyce, the opposition of those whose interests should be identical becomes the "family curse," the "phantom that has haunted us so many years."[29]

Around Lady Dedlock congregate most of the book's ghosts. Her "secret"—her premarital liaison with Captain Hawdon; their child, whom she abandoned and believed dead; and her continuing love for Hawdon despite her marriage to Sir Leicester—hides her distance from those to whom she should be close and causes her distant airs among her present company, while this very aloofness draws suspicion to her. Her marriage to an aristocrat while she loves a man of lower station awakens echoes of the seventeenth-century Lady Dedlock, who chose the revolutionary cause despite her husband's Cavalier sympathies. No less than revolution once did, Hawdon now threatens the upper classes, for from his hideous city burial ground he will be "raised in corruption: an avenging ghost" to pollute the air with disease.[30] Once Esther learns that Lady Dedlock is her mother, she is drawn to Chesney Wold, but the sound of her "warning feet" makes her identify herself with the ghost and feel that she is "haunting" the house.[31] Terrified of herself, she runs away. Thus injustice and secrecy make people incomprehensible even to themselves, while they appear to others as spirits of doom.

To pierce Lady Dedlock's facade, the family lawyer, Tulkinghorn, involves many people in his secret machinations. The house of Snagsby "becomes ghostly,"[32] an object of gossip and rumor. The involvement of Guppy brings him to Krook's shop at midnight, "haunted by the ghosts of sound."[33] Finally, Tulkinghorn himself is shot and becomes a "ghost" to be "propitiated."[34] Unlike Tulkinghorn, who wishes to hoard secrets, Bucket, the detective, makes public both the solutions to the mysteries and the means by which he has solved them. Like the "good spirit" of *Dombey and Son*, he demystifies. Even Lady Dedlock can dispel the ghosts around her by avowing her situation, removing herself from Chesney Wold to seek the grave of Hawdon. As she leaves at dawn, the whole "spectral company" of shadows vanishes into "the realities of day."[35]

Carlyle's book, too, is what Froude called a "spectral" history.[36] Like Dickens, Carlyle suggests states of alienation through the code of the supernatural. People need to comprehend their experience, and if they cannot find some explanation in themselves, they will seek to interpret every event as part of some mystery. Thus Dickens's Snagsby "always is . . . under the oppressive influence of the secret that is upon him. Impelled by the mystery, of which he is a partaker, and yet in which he is not a sharer, Mr. Snagsby haunts what seems to be its fountainhead. . . . It has an irresistible attraction for him."[37] Like Snagsby's possessed state is the state of Carlyle's Camille Desmoulins just before the Terror. He has got his head "so saturated through every fibre with Preternaturalism of Suspicion" that he sees "behind, around, before, it is one huge Preternatural Puppet-play of Plots, Pitt pulling the wires. Almost I conjecture that I, Camille myself, am a Plot and wooden with wires."[38]

Carlyle details the popular psychology of suspicion. For example, in 1789 distrust of the economy caused people to hold on to their money. Trade slowed, and food grew scarce in the markets. People discovered that "they need not die while food is in the land" and some arose to help themselves to it, "the Brigands." But this "actual existing quotity of persons" became the object of rumor and so "long reflected and reverberated through so many millions of heads, as in concave multiplying mirrors, become a whole Brigand World; and, like a kind of Supernatural Machinery, wondrously move the Epos of the Revolution. . . . Not otherwise sounded the clang of Phoebus Apollo's silver bow, scattering pestilence and pale terror, for this clang too was of the imagination; preternatural; and it too walked in form-less immeasurability, having made itself like to the Night."[39]

Carlyle likens the "Great Fear" to the plague that opens the *Iliad* and reveals the social genesis and propagation of a moral epidemic. The social disorder and political unrest accompanying the first great European out-break of cholera around 1830 strengthened the links in the cultural code between epidemic disease and revolution. For reasons of nutrition and sani-tation, the disease killed mostly poor people and thereby set social inequality in high relief. It appeared to the poor like a murderous conspiracy against them by the rich, and it exacerbated the awareness of the rich that the very existence of the masses threatened them. Perhaps the most explosive dem-onstration in nineteenth-century London was the popular protest against the cholera Fast-day, March 21, 1832.[40] The renewed outbreak of cholera in 1848–49 deepened these connections. Dickens and Carlyle resemble each other and typify their time in trying to show the particularities of social me-diation through which the plague, both physical and moral, spreads. Carlyle finds the source of plague in irresponsibility by those in power, which un-dermines popular faith in social institutions. If the institutions no longer work, people will turn to what resources remain to them, form irregular institutions, and thus create the turmoil that generates in turn more suspi-cion and paranoia.

The opening of *The French Revolution* relates physical, moral, and social evil in the code of plague. Louis XV is dying from hideous "confluent small-pox,"[41] and since he is himself France, his condition is also the nation's. As he has lived in an "enchanted . . . Armida-Palace" built by "black-art" and devoted himself to pleasure rather than to administration, the nation too is "smitten (by black-art) with plague after plague" and suffers hunger and misery.[42] The king's "putrid infection" spreads,[43] sickening courtiers, while "the cardinal symptom of the whole widespread malady" is that "Faith is gone out."[44] In his review Mill translates from the medical to the sociological code: "The loathsome deathbed of the royal debauchee becomes . . . the central figure in an historical picture, including all France; bringing before us, as it were visibly, all the spiritual and physical elements which there existed, and made up the sum of what might be termed the influences of the age."[45]

To show the same pattern in *Bleak House*, we might analyze the famous opening, in which the anaphora syntactically, the fog visually, and the present participle temporally reduce the condition of England to one hideous atmosphere. But if Chancery is the center of that scene, Tom-all-Alone's is "in Chancery" and is equally central. Despite talk in Parliament, Tom-all-Alone's "goes to perdition head foremost."

> But he has his revenge. Even the winds are his messengers, and they serve him in these hours of darkness. There is not a drop of Tom's corrupted blood but propagates infection and contagion somewhere. It shall pollute, this very night, the choice stream (in which chemists on analysis would find the genuine nobility) of a Norman house, and His Grace shall not be able to say Nay to the infamous alliance. There is not an atom of Tom's slime, not a cubic inch of any pestilential gas in which he lives, not one obscenity or degradation about him, not an ignorance, not a wickedness, not a brutality of his committing, but shall work its retribution, through every order of society, up to the proudest of the proud, and to the highest of the high. Verily, what with tainting, plundering and spoiling, Tom has his revenge.[46]

Dickens personifies this slum quarter as "Tom" and associates the quarter synecdochically with its inhabitants, thereby combining the medical dangers of disease and the political dangers of revolution. The sexuality of "infamous alliance" hints at venereal disease and evokes the liaison of Lady Dedlock and Captain Hawdon and her pilgrimage to his graveyard, itself as loathsome as Tom-all-Alone's. Through its inhabitant Jo, Tom-all-Alone's reveals to Lady Dedlock the spot where she will die and infects her daughter Esther with smallpox. Sir Leicester neglects his political responsibility, and Tom-all-Alone's falls into ruin; Lady Dedlock neglects her moral responsibility, and her lover falls into ruin. Both poison the air.

Dickens gives us not so much a physical description of the slum ("slime," "gas") as an attitude of scientific precision about it ("chemist," "analysis," "atom," "cubic inch"). Dickens's insistence on "truth" in his

"Author's Preface" led him to draw whenever he could on scientific authorities, for he was convinced that there was no conflict between science, rightly understood, and the imagination. The "poetry of fact" was always his aim. But accurate truth included such moral qualities as "ignorance," "wickedness," and "brutality." The most effective vocabulary in such a context is simultaneously scientific and moral: "spoil," "taint," "corrupt," "pollute," "contagion," and "infection." "Infection" is the key to this passage. Etymologically, it derives from the Latin *inficere*: to stain or color, to put or dip into something, especially a dye. *Inficere* also means to mix with something else, especially a poison; to taint, spoil, corrupt. *Inficere* parallels Greek *miaino*, whose nominal form, *miasma*, referred to the mysterious elements that defiled the air and caused plague. The crucial analogy was between a tincture in which a small drop of dye colors the whole fluid and the way that an evil smell from a single source can diffuse through the air, especially the smell from the decay and putrescence of organic bodies.[47] The concept of infection, then, is itself synecdochic in its emphasis on a whole "atmosphere."

In the "Author's Preface" to *Bleak House,* Dickens refers to the lawyers in the book by citing "an apt quotation from Shakespeare" (Sonnet 111):

> My nature is subdued
> To what it works in, like the dyer's hand:
> Pity me then, and wish I were renew'd!

The poem continues beyond what Dickens quotes:

> Whilst, like a willing patient, I will drink
> Potions of eisell 'gainst my strong infection.

The violation that moral nature suffers from degrading employment is like what physical nature suffers from plague. Through this allusion Dickens engages the whole etymological complex of *inficio.* The "dyer's hand" typifies the professional deformation that has often been a source of comic amusement. In *Bleak House,* however, the cause of professional deformation, what Carlyle called the "environment," comes under critical scrutiny. Phil Squod's Vulcanic deformity results from a warping occupational environment, Jo's ignorance and disease from a pernicious physical environment, and Esther's diffidence from an oppressive moral environment. The book offers countless other examples, for such deformations are like a plague ravaging society.

What hope for renewal do the worlds of *Bleak House* and *The French Revolution* offer? Dickens and Carlyle share the ambivalence appropriate to plots that bring about change but frustrate the apocalyptic hope for total change. The revolutionary French sought to cleanse their world with fire. Popular versions of *Naturphilosophie* gave scientific cachet to millenarian expectations, and the revolutionaries shared the apocalyptic hopes of their supporters in Protestant lands.[48] The troubles of the early 1830s again aroused apocalyptic tremors. In England the concurrence of Catholic Emancipation, the second French Revolution, the cholera epidemic, and the agitation for reform led many to look to the "signs of the times." Dr. Thomas Arnold was "half inclined to believe" that the glossolalia in the congregation of Carlyle's friend Edward Irving was a "sign of the coming of the day of the Lord," at least in the sense that "an epoch of the human race was ending."[49]

The possibility of apocalypse permeates *The French Revolution* from its opening, the death of Louis XV: "Thou, whose whole existence hitherto was a chimera and scenic show, at length becomest a reality: sumptuous Versailles bursts asunder, like a dream, into void Immensity; Time is done."[50] Since what is true of the king is true of the kingdom, the people rejoice, "Behold a New Era is come."[51] The hope is located within the historical actors. Carlyle traces throughout his work how millenarian psychology fed into revolutionary activities, but he emphasizes the disappointment. Repeatedly the actors are deceived in their hopes for a new era. The motif of incongruous confrontation, people's failures to recognize themselves as brothers and sisters when social barriers are torn down, articulates this disappointment. When a crowd of sansculottes breaks into the king's chateau, the parties "brought face to face after long centuries" can only "stare stupidly at one another."[52] The traditional apocalyptic figure of Holy Marriage ironically describes another failure. The Festival of the Confederation should have united all France, but Carlyle finds it only mummery: "Think of a . . . Nation of men, spending its whole stock of fire in one artificial Firework!"[53]

The constantly frustrated hope for a final judgment is equally present in *Bleak House*. The first chapter ends with the wish that Chancery and its misery could be locked up "and the whole burnt away in a great funeral pyre." Miss Flite "expect[s] a judgment": "Shortly. On the Day of Judgment. I have discovered that the sixth seal mentioned in the Revelations is the Great Seal."[54] The death by spontaneous combustion of Krook, the metaphorical "Lord Chancellor," only parodies the desired apocalypse, for although totally consumed, he takes nothing with him. His firetrap of a shop remains as it was, even as Chancery itself goes on beyond the exhaustion of Jarndyce and Jarndyce. There is no total judgment, no way to begin the world anew beyond the individual. Both books share a mood of hope and apprehension, and both teach the patience needed when there is no end.

A comic outburst, however, without promising a new world, may afford a temporary renewal within society. Carlyle describes the procession from Versailles after the Insurrection of the Women: "It was one boundless inarticulate Haha;—*transcendent* World-Laughter; comparable to the Saturnalia of the Ancients. Why not? Here too . . . is Human Nature once more human."[55] However transient the hope of such a new beginning, its energy keeps people going. Dickens often builds long stretches of his novels up to comic reversals: Micawber denounces the "HEEP of infamy" in *David Copperfield*, and in *Martin Chuzzlewit* the plots and counterplots end with masks dropped, roles reversed, and the scoundrels driven out, as Pecksniff receives the last of his many knockings.

Bleak House offers no such comic triumph. Only the reaction to the end of the Jarndyce case resembles it. Amid "immense masses of papers of all shapes and no shapes," spectators emerge, laughing "more like people coming out from a Farce or a Juggler than from a court of Justice."[56] Here, however, the blocking figure is an institution, not a person, and this Bergsonian triumph of humanity asserting itself over the dead things that so often control life is still not enough to save Richard Carstone. The case is "all up with at last," but so is Richard. The contrast of the romantic Richard consumed by his smoldering combustion and Rouncewell the ironmaster, who husbands his fire in engines rather than wasting it in torchlight demonstrations, echoes the meaning of Carlyle's "Close thy Byron; open thy Goethe."[57]

For Carlyle to turn from Byron to Goethe was to assert that individuals can and must form their world, their environment, by productive activity: "Whatsoever thy hand findeth to do, do it with thy whole might."[58] The redemption of Bleak House demonstrates human power over what Sartre later called the "practico-inert." Old Tom Jarndyce gave the house its name and "left the signs of his misery upon it,"[59] for as he wasted himself in the family lawsuit, the wind and rain and weeds ruined the house. But John Jarndyce turned from the lawsuit to the work at hand and created a charming home, now ironically misnamed. Dickens's discarded titles show that he closely associated Tom-all-Alone's and Bleak House as alternative images of Chancery-ruined edifices, and the parallel makes clear that the name of Tom-all-Alone's need not determine its nature. The pathbreaking reports on public health of the 1830s and 1840s emphasized equally that action could remove the atmospheric impurities that caused disease.[60]

In asserting through narration that Esther, Woodcourt, Rouncewell, and others can do productive work despite the politicians, Dickens echoes Carlyle's recognition that "the true Constitution" was not "made . . . by Twelve hundred august Senators," but grew "unconsciously, out of the wants and the efforts of these Twenty-five Millions of men."[61] For Carlyle went beyond Burke or Scott in recognizing that, since France survived the Revolution, there must have been principles of social cohesion within the chaos. In the idiom of *Naturphilosophie* Carlyle visualizes the Reign of Terror as an eddying circulation of energy, flowing outward to fight aristocratic invasion and inward to fight domestic subversion. Although his explanations are not scientific by our standards, Carlyle felt that history's task was not to "shriek" but, with its "imaginative organ,"[62] to see and articulate the realities of the human past.

Carlyle's moral dynamics locate human beings between the cultural realm and the physical. Symbols, "Realised Ideals," compose the upper realm. These have been conceived and achieved by human beings for human beings, to embody and channel human energies. Energy itself makes up the lower realm. It is unformed, destructive in itself, but the source of all life, all *being* and *doing* and *reality*. These two realms must be in touch with each other. Otherwise the upper realm dies, rots, burns, and spreads its infection to human life: "As for Falsehood . . . what should it do but decease, being ripe; decompose itself, gently or even violently . . . too probably in flames of fire?" Furthermore, when the two realms are out of touch, the lower breaks loose as ravaging fire or electricity. Nonetheless, human effort reorganizes this energy into a new realm of symbols and institutions. Again and again Carlyle sets out his terms: "French Revolution means here the open violent Rebellion, and Victory, of disimprisoned Anarchy against corrupt worn-out Authority: how Anarchy breaks prison; bursts-up from the infinite Deep, and rages uncontrollable, immeasurable, enveloping a world; in phasis after phasis of fever frenzy;—till the frenzy burning itself out, and . . . elements of new Order . . . developing themselves, the Uncontrollable be got, if not reimprisoned, yet harnessed."[63]

The skepticism and loss of faith that precipitated the Revolution prevented the "unconsciously" acting participants from seeing significances as clearly as Carlyle can. Tragically, their failure to comprehend the events that caught them up led to the conflicts that exacerbated the process of dissolution and increased the total suffering. Carlyle, however, does not consider it impossible to understand one's own historical environment: "Had they understood their place, and what to do in it, this French Revolution, which went forth explosively in years and in months, might have spread itself over generations; and not a torture-death but a quiet euthanasia have been provided for many things."[64] Sir Leicester Dedlock is not carried off by apoplexy but is doomed nonetheless. Carlyle and Dickens both offer the understanding of their physical, moral, and historical environments that will allow the English to avoid the frenzy of revolution by avoiding the decay of conservatism.

Both books express the wish for apocalypse, but both ironically expose the hope for total transformation to reductive laughter. The gothic language in both expresses the fear that people are prey to incomprehensible forces of the past, but gothic appearances are reduced to social and psychological processes in the present. *Naturphilosophie* provides a synecdochal view of the world, by which the works assert that human energies are at one with the forces of nature and that human beings can therefore change the world. The spatializing power of narrative overview demonstrates the human ability to comprehend the world, while the personal narratives ensure that such "philosophical" comprehension is constantly tested by juxtaposition with "experience." The heterogeneous narrative technique that encompasses such diverse voices constantly draws attention to the writer at work, who at every moment determines by choice the form of the book's world, and by synecdochic magic suggests the validity of the writers' appeals that readers change their "fictile world" through "fingent plastic" activity.[65]

7.   *Rhetoric and Realism: Hyperbole*
      in The Mill on the Floss

My title does not signal a contrast between rhetoric taken as empty and deceitful words and realism taken as the novelist's attempt to present life "as it really was." Rather, it suggests the cooperation of rhetorical self-con-sciousness in making the modern Western tradition of prose fiction. The later-twentieth-century age of French newer criticism seemed no more willing than that of midcentury American New Criticism to recognize the energetic duplicities of language that activate nineteenth-century novels fully as much as they do more recent experimental writing. Despite Frank Kermode's attempts to demonstrate in "pre-modern," "readerly" works the textual plurality and heterogeneity that Roland Barthes characterized as modern, as "writerly,"[1] nineteenth-century fiction remained a straw man in some of the most outstanding work on the criticism of narrative. It is taken as willfully naive and blind to the fictionality of literature, wishing instead to assert the reality of what it represents.[2] I find, however, that the naive faith charged against the major nineteenth-century novelists quickly dis-solves into theoretical and textual complexity.

In beginning to demonstrate this contention through reading an early novel of George Eliot, I have drawn from that work a rhetorical term as my tool for analysis in order to insist upon the self-consciousness in and about the language of the work. My figure of *hyperbole* bears the same name as a geometrical figure defining a shape generated from dual foci but from no center, suggesting the complexity and instability I wish to emphasize.[3] Fur-thermore, I find useful the arbitrary excess of such a geometrical metaphor for the form of a literary work; as a term it is so alien, falls so far short of our usual critical metaphors, that its tentative, purely exploratory value remains always in view. Such an analogy is much less likely to mislead us into false consequences than the organic, architectural, or textile metaphors that are more common. The barrenness may be fruitful as fresh provocation.

Such sidestepping of conventional linguistic models marks the realistic tradition in our fiction since its starting point in Cervantes's *Don Quixote.*[4]

Realistic novelists aim at the truth of life not by a direct and necessarily failed attempt at representing it, but through indirection, through exposure and criticism of alternative claims and strategies whose failures are exposed, leaving a residual sense of unstated truth. Cervantes does not tell us that the reality of Spain in his days was inns and windmills; instead he shows us the consequences of Quixote's trying to live in a world of castles and giants. We come to know the reality of Quixote's world as what exceeds and contradicts his model of romantic chivalry. So in the Quixotic tradition of the realistic novel, "reality" is what escapes all rules and models.[5] The novel does not directly take on reality, and it carries along inside it the false models that must be overcome. If literature in general is a criticism of life, realism is that part of literature that begins through criticism of art, including its own.

The parodic presence of discarded models of action, expression, judgment, and feeling within a novel poses special problems for its critics, for "viewed from a distance," a novel will look like a romance. This power of distance to romanticize motivates the constant new production of realistic works. The last word never lasts; an exposé of the follies of an age comes to seem itself one of the follies of that age. Thus the temporal distance that separated the romantics from Cervantes permitted their new interpretations that ennobled Quixote.[6] A similarly distanced reading may encourage us to find in *The Mill on the Floss* a perfect romantic spiral journey of circuitous return.[7] For the book moves from an initial unity of "Boy and Girl" (title of Book First of the novel) through the alienation of "Downfall" (Book Third) to the reunion of the "Final Rescue" (Book Seventh), which raises the initial union to a higher plane through the dignity of the final biblical epigraph ("In their death they were not divided"—identical to that on the title page). Not on such a broad pattern, but only in the intimacy of local interplay, can the realistic challenge to cultural models be read effectively. Only close reading preserves the critical dimension that Friedrich Schlegel demanded of modern literature and found typified in the novel.[8]

From a work like Erich Auerbach's *Mimesis*, critics have all too easily taken only the emphasis on sociohistorical particularity, the documentary aspect, and neglected the stylistic observations that define the recurrent problematic of the work.[9] Auerbach devotes his own major concern, however, to the break in linguistic principles of literary decorum. A social level appears that would once have demanded the "low style" but now exists in language of "tragic seriousness." The "mixture of styles" that permits the entrance of seriousness into "everyday reality" is the real novelty in the real-istic novel. A new freedom of language charges with the most moving sig-nificance a scene that previously "would have been conceivable as literature only as part of a comic tale, an idyll, or a satire."[10] The position of such a scene within the system and hierarchy of literature makes it truly revolu-tionary. Auerbach's sensitivity to "levels" in the immediate texture of lan-guage allows him also to discriminate "levels" in the narrative technique. The narrator has a power of linguistic formulation that exceeds the charac-ters'. This discrepancy between different ways of forming the world in words shapes novelistic form. Such splits between the book's norms and the norms of traditional literature, between the narrator's norms and those of the characters, between the chief character's norms and those of the world in which she lives, all create a heterogeneous texture in the book's prose and a complexity in the book's structure. It becomes difficult to grasp by what principle the work is to be integrated, unless we are willing to accept a definition of the clashes and demand nothing more definitive.

Himself aware of such splits, Henry James insisted on the artist's need for a "geometry of his own" by which to "draw the circle" that shall "happily *appear*" to contain the relations established within the work.[11] Yet James rec-ognized as well that such appearances would not hold, that for the writer the "inveterate displacement of his general centre" demands the production of "specious and spurious centres to make up for the failure of the true."[12] As critics no less than as novelists, we desire formal clarity, and we realize nonetheless that to impose such clarity in reading falsifies and omits much of what is most important. Let us begin with a harmonious reading of *The Mill on the Floss* in relation to a center and then attend to the waywardnesses that undo the pattern the geometrical eye has defined. Our path will lead out from a central fullness into increasing alienation and discrepancy, until finally a return to the center reveals the splits that had already from the start fractured it, making it "specious and spurious."

I

One of the most striking patterns woven into *The Mill on the Floss* presents a world of astonishing harmony and completeness, in which intuitions that we usually consider primitive are justified by the modern developments of science. The breadth of vision that encompasses all aspects of this world re-moves the terror of the disruptive. Not the extraordinary "proverbial feather" and its terrifying ability to break a camel's back should concern us, but the "previous weight of feathers" that has already placed the poor beast in imminent jeopardy.[13] The "cumulative effect" of "everyday things" (69), the "apparently trivial coincidences" and subtly nuanced "incalculable states of mind" that are "the favourite machinery of Fact," rule the world, not the "terrible dramatic scenes" (295) that haunt our fearful imaginations. If it is "unaccountable" (55) within the Dodson circle that Lucy should look so much as if she were a child of Mrs. Tulliver's, while Maggie looks like no Dodson at all, the mystery is resolved when we remember that a child has two parents and that Maggie will grow up into the image of Mr. Tulliver's mother (233). The quest of science for "a unity which shall bind the smallest things with the greatest" (239) makes the world comprehensible as our home. Even in our little towns by our own hearths the principles and developments of nature and history are "represented" (239) as surely as within the Elizabethan microcosm. The reductive methods of scientific analysis (the "Mill" of Enlightenment as seen by Carlyle and Novalis) combine with the flow and flux of nature (the "Floss") in a familiar order.

Continuous development from a "traceable origin" (63) marks this world, whether in the historical and political sphere of the British Constitution or the astronomical sphere of the solar system and fixed stars. Whatever certain idealists may claim about the mind's capacity to transcend its environment, one finds that "the Basset mind was in strict keeping with its circumstances" (70). The wordplay that joins in the name "Basset" a technical geological term and a familiar hunting dog suggests the complete interrelation of levels, just as do the book's innumerable comparisons between human actions and characteristics and those of animal nature. If it is "humiliating" (36) that Tom and Maggie Tulliver, as they take together their sacrament of cake, resemble "two friendly ponies," it is also a bringing back to earth that renews their vitality.[14] Social developments may sometimes make people "out of keeping with the earth on which they live" (238), but this disproportion can be cured by a return to the privileged "spot" where our childhood sight of nature in its "sweet monotony" of the "same" fixed forever for us the "mother tongue" of our "imagination" (37–38). Through fidelity to such a past, and only through it, can Maggie be sure in life of a ground "firm beneath [her] feet" (420).

The description of the mill at the book's opening adumbrates this pattern of unity in the processes of mankind and nature as it evokes the "dwelling-house . . . old as the elms" and the coincidence of perspective that unites the "masts" of "distant ships . . . close among the branches of the spreading ash" (7). Language itself appears to testify to this relation in the sentences describing the Ripple. It first is "lively" in its current and "lovely" to see, and then at once it seems "living" and its sound like the voice of a "loving" person.

In the description of St. Ogg's, this pattern emerges most compactly as a mass. St. Ogg's is "one of those old, old towns which impress one as a continuation and outgrowth of nature, as much as the nests of the bower-birds or the winding galleries of the white ants: a town which carries the traces of its long growth and history like a millennial tree, and has sprung up and developed in the same spot between the river and the low hill" (104) since Roman times. Echoing a phrase from Wordsworth's *Excursion* that describes the Wanderer's growth among the presences of Nature, Eliot summarizes the town as "familiar with forgotten years."[15] This family intimacy, based on the bonds of the physical, yet affecting as well every other aspect of human life, links that life to nature, and to its own past, as the source of sustenance and value.

This pattern emphasizes the fundamental importance of childhood experience in the development of our mature selves and thus protects the book against the charge of excessive attention to nursery trivialities with which some contemporary reviewers greeted it.[16] It provides as well, however, the basis for expectations of stability and continuity and of an emphasis upon the small and subtle, and many readers have seen the latter portion of the book as deviating from this basis into excess of emotion and action alike. This discrepancy is attributed to extratextual causes, whether a psychological overidentification with Maggie that destroys control or the author's necessity of finishing within the canonical three-volume size after having already lavished upon the earlier portions an "epic breadth" that could not be maintained.[17]

Within *The Mill on the Floss*, however, even within the first two-thirds of it, another pattern can be found that has no priority over the pattern that I have just defined but is different from it and incommensurable with it. One can see in this second pattern "romantic" excess contrasted to the "realistic" fine grain of the first, or one may see the first as a compensatory, romantic myth of order built up by the mind's attempt to defend itself against the real violence of the second. I call this second pattern the hyperbolic. It breaks up the smooth continuity of linkages we have been examining. It is hard to regulate a force that breaks order, but I shall try to specify the hyperbolic in three stages. First, I explore the most literal, "grammatical" cases of hyperbole, when an inappropriately excessive word disrupts the continuity of perception and expression. This involves primarily the language of the characters—both in their speech and thought—and the narrator's relation to that language. Next, I analyze the place of the hyperbolic in the narrator's deeper investigation of human psychology and of our attitudes toward character. This involves primarily the narrator's language and its relation to the language of the audience. Finally, I emphasize the philosophical implications of the hyperbolic as a force disfiguring the harmonious notions of origin, cause, and truth.

II

The narrator introduces the notion of "hyperbole" early in the book during Bob Jakin's quarrel with Tom Tulliver: "To throw one's pocket-knife after an implacable friend is clearly in every sense a hyperbole, or throwing beyond the mark" (48). This comment is itself an instance of rhetorical hyperbole, for it overstates the case. As Maggie insists, "Almost every word . . . may mean several things" (129). "Throwing beyond the mark" is not a hyperbole in "every sense," for there are in the *OED* three other senses of "hyperbole": the rhetorical, "a figure of speech consisting in exaggerated or extravagant statement, used to express strong feeling or to produce a strong impression, and not intended to be understood literally"; a rare general sense, "excess, extravagance"; and an obsolete geometrical sense, "hyperbola." Indeed, so far is Eliot's usage from being "clearly" the sense that it is not even recorded in the *OED*. It is evidently a nonce usage, derived etymologically from the Greek *hyperbolé*, for "throwing beyond"; "overshooting" is the primary sense given in Liddell and Scott, which then gives further meanings that parallel the usual English senses. There is one more Greek sense that is especially noteworthy, for it suggests a strange split within the word; it is one of those words that seem to mean almost opposite things, for it also means "deferring, delay," an undershooting as well as an overshooting, inhibition as well as excess. It is finally worth remarking that the verb *hyperbállo*, from which the noun derives, has a specialized sense with regard to water, "to run over, overflow." The Floss and its floods make an important part in the hyperbolic pattern of the book.

This narrative foregrounding of the term, naming, defining, and exemplifying it all in one sentence, in itself calls our attention to the term's significance. This setting of learned wordplay in close proximity to the movement of Bob Jakin's unlearned mind exemplifies one of the book's major techniques, the exploitation of a discrepancy between narrator and characters, presenting characters' minds in words that they would never themselves use, offering an interpretation of their world unlike any that they could make. The narrator regularly hyperbolizes in going beyond the bounds of the characters' intellectual limitations. This gap established between the world and powers of the narrator and those of the characters contradicts our harmonious reading of Dorlcote Mill in the narrator's dream, in which there had seemed to be a smooth continuity between that past world, so available to memory, and the present standpoint of retrospection. There is then a danger of violence, of forcing, in the narrator's relation to the represented world of the book.

The etymological play of superiority in this "hyperbole" passage clearly relates it to the discussion of metaphor that occurs in the course of Tom's schooling. In trying to teach Tom etymology, Stelling is guided himself by an etymological pun, taken seriously as a paradigm for action. He considers the cultivation of Tom's mind like the "culture" of fields, and thus the resistant mind, like impervious earth, must be "ploughed and harrowed" all the more by the means it resists. The violence here is evident as the narrator compares the situation to making Tom eat cheese "in order to remedy a gastric weakness which prevented him from digesting it." Reflecting on this new analogy, the narrator observes, "It is astonishing what a different result one gets by changing the metaphor!" This change in the model for thought totally reverses the obvious course of remedy. The narrator concludes by lamenting "that we can so seldom declare what a thing is, except by saying it is something else" (124).[18] When we aim our words at a thing, we're always off the mark. All language contains a hyperbolic potential.

The geometric figure of the hyperbola condenses into an emblem many of the most important aspects of the hyperbolic pattern of the book and its difference from the first pattern of centered wholeness that I described. The hyperbola is a discontinuous function; it is not a closed figure but open, and split into two parts; it is a set of points related not to a single origin but to two given points (the foci), and the defining relation is a constant difference.

Linguistic hyperbole demands attention at many points in the book beyond the place where it is named. Bob Jakin admires Tom's control of his speech: "His tongue doesn't overshoot him as mine does" (340). This comment establishes the same contrast between Bob and Tom that marked the earlier scene of their quarrel, but more frequently Maggie is contrasted with Tom in this respect. In "The Family Council" at the time of the Tulliver "Downfall," Tom behaves with earnest restraint, "like a man." In contrast, Maggie suddenly "burst[s] out" like a "young lioness" and in a "mad outbreak" (190) denounces her relatives. In these instances the hyperbolic marks its user as belonging to the wrong class or sex, or even species, as falling outside the charmed circle of respectability and masculinity, though Tom is himself caught up at other moments in the hyperbolic pattern. Just as the first pattern follows the emphasis of Maggie's wishes for the firm ground of the sacred spot and its memories, so in the hyperbolic pattern Maggie's wish for "more" (250) predominates.

Maggie's unfamiliarity with the heights of provincial society makes her "throw" "excessive feeling" into "trivial incidents" (329). Maggie's imagination leads her also into perceptual hyperbole, an atmospheric heightening that melodramatically colors a scene of no outer significance. As she is led back from the gypsies to home, she is "more terrified" than Leonore in Bürger's spooky German poem, and for her, "The red light of the setting sun seemed to have a portentous meaning, with which the alarming bray of the second donkey with the log on its foot must surely have some connection" (102). This deluded, obsessively precise, and symbolic view of the world here is deflated by the pattern of stability and everyday causality; elsewhere in the book, however, it is not always canceled but may also prevail.

Bob and Maggie are not the only hyperbolists. The whole speech-community of St. Ogg's agrees in calling "the 'Hill'" what the narrator tells us is only "an insignificant rise of ground," a "mere bank" (260) walling off the Red Deeps, where Philip and Maggie have their clandestine meetings. Just as Aunt Pullet had earlier "unconsciously us[ed] an impressive figure of rhetoric" (52) in substituting "gone" for "dead," so her unconscious hyperbole, in what the narrator calls a "wide statement" (297), triggers the revelation to Tom of Maggie's meetings with Philip. The narrator describes Tom's consequent state of mind in terms that relate it to Maggie's as she returned from the gypsies. He was "in that watchful state of mind which turns the most ordinary course of things into pregnant coincidences" (298). The tone of irony in this statement works only against any reader trustful enough in the stability of things to believe that the "ordinary course" will prevail. For a comment of Bob's about Philip sends Tom off to intercept Maggie and to accompany her to the Red Deeps, there to denounce Philip.

In that terrible scene of humiliation, Maggie's imagination, "always rushing extravagantly beyond an immediate impression" (301–2), superadds a phantasm of "her tall strong brother grasping the feeble Philip bodily, crushing him and trampling on him." This further heightening of the original "terrible dramatic . . . scene" of confrontation that had "most completely symbolised" (295) her fear still does not prepare Maggie for the repetition soon thereafter, in which father Tulliver flogs father Wakem until Maggie, as if in compensation for the helplessness that she suffered in the earlier scene, rescues both men. In such moments life again knows "those wild, uncontrollable passions which create the dark shadows of misery and crime" (238), those "giant forces" that used to "shake the souls of men" as they "used to shake the earth" (106). Uniformitarianism has not wholly removed the possibility of catastrophe.

This possibility exists within the force of language as it exists within the forces of nature. In considering Mr. Stelling's violent metaphor of "culture," humor held the dangers in control, but our superior amusement at Mr. Tulliver's entanglement in language dwindles as we realize that words are the immobilizing net that binds him for the kill. The narrator notes the dangers to life inherent within the necessary excesses of language as he summarizes the situation after Philip and Maggie have begun to declare their love in the Red Deeps: "It was one of those dangerous moments when speech is at once sincere and deceptive—when feeling, rising high above its average depth, leaves flood-marks which are never reached again" (294). The duplicity of speech emerges clearly, along with the resemblance of this duplicity to the vagaries and discontinuities of the river. This example might suggest a polarization of place in the novel, the Red Deeps being the "place of excess," set against the central scene. But the language here resonates with Maggie's being "Borne along by the Tide" (401) with Stephen and swept along by the flood with Tom at the end. There is no special place of excess in the book. Like a field of force, a force of displacement, the hyperbolic traverses the whole world of the book, wherever the "fluctuations" of a "moral conflict" reveal a "doubleness," wherever "inward strife" wishes to "flow" (380) into release. The "demon forces for ever in collision with beauty, virtue, and the gentle uses of life" are not restricted to the bygone days of the "robber-barons" (237) on the Rhine.

Is it possible for a "secret longing" of which we are not "distinctly conscious," and "running counter" to all our conscious intentions, to "impel" our actions? The narrator urges us, "Watch your own speech, and notice how it is guided by your less conscious purposes, and you will understand that contradiction" (402–3). We must double ourselves into an actor and observer in order to achieve the full, if transient, self-consciousness necessary to allow us to judge the splits within others. Even being "thoroughly sincere" does not protect Maggie from duplicity in her conversation with Lucy, for by revealing her love history with Philip, Maggie unwittingly tempts Lucy to see nothing of significance in the strange vibrations between Maggie and Stephen: "Confidences are sometimes blinding, even when they are sincere" (338). In a book that has invoked Oedipus (117) and that broods on the Oedipal contrast between the "earth-born" and those out of harmony "with the earth on which they live" (237–38), such an observation suggests a relationship between the force of words here and the literally blinding consequence for Oedipus of the words that reveal his ancestry.[19]

In a similar way, Semele is invoked humorously early in the book (153), with Tom in her place and Poulter, like Jove, withholding his immediate glory by not showing his sword. But Maggie's "perpetual yearning," with "its root deeper than all change," to have "no cloud between herself and Tom" (398) proves like Semele's to find full immediacy only in the permanent embrace of death. Conflict is the stuff of human life, for "all yielding is attended with a less vivid consciousness than resistance" (410). Only in the state of strife, of duality, of hyperbolically saying more than we mean, though not all that we mean, do we remain human. What are the other possibilities? The silence and unconsciousness of death, the total yielding to the flow of unconsciousness in madness, or the purity of sainthood. In the book's only perfect act of communication, Ogg names the force and source of the Virgin's wish, "It is enough that thy heart needs it," and she accepts as complete his definition of her "heart's need" (104–5).[20]

III

Yet what place has a saint's legend in this story of provincial mediocrity? The narrator recognizes that any suggested elevation, whether beatific or tragic, jars with the chosen level of milieu and action (in ways like those that Auerbach investigates). The narrator must therefore try to come to terms with this discrepancy between the world evoked and the world represented, this hyperbolic tendency of comparison. The narrator must find ways of mediating between the characters' psychologies and the audience's psychological expectations and levels of sympathy. One strategy uses the principle of the everyday, stable, and continuous. It reduces the hyperbole by devaluing the excessive term. Thus at one point the narrator compares the "unwept, hidden . . . tragedy" of Mr. Tulliver and "other insignificant people" to the "conspicuous, far-echoing tragedy" (173–74) of the royal. The fundamental base of comparison, however, is not greatness but weakness: "Mr. Tulliver, . . . though nothing more than a superior miller and maltster, was as proud and obstinate as if he had been a very lofty personage." The vices of pride and obstinacy join low and high in moral equality that negates distinctions of status. Eliot adds a further element to the comparison. The tragedy of high life "sweeps the stage in regal robes," while we pass obscure tragedy "unnoticingly on the road every day." High tragedy is obvious, showy, in fact is only art, while to appreciate everyday tragedy shows our discernment of reality. Thus the hyperbole is erased; everyday suffering is realer and deeper than that of the exceptional monster; we are back within the domestic circle of continuity and security, even within suffering.

Quite different is another moment in which the narrator begins with hyperbole and then transforms it by estranging us from the familiar term. Rhetorical hyperbole, in which an excessive term is contrasted with one of common measure, yields to a vision of a hyperbolic world, in which everything exceeds common measure. After Maggie has cut off her hair, the narrator hyperbolically compares her sitting "helpless and despairing among her black locks" to "Ajax among the slaughtered sheep" (59). Recognizing that Maggie's "anguish" may seem "very trivial" to adults,[21] the narrator suggests that it may be "even more bitter . . . than what we are fond of calling antithetically the real troubles of mature life." Rather than simply exploiting the antithesis of imagination and real life, the narrator calls it into question, even suggests that there may be no reality except that arbitrarily created by drawing a bar of antithesis. Without the axial coordinates we could not say that one branch of a hyperbola is positive and one negative. Furthermore, the narrator goes on, the discontinuity that establishes reality in the world of value may correspond to a necessary developmental discontinuity within the growth of the individual to maturity:

> We have all of us sobbed so piteously, standing with tiny bare legs above our little socks, when we lost sight of our mother or nurse in some strange place; but we can no longer recall the poignancy of that moment and weep over it. . . . Every one of those keen moments has left its trace, and lives in us still, but such traces have blent themselves irrecoverably with the firmer texture of our youth and manhood; and so it comes that we can look on at the troubles of our children with a smiling disbelief in the reality of their pain. Is there any one who can recover the experience of his childhood, not merely with a memory of what he did and what happened to him . . . but with an intimate penetration, a revived consciousness of what he felt then? . . . Surely if we could recall . . . the strangely perspectiveless conception of life that gave the bitterness its intensity, we should not pooh-pooh the griefs of our children. (59–60)

The significance of this passage in relation to Wordsworth, Freud, and Proust is beyond the scope of my present discussion. I want only to emphasize that the project of recovering the past is set under the sign of impossibility. We usually read that impossibility as a modest irony, disclaiming the narrator's actual achievement of this goal. Even so, we must recognize that just as a psychoanalytic cure requires "transference," so here too there is a necessary displacement. Only through George Eliot can Marian Evans recover her past, and only through Maggie Tulliver can we recover ours.

In contrast to the analysis of Mr. Tulliver's tragic status, the discrimination of two states here is made not through contrasting life and art, but rather through comparing two kinds of art, our adult art of perspective and the "perspectiveless" primitive art of children. The flatness of this original art hides from us the "intensity" within it. Thus a radical challenge is posed to both our sense of reality and our canons of representation. In perspectiveless art no single point organizes the whole into a continuum, and the process of maturation forces us to lose consciousness of the continuity of our present feelings with our past. Nonetheless, Eliot's art is not itself perspectiveless; perhaps most clearly in such moments of circumspection and direct appeal, her art keeps its distance. To speak of childhood's sense of the "measureless" space from summer to summer, one must be capable of measurement.

IV

From the grammatical to the psychological to the more largely philosophical, the force of hyperbole pervades the book, leaving intact none of the certainties with which we were familiar in the first pattern. Thus, the hyperbolical description of Maggie moves beyond the bounds of rhetorical hyperbole to show the hyperbolic principle at work in the realm of cause, effect, and intention. In the sequence in which she pushes Lucy into the mud, Maggie is twice compared to a "Medusa" (88, 91), a disproportion all the more exaggerated because Maggie's hair is cut, depriving her of the primary Medusan attribute. The narrator justifies the comparison: "There were passions at war in Maggie at that moment to have made a tragedy, if tragedies were made by passion only; but the essential μέγεθος, which was present in the passion was wanting to the action" (90). The book's first pattern showed a regular harmony between cause and effect, circumstance and mind, but the hyperbolic pattern constantly signals discrepancy. Any possible explanations to flatten out these discrepancies are unknown or incomprehensible, and this "mystery of the human lot" drives men to the consolations of "superstition" (238).

Maggie's tremendous childhood passion can express itself only in trivial actions, and the same gap between spirit and world prevails elsewhere. Some of the results that she most laments arise from no conscious intention. She "never meant" (33) Tom's rabbits to die from neglect, any more than she "really . . . mean[t] it" (78) when she toppled Tom's "wonderful pagoda" of cards. This disproportion holds in the adult world as well. We "spoil the lives of our neighbours" unintentionally, and the "sagacity" that seeks to reduce these results to causes in "distinct motives" and "consciously proposed end[s]" is in fact hyperbolic, "widely misleading," for such proportions hold only in the "world of the dramatist" (23). The same tactic of setting life against art that reduced the hyperbolic relation between royal and domestic tragedy here insists upon the excess of suffering over aim. The stable, continuous world is a fiction. In the same way, "small, unimpassioned revenges" have an "enormous effect in life, running through all degrees of pleasant infliction, blocking the fit men out of places, and blackening characters." Since there is no appreciable source of agency, we surmise that "Providence, or some other prince of this world . . . has undertaken the task of retribution for us" (223). If we wish to avoid such superstitious metaphors, then we may think of "apparently trivial coincidences and incalculable states of mind" as the "machinery of Fact" (295) rather than of fate, but the metaphor of machinery only gives us the illusion of comprehensibility. We still have no way of calculating the results.

The narrator tries to demystify the "hypothesis of a very active diabolical agency" that Mr. Tulliver requires to explain his "entanglements" by changing the metaphor and proposing that Wakem was "not more guilty" toward Tulliver "than an ingenious machine, which performs its work with much regularity, is guilty towards the rash man who, venturing too near it, is caught up by some fly-wheel or other, and suddenly converted into unexpected mincemeat" (218–19). We laugh at this analogy, and thus laugh at Mr. Tulliver, but the comedy depends precisely upon the disproportion, the sudden excess of the result, postponed until the end, which we could never have expected. How are we to know what is "too near," before it's too late, and does the reference to "some fly-wheel or other" indicate any more real knowledge of the process than Mr. Tulliver has? Indeed, the very phrase "ingenious machine" carries paradoxically animistic overtones. At the end of the book "some wooden machinery" appears as the agency of Tom and Maggie's drowning, but the narrator cannot resist transforming it into an active agent, "huge fragments, clinging together in fatal fellowship" that overwhelm the boat and then are seen "hurrying on in hideous triumph" (456). The hyperbolic pattern escapes our analogies, which are rooted in the will for a natural continuity that this pattern denies, and which demonstrate the pattern in failing to master it.

Even our most cherished cultural institutions work hyperbolically: "Allocaturs, filing of bills in Chancery, decrees of sale, are legal chain-shot or bomb-shells that can never hit a solitary mark, but must fall with widespread shattering" (215). Thus it is no real amelioration of human life that the "floods" of old have yielded to "fluctuations of trade" (106) as the cause of uncertainty. For "so inevitably diffusive is human suffering, that even justice makes its victims, and we can conceive no retribution that does not spread beyond its mark in pulsations of unmerited pain" (215). Justice itself is unjust, as indifferent as the river is to the excess in what it sweeps away. Our machinery does not serve our purposes. The very idea "which we call truth," the finest tool of our cultural creation, crumbles into a "complex, fragmentary, doubt-provoking knowledge." Truth can no longer be the satisfying goal of our inquiry but will only further provoke us, and it is not even at one with itself, any more than is our memory of our past. Only "prejudice" is the "natural food" of our "tendencies" (400) toward wholeness and uniformity. If earlier we saw Enlightenment and nature reconciled, here we recall the hyperboles of Burke's polemic intransigence.

V

Now we may return to the familiar, family world of living and loving together at the mill on the Floss, which formed the basis for our sketch of the book's pattern of harmony. But those figures of harmony are now disfigured, while in a new reversal the force of hyperbole proves productive as well as disruptive. The split between truth and prejudice that we have just noted echoes that between Tom and Maggie, the once-united "Boy and Girl." Tom is the man of prejudice, while to Philip, Maggie "was truth itself" (409), although he is unaware of the terrible revelation that awaits him of what truth is really like. Tom is "a character at unity with itself" (271), while Maggie must fear, yet constantly find herself in, "doubleness" (265). While Tom is "concentrating" (242) himself on recovering his father's position in life and matching his father's "concentration" (243) on the same purpose, the two of them are falling into a "perpetually repeated round" (245) of mechanical recurrence. Maggie in contrast feels "the strong tide of pitying love almost as an inspiration" (243). Thus the harmony of the mill and the Floss that marks the first pattern of the book is contradicted by a contrast of the "mill-like monotony" (166) of deadening singleness with the dangerously double eddies of passionate fluxes and refluxes. The "habitual . . . deepening . . . central fold" (299) in Tom's brow is the disfiguring mark of his commitment, his attachment to his place. Maggie's dream on her way back after floating away with Stephen shows the profound wish for a wholeness to unite the mill and the Floss, for in it she capsizes her boat in reaching out after Tom, but as she begins to sink, she becomes "a child again in the parlour at evening twilight, and Tom was not really angry" (413). But the book's ending grants such wholeness only in death.

The "parlour" itself, if it were as available to the full, "intimate penetration" of Maggie's memory as it is to the reader's, is from the beginning a scene of conflict and discontinuity. There Mr. Tulliver conceives the book's initially disruptive act of overreaching, his hyperbolic "plan" for Tom, which Mrs. Glegg defines as "bringin' him up above his fortin'" (64). Mr. Tulliver explains his intention in terms of that fundamental paternal ambivalence that to modern readers is the most striking link between him and Oedipus: "I don't *mean* Tom to be a miller. . . . [H]e'd be expectin' to take to the mill an' the land, an' a-hinting at me as it was time for me to lay by an' think o' my latter end. . . . I shall give Tom an eddication an' put him to a business, as he may make a nest for himself, and not want to push me out o' mine" (15). Thus the principle of generational continuity is split at its center; the "nest" has no place for two and therefore demands displacement.

Tom himself manifests similar ambivalence toward his father. Even while working to redeem his father's credit, he keeps his efforts secret from a "strange mixture of opposite feelings . . . that family repulsion which spoils the most sacred relations" (283). Maggie also suffers from this split within Tom, for he feels a "repulsion" towards her that "derived its very intensity from their early childish love" (437). She finds that he always "checked her . . . by some thwarting difference" (252). This split within family feelings echoes the opening description of the "loving tide," which with its "impetuous embrace" does not welcome the Floss but rather "checks" (7) it. There is a split in the very source of love, for the loved one's difference from us makes "fear . . . spring . . . in us" (422). Maggie, then, is terrified at the "anger and hatred" against her family that "would flow out . . . like a lava stream" (252) within her. From such contradictions proceeds "that partial, divided action of our nature which makes half the tragedy of the human lot" (439). But the book makes clear also that the other half of the tragedy comes from the concentrated singleness that seems the only alternative.

If both wholeness and division make life tragic, each also makes life livable. The pattern of orderly growth and causation is not the only source of positive value. Dr. Kenn may seem to speak with the authority of the whole book when he laments the present tendency "towards the relaxation of ties—towards the substitution of wayward choice for the adherence to obligation, which has its roots in the past" (433). But his own relation to Maggie has begun through a chance encounter at the charity bazaar, "one of those moments of implicit revelation which will sometimes happen even between people who meet quite transiently. . . . There is always this possibility of a word or look from a stranger to keep alive the sense of human brotherhood" (381–82). This brief confluence between him and Maggie echoes the kindness shown her in her need by Mrs. Stelling, who was not generally a loving woman and "whom she had never liked." In kissing Mrs. Stelling, Maggie first feels a "new sense" of "that susceptibility to the bare offices of humanity which raises them into a bond of loving fellowship" (170). An extravagant comparison marks the point: "To haggard men among the icebergs the mere presence of an ordinary comrade stirs the deep fountains of affection." Thus the wayward and the transient have the same potential for enriching and sustaining life as do long-established ties and deep roots. "Brotherhood" is a matter of contiguity as well as of genealogical continuity, something people may find, or make, for themselves as well as receive from nature. Such a hyperbolic pattern is not, however, easy to grasp. Tom finds Maggie's life a "planless riddle" (343), and in despair he can only expect that in her life one "perverse resolve" will "metamorphose itself . . . into something equally perverse but entirely different" (400). From that metamorphic point of discontinuity, the hyperbolic springs as a constant source of difference, of change, in contrast to the orderly growth of the same from a fixed and presently revisitable center.

This wayward, hyperbolic energy ensures that all the literary types that help to structure the book are different in their return, whether Oedipus or Semele or St. Ogg, or Saul and Jonathan, the father and son whose memorial lament serves as epitaph for brother and sister. If one pattern of the book depends on the recurrence of the "same flowers . . . the same hips and haws . . . the same redbreasts" and is best fixed in a landscape description of a town "familiar with forgotten years," another landscape best carries the hyperbolic pattern: "Nature repairs her ravages—but not all. The uptorn trees are not rooted again; the parted hills are left scarred: if there is a new growth, the trees are not the same as the old, and the hills underneath their green vesture bear the marks of past rending. To the eyes that have dwelt on the past, there is no thorough repair" (457). I have used the tag quotation from Wordsworth ("familiar with forgotten years") to recall the first pattern of the book, which in many ways corresponds to what we call the Wordsworthian in George Eliot and in nineteenth-century culture generally, but within Wordsworth's text itself the same kinds of conflict and contradiction occur. In its context the quoted phrase also evokes hills "scarred" from "past rending." In describing the youth of the Wanderer, as he turned his eyes from the books he was reading to the book of nature, Wordsworth says he saw:

> some peak
> Familiar with forgotten years, that shows
> Inscribed upon its visionary sides,
> The history of many a winter storm,
> Or obscure records of the path of fire.[22]

Such violence sets in action the conflict between contrasting linguistic registers (and associated forms of experience and action) that makes *The Mill on the Floss* realistic in its attempt to unsettle cultural complacencies yet allows it as well to avoid the merely prosaic and routine. Eliot's awareness of this conflict makes her book an active clash between the hope of a fitting language and the recognition that language is never at one with reality, any more than the world is at one with itself. Rather than trying to heal such splits through formulas of artistic integration that weld the book into a specious wholeness, or trying to naturalize them through a biographical interpretation of George Eliot, I find it most fruitful to confront the complexities of *The Mill on the Floss* within the larger history of the realistic novel, which takes its beginning and elaborates its practice from just such splits.

8.   *Rhetoric and Realism; or, Marxism, Deconstruction, and* Madame Bovary

I

The terms of my title suggest certain kinds of questions that are asked nowadays by serious critics of novels. These questions were not asked, or considered serious, in America when the premises of New Criticism still dominated the agenda, not even by critics like Harry Levin or Lionel Trilling, who resisted the most extreme claims of literary autonomy.[1] For these questions detract from the formal integrity of individual works. They threaten both to disarticulate works internally and to open works to external relations, and they thus participate in that active unbounding to which this volume is devoted through its concern with impure worlds.

Such questions might ask about instances, single or recurrent, of language that is not clearly under aesthetic control, that does not conduce to greater beauty or intelligibility when it is focused upon. Such inquiry, indissociable from the work of Paul de Man, may be related to further interrogations of the ways in which a work may be seen not to fit together, such as the "generic discontinuity" that Fredric Jameson has made a special focus for his thinking about the novel. Whether for Jameson or de Man, such unsettling of formal integrity will then be related to comparable cases in the worlds of thought or action; they turn from literature in itself to its relation with philosophy and history.[2]

For my present purposes, I am taking "deconstruction," for which de Man is exemplary, in relation to questions of "rhetoric." By "rhetoric" I mean here a system of relations within language that tampers with meaning in ways that have at least since Plato been considered antagonistic to the goals and procedures of philosophy. At the same time that it is deviant, however, rhetoric is not idiosyncratic, for as a systematic repertory it preexists the individual shaping of a single writer or work. That is to say, rhetoric appears literary compared to philosophy but mechanical compared to literature. For my second set of terms, I am relating "Marxism" to questions of "realism," by which I mean, broadly, inquiries that relate literary works to history, society, politics, the economy. One advantage I find in the terms of "rhetoric" and "realism" is that in ordinary usage they form a pair whose relative evaluation is unstable. Realism is the stuff of life that saves literature from the mere artifice of rhetoric; rhetoric is the fictionality that saves literature from the quotidian banality of realism.

Under the sway of New Criticism, following a process that had run through the whole nineteenth century, rhetoric was reduced to the vagueness of "paradox" and the catchall of "metaphor." Such elements were understood as necessarily present in any successful work and thus became merely defining features of the literary, rather than allowing for the differentiation of one work or corpus or genre or period from another. For New Criticism, realism was simply banished in favor of autonomy. However disingenuously, the themes and imagery of literary works were understood to inhere uniquely within them, unrelated to other forms of knowledge or action.

The realism that by the 1960s was less opposed than considered beyond the pale of discussion was taken as a servile, transparent copying of the world. The fate of the notion of representation in European theoretical debates of the twentieth century is too complex to address here, but it is worth noting that in the United States, too, a complex genealogy overdetermines the New Critical dismissal of realism. In the early decades of the twentieth century, the question of realism arose polemically as part of a generational conflict within bourgeois high culture, with those we now call modernists opposing realism as part of a rejected "Victorianism." Beginning at about the same time but coming to a head somewhat later, in the twenties and thirties, the question of realism functioned in a larger class conflict within American society: The agrarian conservatism of the New Critics stood against the populist democracy that V. L. Parrington's work served intellectually to legitimize. In the thirties and forties, the question of realism was contested within the American left: The so-called Trotskyites of *Partisan Review* furthered modernism against the so-called Stalinist culture of socialist realism and the Popular Front.[3]

Thus the "Truants," as William Barrett named the group around *Partisan Review,* joined the "Fugitives" along with the British "Bloomsbury" in supporting what Ortega y Gasset had described as "the dehumanization of art." For the question of realism, I find especially telling Ortega's optical metaphor: Writers had ceased to look through the window, focusing instead upon the faint internal reflections that play upon the pane's surface. In

Anglo-American literary culture, this dehumanization could be seen in Joyce's dissolution of the everyday into myth, in Eliot's fragmenting of the lyric subject into myth, in Yeats's stirring turn to the barbaric violence of myth.

Myth, however, provided the ground from which arose the intellectual breakthrough that displaced New Criticism. Through attention to myth, the Canadian structuralism of Northrop Frye turned New Criticism into poetics, and his *Anatomy of Criticism* (1957) stimulated a lively interest in literary theory. More important for the story I am telling, however, is the work of Claude Lévi-Strauss, and I can understand the eager attention to the work of Lévi-Strauss in American literary culture—far more than among professional anthropologists—only by the apparent congruity of his concerns with theirs. That is, New Criticism had taught students of literature to value the study of myth, and Frye had whetted the appetite for theory. Thus the enthusiasm for Lévi-Strauss and for structuralism generally. Meanwhile in France, structuralism spread quickly from the study of myth to the broader study of "collective representations." In the 1960s appeared pathbreaking exemplars of structuralist studies of popular culture (Roland Barthes on James Bond), of ideology (by Louis Althusser), of literature (by Gérard Genette and Tzvetan Todorov). These works, along with the more epistemological inquiry of Michel Foucault, all made clear that the relations between cultural products and the world were neither immediate nor transparent nor reduplicative. Literature related to the world through the relations it held to other systematic means of coding, of organizing.[4]

To leave this somewhat breathtakingly high road of rapid summary, let me offer a moment of reading from *Don Quixote*, the novel that continues to stand as the founding instance of the genre, to illustrate what I mean by starting to think of realism—the relation of literature to other sectors of life—in terms of the relations between different systems or codes.

Recall the encounter between Don Quixote and the barber. Quixote insists that the barber has the famed golden helmet of Mambrino; the barber retorts that it's just his brass shaving basin. But all the other "honorable gentlemen"—to humor Quixote—take a vote, and the barber finds his basin "turned into Mambrino's helmet before his eyes." The barber can only grant that "might makes right." Against this conspiracy of gentlemen, however, a servant speaks his opinion that the basin is a basin and nothing else, and a trooper of the Inquisition insists likewise—"as sure as my father's my father"—provoking a brawl.[5] Here the question of "black" and "white," of "truth" and "lie," the nature of reality as designated by words, is contested.

It remains comic in the *Quixote*, but Nietzsche would argue that "the lordly right of bestowing names is such that one would almost be justified in seeing the origin of language itself as an expression of the rulers' power." And Virginia Woolf poses the fundamental questions of the novel as a form: "What is reality?" and "who are the judges of reality?"[6]

In this passage from the *Quixote*, it takes the authority and power of the class structure, the church, and patriarchy to fix words to things in a way that makes them stick. Yet for Cervantes the novel itself is a "step child," a deviant from the paths of these authoritative transmissions. The novel thus takes a distance from the powers that ground our ordinary life. They all claim authority from the way things naturally are, and the novel opposes them by showing that things may be otherwise. This is a fundamental criticism of life, achieved through a criticism of linguistically modeled codes of culture and literature.

We face then a double revision, both in our understanding of the works we have considered realistic and in our understanding of the critical practice that we might consider realistic. Works are no longer to be treated as mirrors; the task of criticism is no longer to "replace" the work, substituting for it a past author's intention or social origin. Rather a contemporary realist criticism will strive to place the work in action, to elucidate what it did and does. Such criticism will therefore ally itself with studying the "effective history" of works in their reception and institutionalization.[7]

I would like to conclude the framework I have been offering with a typological sketch and a bemused warning. I have been characterizing four types of criticism, which may be compared with regard to the critical actions and objects that make them up, critical action as a matter of both tone and gesture, critical object as both internally and externally construed. The tone of New Criticism is admiration and its gesture is to individualize, taking its object internally through its formal integrity, and externally through its uniqueness. If New Criticism admiringly individualizes, structuralism carefully socializes: While it grants the formal integrity of works considered internally, its major concern is the intelligibility that only becomes possible through establishing the systematic relation of a work to other cultural forms. Deconstruction quizzically fractures, exposing a formal heterogeneity that cannot be separated from intertextuality and thus renders unworkable the distinction of internal and external. Marxism militantly remolds: Recognizing a formal heterogeneity that cannot be contained as a philosophical contradiction but must be related to social conflict, it strives to establish lines of struggle where deconstruction had left only permeable membranes. My bemusement comes from a sense that the single critic whose work bears the fullest—necessarily complex—relation to all these issues is Mikhail Bakhtin,[8] but he did his work several decades before the period I have been attending to, and therefore my warning: There is more to the story than I have been able to tell here.

II

I would like to turn now to some critical reading. I take *Madame Bovary*, a work no less essential than the *Quixote* to understanding realism, rhetoric, and the novel as they have figured in our culture. I begin from a matter of textual spacing, go on to consider a related rhetorical figure, and move toward matters of historical judgment that engage the crucial grounds of debate in contemporary cultural politics.

One of the most striking aspects of *Madame Bovary* is Flaubert's extraordinary economy in the use of direct speech. Recall that, between the first meeting of Charles and Emma and the time some twenty pages and twenty months later that they go to the fancy ball at Vaubyessard, there is no dialogue between Charles and Emma. When dialogue does occur, one of the striking stylistic features is the frequent use of ellipses. At such crucial points in the book as Emma's last night with Rodolphe before their planned elopement, or her last, desperate appeal to him for money to save her from financial ruin, there stand prominently on the page the three dots (. . .) that mark the incompletion, the fragmentation of their sentences, their inability to proceed, to get anywhere. We sense within this device not only the characters' inadequacy but the writer's impatience with them. Our participation in the illusion of character and story makes us feel that even if the characters lack the fluency of the heroes and heroines of romance and melodrama, they nonetheless would be saying something more than they do if the writer were not cutting them off, giving us only the minimum necessary to make the book comprehensible. The narration of the famous agricultural fair scene exemplifies this aspect most fully. There the ellipses that truncate the speech of the councillor precisely mark the will of the author, who shifts from this stream of fatuity to the no-less-fatuous love talk by which Rodolphe is seducing Emma, and as we readers can be trusted to get the point, the fragments become shorter and shorter.

By his ellipses Flaubert not only exposes but also plays with other forms, such as melodramatic romance. After they have ridden off into the woods, and he has started to urge Emma on to love, Rodolphe pleads with her not to return, but to "Stay a minute longer! Please stay!"[9]

> "I shouldn't, I shouldn't!" she said. "I am out of my mind listening to you!"
> "Why? . . . Emma! Emma!"
> "Oh, Rodolphe! . . ." she said slowly, and she pressed against his shoulder.[10]

If we know what's happening now, it's not from the actors' words but because we recognize the convention that passion strikes mute, that love is beyond words, a convention that Flaubert simultaneously mocks and employs.

Rodolphe's later reflections upon Emma's attempts at romantic eloquence, which the narrator spares us from having to read, lead to one of the most famous passages on speech in all of Flaubert's writing:

> He had so often heard these things said that they did not strike him as original. Emma was like all mistresses; and the charm of novelty, gradually falling away like a garment, laid bare the eternal monotony of passion, that has always the same shape and the same language. He was unable to see, this man so full of experience, the variety of feelings hidden within the same expressions. Since libertine or venal lips had murmured similar phrases, he only faintly believed in the candor of Emma's; he thought one should beware of exaggerated declarations which only serve to cloak a tepid love; as though the abundance of one's heart did not sometimes overflow with empty metaphors, since no one has ever been able to give the exact measure of his needs, his concepts, or his sorrows. The human tongue is like a cracked cauldron on which we beat out tunes to set a bear dancing when we would make the stars weep with our melodies.[11]

In defining a sense of incommensurability between needs and words, Flaubert emphasizes the deficiency. In George Puttenham's terms, Flaubert favors the "figure of default," "eclipsis."[12] If ellipsis is most literally the mark used in writing or printing to indicate the omission of a word or words, it is also a rhetorical figure by which words are omitted, "which would be needed to complete the grammatical construction or fully to express the sense" (*OED*). Thus even when the marks of ellipsis are not physically present and when grammar is observed, we still may find Flaubert's language regularly elliptical, missing something that would be needed fully to express the sense. One strains to hear celestial music behind the clattering of kitchenware.

Characters within the novel sometimes find themselves in this position. During his first acquaintance with Emma, as he went home at night, "Charles went over her words one by one, trying to recall them, trying to fill out their sense, that he might piece out the life she had lived."[13] But more often, as in the passage cited here, the metaphor of cloak or garment suggests the concealment that language throws over feeling, so elsewhere, too, speech is characterized as "a rolling-wheel that always stretches the sentiment it expresses."[14] This drastic literalization of the etymological sense of "express" seems thoroughly to doom any hope for truth in expression. If Emma was the victim of Rodolphe's unbelief in her love, similar metaphors describe the advantage that she later takes of Charles through her use of language. Her existence becomes "one long tissue of lies, in which she wrapped her love as under a veil in order to hide it."[15]

Thus expression is, if sincere, doomed to failure and is otherwise merely a tool of deceit, as when Rodolphe in his conversation with Charles "fills with banalities all the gaps where an allusion [to Emma] might come in."[16] The writer, therefore, must try another strategy, not that of expression but of implication. If the Greek *elleípo* comes to mean to "fall short" and to "leave out," its original meaning is to "leave in." The *OED* quotes Cowley on ellipsis as "leaving something to be understood by the reader." This procedure has many variations. We may have a simple ellipsis of time, as after Emma has fainted, we read:

> "I'll run to my laboratory for some aromatic vinegar," said the pharmacist. Then as she opened her eyes on smelling the bottle:[17]

This passage omits the time and action of getting the bottle, but no reader fails to follow, even though the continuity of the scene has been thus subtly disrupted. The same technique marks the scene in which Emma and Rodolphe first make love. After "she abandoned herself to him," a new paragraph begins, "The shades of night were falling." All description of their physical love has been passed over, but the suffusive interanimation of Emma and nature in the paragraph suggests clearly enough that it has been very satisfying to her, even though all direct description of her emotional response is also omitted:

> The shades of night were falling; the horizontal sun passing between the branches dazzled the eyes. Here and there around her, in the leaves or on the ground, trembled luminous patches, as if humming-birds flying about had scattered their feathers. Silence was everywhere; something sweet

seemed to come forth from the trees. She felt her heartbeat return, and the blood coursing through her flesh like a river of milk. Then far away, beyond the wood, on the other hills, she heard a vague prolonged cry, a voice which lingered, and in silence she heard it mingling like music with the last pulsations of her throbbing nerves. Rodolphe, a cigar between his lips, was mending with his penknife one óf the two broken bridles.[18]

This passage may stand for the way in which expression yields to implication in two senses: first in the way that Emma's emotional state emerges through language of perception and through analogies worked upon that, so that nature rather than Emma receives the direct description; second in that we know from Flaubert's correspondence that this scene was one in which he felt himself directly participating, but only in Emma's sense of oneness with the scene do we find traces of Flaubert's experience.

The last sentence of the passage poses a further question about the implications of ellipses in the book. It puzzles me at least; I've never been at all sure how to take it, and my reading in criticism suggests that disagreement persists. Most simply we are offered the choice of taking the last sentence as the deflation of the reverie into the humdrum world of the everyday, through such contrasts as that of the far-off and the near, the ecstatic woman and the practical man, the world of nature and the world of man bridling nature; or else we may feel that here this everyday sight and activity are transfigured through the context, that for Emma the halo of the scene surrounds Rodolphe. We may take the difference between these two interpretations as the difference between understanding the last sentence as part of Emma's perception and understanding it as the narrator's withdrawal from Emma to a blank registration of the scene, freed from the veils of her ecstasy.

The book's whole technique of juxtaposition without any explicit clues as to why the juxtaposition has been made leaves us often at a loss, and no less puzzling are the disconnections that are typographically introduced between items that we might ordinarily expect to be part of a continuous series. After Emma and Rodolphe have made love, we read:

> She was charming on horseback—upright, with her slender waist, her knee bent on the mane of her horse, her face somewhat flushed by the fresh air in the red of the evening.
>
> On entering Yonville she made her horse prance in the road.
>
> People looked at her from the windows.[19]

If the sentence of entry into Yonville takes a paragraph of its own to emphasize that it is a new phase of the trip between the woods and the town, we still must scratch our heads to come up with an explanation for why the next sentence is a new paragraph. Of course we can always find some reason—say the disjunction between the censorious community and the individual striving for a freedom beyond its confines, the outdoors versus the indoors—but it will always seem arbitrary. Such paratactic sequences seem rich and precise in the obvious willful care that has gone into their construction, yet they are also curiously uncontrolled, for there is no narrator whose reassuring presence we can refer all these moments back to. It is for this reason that it was necessary in making so many of my points along this argument to say "we read" and that my initial observations began from a matter of typography. With Flaubert we are in the realm of the textual. His elliptical style creates the default of any constant narrative presence and leaves us warily by ourselves in making the necessary interpretations to tease out the implications and thereby show our understanding.

The contrast between the bumbling incapacity in his characters' ellipses and the magisterial authority in Flaubert's elliptical procedure begins from the first use of ellipsis in the book, in the account of Charles Bovary's first day in school. As a newcomer with a grotesquely elaborate headgear and a shy inarticulacy, Charles has provoked the ridicule of his classmates:

> "What are you looking for?" asked the master.
> "My ca . . ." Charles replied.[20]
> "Five hundred verses for all the class!" shouted in a furious voice, stopped, like the *Quos ego*, a fresh outburst.[21]

Flaubert sets against Charles's helplessness the master's power, likened to that of Neptune calming the winds in the *Aeneid*.[22] The master's power, however, is neither divine nor natural; it is strictly literary and disciplinary—a task of book Latin.[23] The Virgilian model to which it refers long served as a textbook instance (e.g., in Quintilian) of a rare and impressive figure of speech—itself an instance of literary default—aposiopesis, "silencing." *Quos ego*, Neptune's threat, is not a full sentence and so might be translated best by Elmer Fudd: "Why, you, I'll . . ." But in this case divine or literary power makes the words wholly effective at calming the "outburst."

We may conclude the examination of ellipsis in *Madame Bovary* by invoking the geometrical figure of the ellipse, a regular oval, smooth and continuous and enclosed, that nevertheless "falls short" of the harmony of a circle because it is determined not by one unique center but by two foci, the sum of the distances from which is a constant for any point on the curve. Much in the book relates to the failure of centering in Emma, and we may now emphasize the duality within her. If her attempt to make a center of her love for Leon failed to establish a center of spiritual value in the midst of the surrounding bleakness of small-town domesticity, it is perhaps, in the logic of the book, because there is a simultaneous yet different attempt at centering within her, one that values the concreteness of her surroundings over any supposedly higher values. Her "nature" is also "positive in the midst of its enthusiasms" and "loved the church for the sake of the flowers, and music for the words of the songs."[24] Thus she can believe not in the possibility of creating a place of happiness within herself, but rather "that certain places on earth must bring happiness, as a plant peculiar to the soil, and that cannot thrive elsewhere."[25] Thus she materialistically confuses "the sensuous Pleasures of luxury with the delights of the heart."[26] There is no center from which she lives, and the oscillation between foci deforms her life.

The sentence that best emblematizes this elliptical pattern is the famous "She wanted at the same time to die and to live in Paris."[27] The sentence establishes no opposition between the two points; different as they are, together they work to define the limits of her aspiration. They also mark the two foci from which interpretations of the book have worked. The absolute of death marks the perspective from which the worldly desires of the book must seem vanity, whether in the framework of traditional Christian morality, for which Emma is, as for Homais, "a lesson, an example, a solemn picture,"[28] or from the modernistic, neo-romantic perspective of absolute irony, which equally sees her life as blind, self-mystifying delusion. At the same time, the sense of a full life in a specific place suggests such critics as Poulet and Richard in their analyses of the rich interplay of consciousness and materiality in the language of the book, in the experience of Emma and Flaubert both.[29]

The book itself defines these terms of response within Emma as she watches *Lucie de Lammermoor* and feels both the life within the work and the death within the work, its relation to human experience and to inhuman form. At first she "recognized all the intoxication and the anguish" of her affair with Rodolphe: "The voice of the prima donna seemed to echo her own conscience, and the whole fictional story seemed to capture something of her own life." But from this participation she begins to slip away, or to rise, into the distance: "But no one on earth had loved her with such love. . . . Such happiness, she realized was a lie, a mockery to taunt desire. She knew now how small the passions were that art magnified." In her attempts at "detachment" she achieves a perspective that corresponds closely to the defenses of much modern criticism and sees "this reproduction of her sorrows" instead as "a mere formal fiction." Thus she is freed to "smile . . . inwardly in scornful pity, when from behind the velvet curtains at the back of the stage a man appeared in a black cloak." Her attention is on the literal details of the theater, the "stage," the "curtains," not Edgar but only "a man in a black cloak." This superior position, however, proves no more stable than had the previous one, and "swept away by the poetic power of the acting, and drawn to the man by the illusion of the part," Emma returns to projection and "tried to imagine his life."[30]

Our presumption of superiority to Emma, the "scornful pity" that we may feel for her, and that Flaubert may have also felt at moments in composition, should not blind us to the fact that as readers we are involved in the same difficulties as she is. Without some participation and feeling on our part, the work will remain a "mere formal fiction."

This sequence may remind us that Flaubert's distrust of speech, as rolled fabric, is also related to a distrust of narrative, considered equally inadequate to the complexities of reality. In his writing, narrative tends to behave like the guests at Emma's wedding: "The procession, first united like one long colored scarf that undulated across the field, along the narrow path winding among the green wheat, soon lengthened out, and broke up into different groups that loitered."[31] The attempt at what we now call spatial composition is suggested in Flaubert's own metaphor of composition, which refuses both passion and the linear time of organic continuity: "Books are not made like babies but like pyramids, with a premeditated plan, by placing huge blocks one above the other."[32] This observation, reflecting the tension between the "quest for origins" and the "discovery of the mausoleum" that Edward Said elucidated for the nineteenth-century novel in general, may be supplemented by one of the most teasing moments in the book, the short paragraph that forms the hinge between the introductory description of Yonville and the narration of the Bovarys' arrival within this prepared scene: "Since the events about to be narrated, nothing in fact has changed at Yonville. The tin tricolor flag still swings at the top of the church-steeple; the two streamers at the novelty store still flutter in the wind; the spongy white lumps, the pharmacist's foetuses, rot more and more in their cloudy alcohol, and above the big door of the inn the old golden lion, faded by rain, still shows passers-by its poodle mane."[33] No history has intervened to change the visual relation of church and state (and thus the Revolution of 1848 and coup d'état of 1851 are denied); the forces of nature have not been able to tear away the streamers; preservatives have slowed the organic to a virtual standstill; and the discrepancy between the splendid name of "Golden Lion" and the image that absurdly fails to represent it stands as a static emblem of what Emma is to experience in narrative. But that narrative changes "nothing in fact."[34]

This remark, one of the very few places in the book that draws explicit attention to the act of narration, is puzzling, for at the end of the book not only is Emma dead, and also Charles, but Lheureux and Homais have achieved new triumphs. We may take it that these deaths and triumphs mark no change, but only the continuation of the "mœurs de province" to which the book's subtitle devotes it. Nonetheless, it seems to be better to take the statement very literally, rather than trying to claim that some changes are really no changes, and to recognize in "the events about to be narrated" a definition of the whole rest of the book. The unconscious processes of linguistic change that have transformed "in fact" (it works the same for the French *en effet*) from an assertion about the "real world" to a mere introductory turn of phrase—made it in Roman Jakobson's terms more a matter of code than of context[35]—are here brought to consciousness by the pressure of Flaubert's writing in its attempt to deny referentiality and to privilege the systematic self-reference of the book. "In fact" nothing he describes will ever change after "the events about to be narrated" because they exist only in the fiction of the book. Every word of it to the end is one of those events, and when the book has ended nothing changes within it.

III

Having called on the resources of rhetorical analysis made possible by deconstructive criticism, a realist criticism must now question the Flaubertian positions that we have succeeded in specifying. If in this literature the *Quos ego* of Flaubert's ellipsis silences history's outbursts, there may yet be more to the story. We may share Flaubert's scorn for narrative eventfulness, and we therefore laugh at a satirical description of *Madame Bovary* as a moralistic antiromance, "the history of a wicked woman who goes from one abomination to another, until at last the judgment of Heaven descends upon her, and, blighted and blasted, she perishes miserably."[36] Yet when the book was prosecuted upon publication, essentially this view of it was offered by the defense attorney (to whom Flaubert subsequently dedicated the book). *Madame Bovary* was rescued and legitimated by the vestigial narrative structure that it wishes to mock. The critic who emphasized the book's disconnections, its refusals to reach full, satisfactory, conventional expression, was the prosecutor. He was the one to charge Flaubert with presenting "the poetry of adultery" and to insist that a bad ending could not be tacked on to redeem such initial excess.[37]

Both attorneys seem rather clownish to us, yet the issue between them is one of the oldest and most complex in cultural theory: the relations of part and whole. Both Longinus, who approved, and Plato, who disapproved, agreed with the prosecutor's premise that literature moves us most powerfully at *moments*, which are fragments separate from any totality. On the other hand, from Aristotle's *catharsis* to I. A. Richard's "stable poise," theories of formal wholeness are immobilizing.

It is tempting to extend these claims politically. In the earlier nineteenth century, Shelley and Hazlitt, as Longinians, supported political radicalism, against which Coleridge the Aristotelian stood conservatively.[38] In the 1930s, Walter Benjamin's Longinian politics of agitation opposed Lukács's Stalinist Aristotelianism.[39] Such analogies have been very important in recent decades in making certain critical positions seem more, or less, attractive. I have argued elsewhere,[40] but can only assert here, that culture is related to politics—and a task of what I call "realist" criticism is to study and specify such connections—but that there is no reason to think that the relation is a simple analogy. There are more complex figurative relations than that of metaphor; relation does not consist only in likeness. If a notion like "reification" means anything, it means that Marxists cannot assume a transparent resemblance between sectors that have been socially produced as distinct.

One value in studying Flaubert is to recall us to these difficulties. Jonathan Culler's deconstructive reading of Flaubert hails his "achievement" as "revolutionary," but it goes without saying that the effects are limited within the institution of literature. Jean-Paul Sartre's Marxist analysis brings home the success of *Madame Bovary* as ideology: It helped to constitute a class fraction of the upper bourgeoisie who shared a position toward the Second Empire of cynical support, which the book allowed to reach articulation. In a further twist, Fredric Jameson's Marxism is more difficult, dubious, and challenging, neither euphoric like Culler nor censorious like Sartre. While dismissing the anarchist political claims of the deconstructive reading, Jameson would see in the socially formative power that Sartre exposes just what a left-wing critic should most value—if only one makes the *allegorical* transformation that cancels the empirical content in favor of a utopian projection of a world wholly *different*.[41]

I would like to conclude with a final observation that I hope has been clearly implicit—yet I shun ellipsis to spell it out. The narrative responsibilities of intellectuals became in the later twentieth century a major topic for debate and exhortation, whether in the work of establishment historians like Lawrence Stone and Bernard Bailyn, of maverick philosophers like Alasdair MacIntyre and Richard Rorty, or of radical critics like Jameson and Edward Said.[42] The challenges have not disappeared. In trying to come to terms with the complexities of this issue, I find it salutary to explore the comparable, though far from identical, cases of the novelists of the nineteenth century. Like them, as cultural intellectuals, we are participating in a hegemonic practice, more deeply than we can ever fully know, yet we also understand ourselves in our activities as teachers, scholars, and writers to be doing counterwork that not only aims but somewhat succeeds at making an opening where alternative views and practices may emerge. From a certain demographic perspective, it is surprising that the novel of the nineteenth century reached a smaller proportion of the population, certainly in the United States, than college English courses do today; that is, statistically, the novel was more elitist than contemporary literary higher education. On the other hand, there is an immensely greater state investment in authorizing higher education now than there ever has been in fiction. These contrasts demonstrate that the differences are interestingly complex, rather than easy, and they underline my fundamental emphasis. The refinement of textual inquiry can aid but should not replace the questions of uses and effects: rhetoric, yes, but realism too.

9. Baudelaire's Impure Transfers: Allegory, Translation, Prostitution, Correspondence

This chapter arose from the challenge of presenting a difficult author in lucid, clear text for a standard reference work. Light annotation has been added for this revision. In focusing on the complexities in Baudelaire's experience, criticism, and poetry, I elaborate his lexicon of impurity, the terms that chart the process of making connections by breaking bounds.

The Life

Charles Baudelaire lived in a world even more aware than our own of rapid transformations in every aspect of life. The very term "modernity," which figures importantly in his writings, only came into the French language during his youth. By the time he published *Les fleurs du mal*, in 1857, he had already lived under four political regimes. He was born in 1821 under the Bourbon monarchy, which the allies had restored to the rule of France after they defeated Napoleon in 1815. In 1830 a revolution brought in a constitutional monarchy under the Orleanist Louis-Philippe. This bourgeois monarchy yielded in 1848 to further revolutionary activity, and the Second Republic (the first had been under the Revolution, 1792–1804) was instituted, only to succumb to the coup d'état of Louis Napoleon, nephew of Bonaparte, on December 2, 1851, which brought in the Second Empire. Titles like "restoration," "second" republic, and "second" empire suggest repetitiveness; the term "revolution" originally characterized the planets' movements in their orbits. In contrast to these political cycles, the social and economic innovations showed no signs of return. Baudelaire's contemporaries understood that there had occurred a change from an aristocratic to a bourgeois society, from a domination of landed wealth to the predominance of commercial and industrial interests. A more democratic polity and more dynamic economy made available for writers vastly greater means of publication, particularly in the newly flourishing periodical press, yet it was not clear that the dominant bourgeoisie cared for the literary enterprises that writers might undertake. Baudelaire and his contemporaries therefore both cast nostalgic glances back to aristocracy and also empathized with the new workers' movements—for both represented alternatives to the bourgeoisie.[1]

All this change could seem the falling away from a valued past, or progress toward an ever-improved future. One's status in life was no longer fixed. The government official François Guizot, faced with complaints about the property qualification that limited voting rights under Louis-Philippe, could answer simply, "Make yourselves more money" ("Enrichissez-vous"). The power of money in a world of increasingly free markets, in which not only goods but also "free labor" were sold, destroyed traditional values. *The Communist Manifesto* (1848) characterized the bourgeois age as one in which "all that is solid melts into air."[2] After 1849, the great capital city of Paris itself dramatically exemplified this mobile fluidity. Under the direction of Baron Haussmann, old quarters of the city were torn up— especially those that had been rebellious—and wide new avenues regulated and accelerated the flow of traffic, while facilitating also free lines of fire and rapid deployment for troops against an uprising.

Baudelaire's own family offers a vivid emblem of this messy historical layering. His father was an old man, born in 1758, under Louis XV. His life had been shattered and remade by history: He studied in a seminary and was ordained a priest, but during the Revolution he left the Church. His connections included intellectually liberal aristocrats (such as the Marquis de Condorcet, a great visionary of humanity's future, who died in the Terror), and he finally held a sinecure at the Senate under Napoleon's Empire. Baudelaire looked back to his father as a cultured man, who had practiced both poetry and painting. Baudelaire's mother was born in 1793 in London, where many French families emigrated during the Revolution. In his later life Baudelaire recalled the brief period he had enjoyed alone with his mother, after his father's death in early 1827 and before her remarriage in late 1828. The transitions—from life with an elderly father to life alone with his mother to life with a stepfather—must have been startling. His stepfather, Jacques Aupick, born in 1789, the year of the Revolution, was over thirty years younger than his father. Having begun his career with Napoleon's army, Aupick managed to flourish under the newer regimes. He became head of the garrison in Lyon at the time of the workers' rebellion there, rose to general, became head of the Polytechnical Institute (France's West Point) in Paris just before the 1848 Revolution, served the new republic as ambassador in Constantinople and then Madrid, and was named a senator under the Second Empire, dying just before the publication of *Les fleurs du mal* in 1857.

Baudelaire's two fathers represent two eras: an age of religion, philosophy, and the arts, and an age of the army, technology, and politics. They model the contradictions Baudelaire felt within himself, beginning from childhood. Another contradiction also shaped Baudelaire's family life: The extreme propriety of his mother's correspondence with Charles jars against the sensual details by which his autobiographical jottings remember her. Modern research has discovered, however, that only weeks after her second marriage, she delivered a stillborn child. We may surmise the compensatory energy behind her shock at Charles's choices of life, the mother's hidden fault exaggerating the son's faults.

Baudelaire's life after his mother's remarriage may be told as a series of disasters.[3] This is not the whole story, but it helps explain his excitement at the story of Edgar Allan Poe's ruinous life, in which he saw a version of his own. In his last year of secondary school, Baudelaire was expelled for refusing to hand over a note from a schoolmate. While beginning a purely nominal course of legal studies, he contracted venereal disease and many debts. To keep him out of trouble, his family put him on a ship bound for India, a trip that lasted nearly a year and was intended to be longer. Shortly after his return, he began a liaison with Jeanne Duval. The two lived together much of the next decade, did not finally give up trying to do so until 1856, and remained in touch until at least 1864. A woman of color, minor actress, and prostitute, Jeanne stood outside bourgeois norms. At his twenty-first birthday, Baudelaire inherited from his father an estate large enough to give him a comfortable income, but within two years he had reduced his capital by almost half, with further debts impending. His family, as French law allowed, named a trustee to manage the estate, so in 1844 Baudelaire became again a legal minor. The next year, shortly after the publication of his first signed work (1845), he attempted suicide. In 1848 he joined the revolutionary activity—according to one witness, crying, "We must shoot General Aupick!" The coup d'état by Napoleon III so dismayed him that he wrote to his trustee that he was "physically depoliticized" (March 5, 1852).[4] By his middle thirties, his literary career seemed well launched, but in 1857 *Les fleurs du mal* was prosecuted by the state, leading to the suppression of six poems and to a fine. The remaining decade of his life passed in continuing financial difficulty, worsening health, and loneliness. From 1864 to 1866, he tried living in Brussels in order to escape his creditors and to gain lecture fees, but nothing worked out, and he was stranded there when a stroke left him helpless. He was taken back to Paris and in 1867 died there, aphasic. It was widely believed that his debility resulted from syphilis, and medical debate continues. The disease was very common, often caught by schoolboys on their visits to brothels, and the available treatments were ineffective. Beyond these historical facts, it is striking that Baudelaire might have suffered from the same disease and been struck down at the same age as Adrian Leverkühn, Thomas Mann's paradigm of the modern artist in *Doctor Faustus*.

Another version of Baudelaire's life would emphasize his resiliency. The trip to India allowed him a moment of heroism amid a storm and, more importantly, gave him a world of poetic imagery, including sea, ships, and the tropics. So too, the relation with Jeanne Duval was not only, as Baudelaire sometimes insisted, the great love of his life; it was also fundamental to some of his greatest poems. Even the public disgrace of his poetry bore fruit. Baudelaire had considered *Les fleurs du mal* complete as published, and he lamented the necessity to "artificially become a poet again" (February 19, 1858, to his mother), as he felt obligated to do in order to replace the poems struck from the volume. Nonetheless, the work he did for the second edition (1861) was both in quality and productivity unmatched in his earlier career. In order to give positive meaning to Baudelaire's life, I have had to begin discussing his work.

The Corpus

Baudelaire holds his place in world literature as the author of a book of poetry, *Les fleurs du mal*, yet this slim volume occupies only one out of the seven volumes in the posthumous collected edition of 1868–70.[5] The rest of his work greatly rewards anyone drawn to it by the poetry, and it can fascinate even readers who know nothing of the poems. Because the translation of lyric poetry is so difficult, many English-speaking readers know and prefer Baudelaire for his prose. His greatest prose comes in his criticism, his studies of the "artificial paradises" of intoxicants, and the *Petits poèmes en prose* (collected 1869).

Art criticism provided Baudelaire's first publication: He produced commentaries, in the manner of Diderot and extending the insights of Stendhal, on the great annual exhibitions of current painting—the salons. His essay on the salon of 1846, along with that of 1859, "The Essence of Laughter" (1855), and "The Painter of Modern Life" (1863) are extraordinary works. Not only do they capture the widely various artistic energies of Baudelaire's own time—the great romantic canvases of Delacroix, the mad antics of English pantomime, the journalistic illustrations of Constantin Guys—their ideas and judgments also inspire art critics to this day. He wrote less on literature. The high point is a review of Flaubert's *Madame Bovary* (1857), but the essays on his poetic contemporaries are also worthwhile. His one piece of music criticism (1863) won him praise from Nietzsche as Richard Wagner's first intelligent admirer. Baudelaire's criticism analyzes contemporaries with an acuity that gives the critical writing as firm a place in later history as the masterpieces it proclaimed.[6]

The greatest bulk of Baudelaire's prose presents an anomaly to American readers: translations of the prose works of Edgar Allan Poe. The anomaly is double. First, Poe does not seem great enough to merit the labors of a master of world literature. But second, even if we grant that Baudelaire did for Poe what he boasted he had done for Paris—turned into gold the mud he had to start with—there is no way of demonstrating this outside the French language. These translations, however, remain current and classic in French. They have provided an access to Poe for generations of European readers, and they have made of Poe quite a different figure from what he is in the United States. "Translation" is itself a crucial term in Baudelaire's thinking about the arts, which links him to key concerns of the twenty-first century.

Further translation makes up part of *Artificial Paradises* (collected 1860). These essays on wine, hashish, and opium include Baudelaire's version of Thomas De Quincey's *Confessions of an English Opium-Eater*. Problems of translation even haunt Baudelaire's most innovative prose, the fifty "little poems" (also known as *Paris Spleen*) that try to achieve a style responsive to the "countless crisscrossing relations" of modern city life. Several of these "poems" turn into prose verse from *Les fleurs du mal*.

Les fleurs du mal offers a textual problem. After the condemnation of six poems in 1857, Baudelaire wrote new poems to replace them in the second edition. Consequently, there is no single author's edition that published all the poems written for the volume. This would not be important, except that Baudelaire emphasized in 1857 that the collection had to be understood as a whole, and Jules Amédée Barbey d'Aurevilly, with Baudelaire's encouragement, wrote of the volume's "secret architecture." In sending the 1861 edition to Alfred de Vigny, Baudelaire emphasized that it was no "collection": It had "a beginning and an end" and the new poems replaced the suppressed ones within a "singular framework" (letter ca. December 16, 1861). The usual French solution is to publish the 1861 text, followed by the condemned poems, but several American translations fit them back as close as possible to their original locations. This is suspect, however, because in making the second edition, Baudelaire moved a number of poems. Thus location in 1857 is no guarantee of location in 1861. On the other hand, most readers now discount the claim for a "secret architecture." Although there are clearly principles of resemblance and contrast that give particular poems relations to other poems, and there is some sense of progression through the volume as a whole, no one has demonstrated the necessity for every poem to be present in a particular order. (My references follow the numbering of 1861, as in the edition by Pichois.)

To begin characterizing and analyzing Baudelaire's poetry, I take one of the longer poems from *Les fleurs du mal*. It originally appeared in the preview of the volume that Baudelaire succeeded in placing in the prestigious *Revue des Deux Mondes* in 1855. In both editions it comes near the end in the section "Fleurs du mal."

The Corpse: "A Voyage to Cythera"

"A Voyage to Cythera" comprises fifteen quatrains, rhymed *abba*. The line contains twelve syllables, typically with a caesura—a break—after the sixth. In using this alexandrine line, Baudelaire followed the tradition of major French poetry from Ronsard in the sixteenth century through Racine in the seventeenth century, to his own older contemporary Victor Hugo. Baudelaire, however, employs fewer variations on the classic form of the line than did Hugo. As a prosodic conservative in his management of the alexandrine, he thus took some distance from romantic style.

As a "voyage," this poem has a plot, and its movement is more obvious than in some of Baudelaire's poems, which are sometimes deliberately immobilized. Here, however, movement dominates from the beginning: The heart, "like a bird, flutters" and "soars," while the ship too "rolls" over the waves. The first words of the poem, "my heart," suggest a poem of subjectivity, a romantic display of the first-person singular, but instead the narrative leaves aside the first person almost entirely, until the last four quatrains. The narrative represents a series of discoveries, made visually, from a distance.

After the buoyancy of the first stanza, the second abruptly shifts register: "What is that sad, black island?" This contrast to the sunny radiance of the first stanza leads to another jolt, for the gloomy island is Cythera, in Greek mythology the home of the goddess of love. But the glamour is worn. No matter what "people say" and "songs" tell, its magic appeal holds only for "old boys," bachelors whose love lives have become "banal" routine: "Look, after all, it's a poor piece of earth."

Suddenly in the third stanza another voice breaks in to hymn the mysteries of the island in a formal apostrophe: "Isle of sweet secrets and the holidays of the heart!" The happy movement of the heart and ship in the first stanza here carries over to the island's air, with the repetition of the verbs "soar" (lines 2 and 11) and "roll" (lines 3 and 16). The syntax is elevated. Modifiers are placed, contrary to usual practice, before what they modify, delaying the appearance of subject and verb. Such "suspended" effects echo Latin gravity:

> De l'antique Vénus le superbe fantôme
> Au-dessus de tes mers plane comme un arôme.

Very literally:

> Of the antique Venus the proud ghost
> Above your waters floats like a scent.

By the poem's end, when banished Venus returns as a ghost, the smell is not all "roses." The invocation reaches its climax in a rolling of repeated *r* sounds, but then the second voice breaks in again, continuing the sound of *r*, but reversing its import: The "garden of roses" becomes a "rocky desert" (lines 16 and 19). This dramatic dialogue of two voices exemplifies what often energizes Baudelaire's work, the interplay of levels of speech, often wholly different registers of vocabulary—here the language of song against that of sight.

The narrative again resumes; a "singular" object has attracted attention. The next twenty lines specify what has been seen. The description begins in the negative. The sixth stanza repeats the language of ecstatic classical song, a vanishing glimpse of the erotic intensity that the poem holds out only to deny by negating it. In contrast to the "white sails" of the ship stands the "black" shape of a gibbet—like a "cypress," the traditional tree of death, rather than the "myrtle" (line 13), traditional tree of love. The birds too have changed. After the initial resemblances among heart, bird, and ship, in stanza 7 the ship "troubles" the birds, breaking the imagined harmony of man and nature, and in stanza 8 nature takes its revenge, as "ferocious birds" tear apart a hanged man. Rapid shifts of language try to assert mobility against the fixating power of this spot. The understatement of calling the hanged man "ripe" yields to speaking of him as "a thing all rotten"; the birds are rehumanized as full of "anger," but their destructiveness is so inhumanly methodical that their beaks are like "tools."

The ninth stanza is held by the dreadful object: "The eyes were two holes, and from the belly, broken open, the heavy intestines flowed down over his thighs, and his tormentors, gorged with dreadful treats, had with the blows of their beaks absolutely castrated him."

The last movement begins with the speaker addressing the corpse, as he had earlier addressed the island, and in the same outworn vocabulary, "Dweller of Cythera, child of so lovely a sky." Then without any formal mark to indicate a second speaker, the language turns wrenchingly: "Ridiculous hanged man, your sorrows are mine!" From speculation on the other, the speaker turns to himself: "I felt like vomit coming up to my teeth the long river of gall from old sorrows." Are these sorrows the speaker's own, or are they a larger human sorrow, stretching back even to the times of Venus's glory? Facing this "poor devil," initial horror and subsequent scorn yield to sympathy. The speaker himself now feels the "beaks" and "jaws" of "crows" and "panthers," which "used to love so much grinding up my flesh." The outer scene is internalized. The "sky" and "sea" may be "enchanting" and "calm," but "for me everything was now black and bloody," and "as in a thick shroud, my heart was wrapped up in that allegory."

Just before ending, the poem acknowledges its mode. The narrative of events in the Mediterranean Sea is redefined as "allegory." The hanged man has no value in himself, but only as appropriated for another's purposes. No connection joins the present speaker and the classical meanings of Cythera that provide the decor: "On your isle, O Venus, I found nothing standing but a symbolic gibbet, from which hung my image." The voyage to Cythera becomes a voyage into a mirror; the horror is not the object one sees but the subject that it represents. "My image" is an image of me, but also an image I made. Perhaps I could make another one: "Ah, Lord, give me the force and the courage to face my heart and my body without disgust."

Reading this *fleur du mal* (most literally, "flower of evil") helps to define what that violently contradictory title means. The "flowers" of lines 13 and 22, absent from the modern island, nonetheless blossom in the form of the poetry, while the evil we encounter is not "unspeakable rituals" (line 43)—a literary banality like the "Eldorado" of old songs (lines 6 and 7)—but rather the pain of "old sorrows" (line 48). The American modernist Wallace Stevens suggested that his poem "Esthétique du Mal" (1944) was about the relations of poetry and pain, and I find this useful for Baudelaire. *Mal* can also mean "difficulty"—like that of making poetry when all the old songs have already worn out, when even the innovations of romanticism have become clichés.[7]

Baudelaire differs from the norms of romanticism in his management of the "I." This poem makes programmatically clear how little that "I" can be identified with the empirical existence of Charles Baudelaire. Baudelaire never voyaged in the Mediterranean. The poem's setting comes from Gérard de Nerval, who had published in 1844 several journalistic pieces on his disillusion at encountering the old isle of Cythera, now barren under English rule. Here is a sample from Nerval: "I saw a little monument, vaguely standing out against the azure of the sky, and which . . . seemed the still standing statue of some tutelary divinity. But as we approached further, we made out clearly the object . . . which drew that coast to the attention of travelers. It was a gallows, with three branches, of which only one was decorated."[8]

Baudelaire's poem translates the writing of another into his own. This is not unique in his poetry. The sonnet "Bad Luck" (number 11) translates stanzas from Henry Wadsworth Longfellow for its octave and from Thomas Gray for its sestet, yet the poem is both successful and as fully Baudelaire's as any other. Baudelaire's "I," then, is a certain way of negotiating a relationship with literature. Baudelaire felt sure that he had never plagiarized from Poe, because all he had found in Poe was himself. For Baudelaire, the process of reading or seeing was, to the extent that it succeeded, a finding of himself in what he saw or read. This may lead to the claustrophobia of "Spleen" or the self-tormenting, ironic self-observation frequent in his work. Baudelaire could find himself in very uncomfortable ways—the hanged man of Cythera, or Edgar Allan Poe, execrated by the American bourgeoisie and driven to a shameful death—but the process could also be wonderfully satisfying. In all cases, the process is a transfer of properties; something becomes merely a sign for something else, as in allegory.

To see in Baudelaire only the nonempirical "I," the recourse to allegory, the translation of one literary work into another, is to ignore much. For his poetry clearly also relates to the experience of Paris in the Second Empire, the experience of a man with a complex erotic life in a varied social world. The sea of "A Voyage to Cythera" is not wholly alien to Paris. The city itself becomes oceanic: "Tell me, does your heart sometimes fly, Agatha, far from the black ocean of the filthy city, to another ocean where splendor shines?" (number 62). From a Paris garret, chimneys and bell towers seem "masts of the city" (number 86). The "multitude" of the city and the "solitude" of the ocean are "equal and convertible for the active poet" ("Crowds," in *Paris Spleen*). The principle of transfer that makes possible allegory and translation connects diverse elements of life. Baudelaire had himself voyaged, but in thinking of De Quincey, who had not, he turned to the "voyager," the "ancient mariner," as "metaphors that poets use" for a man who has struggled with life (*Artificial Paradises*). James Joyce's figure of Ulysses for the modern city dweller already lurked in Baudelaire.

Two Bodies: "A Corpse" and "Jewels"

The emotional response to seeing a body in a context set by love runs from "A Voyage to Cythera" through many other of Baudelaire's most striking poems, which take very different directions. A dead body focuses attention from the beginning of "Une Charogne" ("A Corpse," or "Carrion," number 29): "Remember the object that we saw, my soul, that sweet and lovely summer morning, at the turn of a path, a foul corpse, on a bed scattered with pebbles, its legs in the air like a lewd woman." The poem's effect comes from the tension between horror and beauty, the past sight and the present address to the beloved. The initial rhyming contrast between "soul" (*âme*) and "foul" (*infâme*) is exacerbated.

Both the positive and the negative are amplified, and the positive becomes an aspect of the corpse itself: "The sky watched the splendid carcass open like a flower." Set against this stands the rhyming second half of the stanza, "The stench was so strong that you thought you would faint on the grass." "Blossom" (*s'épanouir*) and "faint" (*évanouir*) echo each other, and the formal preterite tense of narrated action (*crûtes*, "thought") powerfully distinguishes human queasiness from natural process, described in the imperfect tense. The poem recalls medieval verse in contempt of the flesh, and even more closely baroque poems (such as Andrew Marvell's "To His Coy Mistress") that seek to win a lover through exploitation of what were once religious topics, but the end strikes a new note. The final turn contrasts the body of the beloved, whom the poem reduces from "soul" to corpse, with the achievement of the poet: "Then, my beauty, tell the vermin who will eat you with their kisses, that I have preserved the form and divine essence of my decomposed loves."

The last word of the poem, "decomposed," is not only a term of organic decay; it is also a key term in Baudelaire's aesthetics. In the third section of the "Salon of 1859" he argues that the Imagination is "queen of the faculties" because it "decomposes all creation" and with the "amassed materials" it "creates a new world." In the poem, the process of "giving back" to Nature "all that it had joined together" produces a new flowering and a "strange music." The corpse becomes a "sketch" left for the "artist to finish from memory." Baudelaire's criticism warns against directly imitating nature and urges instead recourse to "memory." The poem thus offers further insight into what *fleurs du mal* might be. Their beauty is not easy, and to achieve it may be a dreadful task that takes all the writer's energy: Your soul threatens to faint along the way. This difficulty emerges again in a prose poem, "The Artist's Profession of Faith." A glorious day at the seashore threatens to overwhelm his capacities—provoking this final formulation: "The study of beauty is a duel in which the artist cries out in fear before he is beaten."

A comparable interplay of mastery and submission shapes the confrontation with another body and another beauty in "Jewels," one of the condemned poems. The loved one, although naked, has yielded to her lover's "heart" and kept on her "sonorous jewels," which give her the "conquering air" that, paradoxically, "moorish slaves" have. She calmly "let herself be loved." She is a "tamed tiger," but her body then "troubles" and "disorders" the speaker's calm. There is no overt violence in the scene, yet the language of power pervades it, and the poem ends ominously with the dying firelight "flooding with blood that amber-colored skin." Within this framework is set the "ecstasy" produced in the speaker by the "sparkling world of metal and stone," the jewels where "sound and light are mixed," and by the "metamorphoses" of the beloved's "poses": "And her arm and her leg, and her thigh and her loins, polished like oil and curved like a swan . . . and her belly and her breasts, those grapes of my vine."

As in "A Voyage to Cythera" and "A Corpse," the eyes encounter the parts of another body, but the "decomposition," the dismemberment here, fully as thorough as in the other poems, is registered positively. Even a mixture that might seem grotesque provides pleasure: "I thought I saw united by a new design the hips of Antiope with the chest of a boy, that's how much her pelvis stood out from her waist." Perhaps the jewels' stone and metal guard this body against decay, making this body hard rather than soft—as elsewhere we see a woman whose "polished eyes are made of enchanting minerals," who is "nothing but gold, steel, light, and diamonds" (number 27). The "statue with jet eyes, big angel with brow of bronze" (number 39) figures as a paradoxical positive (*front d'airain* has also the sense of a bold front, a brazenness). The soft, vulnerable body usually associated with love has little place. At rare moments a fraternal feeling for "the vomit of Paris" (number 105) allows Baudelaire to speak as "The Soul of Wine" and promise to restore to the worker's son his vigor and color, to be for "that frail athlete of life the oil that strengthens again the muscles of wrestlers" (number 104).

In their contrast between disgust and ecstasy, as well as between the soft and the hard body, "A Corpse" and "Jewels" define extremes of Baudelaire's work, and they thus help us understand the contrast of "Spleen" and "Ideal" (the section in which they stood only half-a-dozen poems apart in 1857). *Extremes* defines a major effect of Baudelaire's poetry and of his reputation. If these two poems dramatically contrast with one another, they resemble each other in their divergence from the ordinary norms of love poetry or good taste. Shock is omnipresent in Baudelaire's work. He proclaimed that beauty is always strange (*bizarre*) and that its effect is "astonishment." This sense of beauty is related to his life in Paris, the great capital of choked, foggy streets, where "the ghost accosts [*raccroche*, used often of prostitutes' solicitations] the passerby in broad daylight" (number 90). The "magic" of the city is violent, as "paving stones rise into fortresses" (sketch for epilogue to *Les fleurs du mal*) in the barricades of revolutionary days, times that fill the city with corpses at any turning.

The city forms a basic structure for experience, and it also provides a more consciously felt environment.[9] One resorts to shock to stand out from the crowd, to proclaim one's own life against the surrounding, ghostly wraiths. Among the crowd of all those who have ever written, to differentiate oneself requires something striking. Baudelaire found in Poe, moreover, an argument he made his own: Human incapacity for attention over a prolonged period, the "interrupted reading" imposed by "needs of business," constrains the artist. Commercial culture becomes an argument for short lyrics. So too, in a city where the eye predominates over the ear, where images more than sounds are the stuff of poetry and experience, the short poem offers the advantage of a readily apprehensible, visible form.

Baudelaire's shocks arise from the depths of city life, and they directly respond to some of its circumstances. They also willfully outrage bourgeois decorum. Baudelaire rightly prided himself on the traditional excellence of his spelling, his grammar, his diction, and his verse making, but none of these virtues carried any weight for a public that knew nothing of writing as a craft. Romantic emphasis upon inspiration here conspired with bourgeois ignorance. Baudelaire's poetry shocked by its subject matter of prostitution and perversion. In a society where every day most workers sold their bodies to bring wealth to another, it was considered unspeakable that some women (estimated at 34,000 in Paris of the 1850s) should sell their bodies to bring pleasure to another. This moralistic ideal was one target for Baudelaire. He carried throughout his career Stendhal's formulation from "On Love" that "beauty is a promise of happiness." Therefore he could never accept the idealist aesthetics of disinterest that for the bourgeoisie stood beside capitalist economics, the exploitation of bodies in toil for production. The body that sells pleasure by displaying itself contradicts both bourgeois aesthetics and economics. But, viewed differently, the prostitute paradoxically fulfills bourgeois norms, for the sale of love completes the process of desanctification that reduced every value to the market's. Thus in the poem beginning, "You'd take everyone in the world into your bed," the woman addressed has "eyes lit up like shop-windows" (number 25).

The prostitute has a further place in Baudelaire's poetry. The prostitute not only violates bourgeois decency and criticizes its hypocrisy by taking it to an unacknowledged logical extreme, but she also images the poet. In an early poem, Baudelaire writes of his love, "To have shoes she has sold her soul, but God would laugh if I . . . put on high airs by this disgrace, I who sell my thought and want to be an author" (poem beginning "Je n'ai pas pour maîtresse une lionne illustre"). If the prostitute sells her soul by selling her body, does not the writer do even worse by selling his thought? The new journalistic market in *esprit*—wit, intelligence—made the writer deeply complicit in the bourgeois mechanisms that he also opposed and that also stifled him. The ideal of free thought, confronted with the necessities of the free market, created a conflict that contributed to paralysis, marked by key terms like *ennui* and *spleen* in Baudelaire's work. As a productive writer, one contributed to the din, the traffic, that drowned out value.[10]

Baudelaire's short poems respond to two possibilities within this situation: first, the need for a powerful form to fix, to still, the chaos; second, the need for a sudden opening, a shock that takes you out of yourself. Thus Baudelaire praised the sonnet form; its constraint makes its idea "spring forth more energetically." He then develops an image drawn from urban experience: "Have you noticed that a bit of sky, seen through a cellar window, or between two chimneys . . . or through an arcade, gives a deeper idea of infinity than the grand panorama you see from the top of a mountain?" (February 18, 1860, to Armand Fraisse). The sonnet in France, as in England, had fallen into disuse after the Renaissance and was explicitly revived by romanticism. Yet great romantic poets like Hugo did not much use the form, so Baudelaire's sonnets, while "romantic," still allowed him individuality.

Polarities

Probably Baudelaire's most famous poem is the sonnet "Correspondences" (number 4), which in its narrow space opens out an infinity:

> Nature is a temple, where living pillars sometimes murmur confused words. Man passes through it by forests of symbols that look at him with familiar gazes. Like long echoes that from afar mix themselves into a deep and shadowy unity, vast as night and as day, smells, colors and sounds answer back to each other. There are smells cool as babies' flesh, sweet as oboes, green as meadows, and others corrupt, rich, and triumphant, that have the expansion of infinite things, like amber, musk, benzoin, and incense, and sing the transports of the spirit and the senses.

This poem has long been understood in relation to the subsequent literary movement called symbolism. But Baudelaire does not acknowledge any significant difference between symbol and allegory. In this he differs from such romantics as Goethe and Coleridge, for whom "translucence" distinguishes the symbol. Baudelaire, however, emphasizes "shadowy" confusion. No principle joins any element firmly to any other: A sensory motif returns to the primal unity, and when it comes back it may be transformed into anything else. That is, the principle of "correspondence" unmoors things from their properties. As in allegory, nothing is itself alone and for itself, but it may function as a relay for something else. In his *Intimate Journals*, Baudelaire writes of "prostitution" as the process by which a unity becomes a duality, that is, a unique property becomes the property of another. In this sense of the word, correspondences are not only a mode of allegory but also a mode of prostitution. The infinity opened up is a phantasmagoria of sensory transfer, a free market in the sensual.

Much later in "Spleen and Ideal," Baudelaire offers another version of this state of affairs. "Obsession" (number 79) answers back to "Correspondences."[11] Its last words repeat "familiar gazes" from early in "Correspondences," and its opening image transforms the "temple" of Nature: "Great forests, you terrify me like cathedrals!" Only night might please the speaker, but its stars' "light speaks a language that I know." The speaker seeks instead "the blank, the black, and the bare"—an end to the ceaseless transports by which one property becomes only a sign for another. But the process continues: the "shadows" become "canvases," on which there "live . . . departed beings with familiar gazes."

Both poems depend on correspondences and both might be called obsessive, though the one has the positive tone of mystical experience and the other the negative of Renaissance mad songs. The echo of "familiar gazes" suggests that each evokes family experience, a sense of totality that may begin in the infant's relation to its mother's body as an encompassing world. Such unity precedes self-knowledge as a separate individuality, whether painfully as in "A Voyage to Cythera" or with exhilarating liberation. Baudelaire himself speculated that the power of "genius" is that of "childhood, recaptured through an act of will" ("The Painter of Modern Life," sec. 3). Yet as he recalled childhood, there were not only moments of sensual correspondence like that by which he "confounded" the "odor of fur" with that of womankind; he also found in his earliest experience "two contradictory sentiments" coexisting: "the horror of life and the ecstasy of life" (*Intimate Journals,* "My Heart Laid Bare," sec. 73).

Some of Baudelaire's poems, like "A Voyage to Cythera," move from ecstasy to horror. Others, like "A Corpse," blend the two very closely together. Yet others, like "Correspondences" and "Obsession," are strongly polarized toward one or the other extreme. Our reading of Baudelaire cannot rely on his explicit valuations; the ambivalence of "contradictory sentiments" always functions, and recurrent patterns cut across any particular position. One such pattern is that of disillusion, as in "A Voyage to Cythera," but this very notion is double edged. Disillusion is "strange" (*bizarre,* like the beautiful): "half regret for the vanished phantom, half pleasant surprise at the novelty of the real fact" ("The Rope," in *Paris Spleen*). The confidence of reposing on something solid, no matter how barren and rocky, brings reassurance.

In this light we may contrast "Paris Dream" (number 102) with "The Abyss" (first published in 1862). These two late poems reach opposite extremes. The flashing limbs of "Jewels" moved Baudelaire to figures like those of the Song of Songs (breasts become "grapes of my vine"). His dream vision of Paris elaborates the "world of metal and stone" into a vision like that of New Jerusalem in Revelation, a city that transcends nature: "I had banished from these spectacles the vegetable, which is irregular, and proud of my genius . . . I enjoyed . . . the intoxicating monotony of metal, marble, and water." This "terrible landscape" is both a glorious creation of will and a fright to its creator. It extends Ralph Waldo Emerson's fear, expressed in "Ode, Inscribed to William H. Channing," that "things are in the saddle and ride mankind," that human creation had overreached human control, like Frankenstein's monster. The domination of eye over ear was for Wordsworth at the beginning of the century and Georg Simmel at the end a decisive new fact of city life.[12] The dream's end fulfills this tendency: Over the scene there reigned "(terrible novelty! Everything for the eye and nothing for the ears!) a silence of eternity." Then the dream breaks. Against the dream's "eternity" and "silence," the clock is "brutally striking noon"; the speaker's eyes, "full of flame" from his vision, awake to "the horror" of his shabby room. In "The Abyss" the terrible novelty of vision itself offers only horror, without ecstasy, and produces constant "vertigo." In the "Paris Dream," the enclosure of the room contrasted negatively to the breadth of vision, but in "The Abyss" vision is terror, and waking provides no escape: "I'm afraid of sleep as I would be afraid of a big hole. . . . I see nothing but infinity out all the windows."

"Elevation" (number 3) and "The Wish for Nothingness" (number 80) likewise draw different emotions from comparable situations. "Elevation" clearly fulfills a traditional understanding of the "Ideal." The poet's spirit "moves with agility" above the earth, even beyond the sun and the heavenly spheres. The serene fields of light are a happy change from the fogs of existence, for those "whose thoughts like larks take free flight to the skies in the morning"—like the birds of "A Voyage to Cythera." This happy spirit gains an overview, "soars over life," and "effortlessly understands the language of flowers and dumb things." Yet this overview has little content; contrast Wordsworth's success in substantiating what it means to "see into the life of things" in "Tintern Abbey."[13] If one has soared beyond all life, why should one even be interested in the language of things? In the following poem, "Correspondences," the "confused words" of nature lack the clarity promised here. The poem's energy is in the flight, not the goal; the movement itself produces value. "Elevation" prefigures the bitter wisdom of "The Voyage" that concludes *Les fleurs du mal*: "We want . . . to plumb the depths of the abyss, Hell or Heaven, what difference, to the bottom of the Unknown to find something new!"

Even more closely, however, "Elevation" is answered by "The Wish for Nothingness." Again the speaker is beyond the world, which no longer touches him; even "lovely spring has lost its smell." Again he takes an overview: "I observe from above the globe's roundness, and I don't even try to find there the shelter of a hut." The situation is like that of a stranded mountain climber: "Time swallows me up minute by minute as an endless snow does a stiffened body." The only wish is to end this paralysis, which is, paradoxically, painful in its absence of feeling: "Avalanche, will you carry me down in your fall?" Against the "Ideal" of "Elevation," here is "Spleen." Yet the situation makes possible a new, rich story—that of the descent. If the soaring of "Elevation" and its birds no longer works, there remains the "plunging" so frequent in Baudelaire's world. This is another meaning of *fleurs du mal*.

The path downward has traditionally been painful and evil, but it inspires Baudelaire's most original poetry, even if that poetry starts from the already-worn trappings of romantic Satanism. In helping Baudelaire think about how to defend his poetry from prosecution, the great critic Sainte-Beuve offered a line of analysis familiar to English readers from Keats's melancholy reflections upon the situation of the late-coming poet.[14] As Baudelaire put it in notes for a preface to the second edition: "Illustrious poets had already divided up a long time ago the most flowery provinces of the kingdom of poetry. It seemed to me pleasant, and all the more agreeable because the task was difficult, to draw *beauty* from *Mal* [evil, pain, difficulty]." Or in Sainte-Beuve's terms, "Lamartine had taken the skies. Victor Hugo had taken the earth, and more than the earth. Laprade had taken the forests. Musset had taken passion. . . . Others had taken the home, rural life, etc. . . . What was left? What Baudelaire took."[15]

Baudelaire takes energy from doing what previous poets had left undone, no matter how difficult and painful. Even more, though, the arrangement of *Les fleurs du mal* and the chronology of Baudelaire's works (the two are not identical, but here they tend to confirm each other) suggest that his continuing poetic production depended upon his reading of his own work in order to renew it, bringing out unexploited aspects of situations, feelings, images, and words that he had already used. Self-reading likewise provokes writing in such prose poems as "A Hemisphere in a Woman's Hair," "The Invitation to the Voyage," and "The Widows," which closely correspond to poems from *Les fleurs du mal* ("Hair," "The Invitation to the Voyage," and "The Little Old Women"). We return to translation and the allegorical transfer that assigns fresh meaning, corresponding to a given decor.

Spleen

Baudelaire's "Spleen" is not unprecedented. Coleridge's "Dejection" ode wishes for the violence of a storm to "startle this dull pain, and make it move and live."[16] Nonetheless, Baudelaire made this vein his own, and later poets cannot touch it without fearing his influence. Poems number 75 through 79 bear the title "Spleen," and number 74, "The Cracked Bell," was first published in 1851 under the title "The Spleen." The word *spleen* in French is taken directly from English and denotes a particularly modern and thus somewhat alien form of melancholy. It is related to the more traditional *ennui* (a word English takes from French), which in "To the Reader" Baudelaire allegorically transformed into the deadliest of sins: "Although he does not make a big stir or a big fuss, he would willingly make the earth a ruin, and in a yawn swallow the world. . . . His eye weighted with an involuntary tear, he dreams of scaffolds while smoking his hookah." This "delicate monster" resembles the speaker of the third "Spleen," "the king of a rainy country, rich, but impotent, young and yet very old," who cannot be cheered by "hunting, nor hawking, nor his people dying in front of his balcony." In *The Waste Land*, T. S. Eliot drew upon the opposite imagery, that of drought, to develop a similar feeling.

Spleen is inseparable from a distortion of time. The fourth "Spleen" begins with three parallel stanzas, each invoking and prolonging the same dreary moment, "When . . . When . . . When . . ." The sudden furious howling of bells that breaks this suspense brings only a slow, silent procession within the speaker's spirit. The mood is not dispelled but only exacerbated, and the "Hope" that earlier fluttered timidly "like a bat" now "weeps" in defeat. The decor of everyday life composes the scene: "my cat, trying to make a bed on the tiles" (number 75); "a big chest of drawers loaded with accounts, verses, love letters, lawsuits, romances, with heavy hairs rolled up in receipts"; "an old boudoir full of faded roses, where a mess of outworn fashions lies" (number 76). And this scenery comes to life: "The big bell mourns, and the smoky log sings along in falsetto with the sniffling clock," while in a smelly pack of cards, "the jack of hearts and the queen of spades speak forebodingly of their used up loves" (number 75).

The "language of flowers" in "Elevation" seemed to promise something good, but this language of "mute things" in the "Spleen" poems oppresses the hearer. And in hearing it, one becomes like the things that speak it. Those old desks and dressing rooms are figures for the speaker. The "I" is dispersed among things. The second "Spleen" begins, "I have more souvenirs than if I was a thousand years old," and it takes full advantage of the ambiguity by which "souvenirs" can mean either "memories"—spiritual presences in the mind—or "memorials," "keepsakes," things by which a memory may be provoked. This hovering between the material and mental, this weighting of the spirit together with a discomforting vivacity of things, begins the sequence of four poems, and ends it, in allegory.

The first "Spleen" begins: "Pluviôse, angered against the whole city, lavishly pours from his urn a shadowy cold upon the inhabitants of the neighboring cemetery, and mortality upon the foggy suburbs." The most chilling thing is the complete and indifferent grammatical parallel between what's done to the dead and what's done to the living. But there is some difference: The cemeteries have "inhabitants" (this figure of speech that abuses reality is called *catachresis*), while the suburbs, through the figure of metonymy, have swallowed up their dwellers, so that the poem speaks of the place but not the people. "Mortality" is puzzling; why not simply "death"? Mortality can be properly attributed only to those who are living, and by this logic to "pour out mortality" is to insist upon the life of those it's poured out upon, as if until that moment they had been immortal. Another sense for the term, however, emerges from the newly massive and intensive statistical studies of nineteenth-century Paris, including elaborate tables of mortality drawn up neighborhood by neighborhood. To speak of "mortality," then, suggests the statistical chance of death. Even something so intimate as death becomes common property. A person has a particular probability of death, just as a commodity has a particular probability of being sold. It doesn't matter what happens to the individual, so long as the overall numbers work out properly.

The allegorical figure of "Pluviôse" evokes a traditional image of the water bearer (Aquarius in the zodiac), but the name "Pluviôse" was invented for the calendar designed in the French Revolution. The term was both new—existing in the language only since 1792—and outmoded—since the revolutionary calendar had been put aside and was never revived. The status of this figure to whom such grand power is attributed is no different from that of the "superannuated fashions" in the boudoir. They too were recently invented and already defunct.

The final "Spleen" ends, "Long hearses, without drums or music move slowly through my soul; Hope, beaten, weeps, and dreadful Anguish, despotic, on my bowed skull plants his black flag." To this allegory of the emotions, we might contrast a moment from Petrarch's sonnets: "Love, who in my thought lives and reigns and keeps his principal seat in my heart, sometimes comes armed upon my forehead and settles down there and puts up his banner."[17] The shift from "forehead" to "skull" suggests a graver defeat and exemplifies Baudelaire's anatomical extremity, as in "A Corpse," which Sainte-Beuve called "petrarchizing upon the horrible." Even more striking is the shift from the triumph of love to that of anguish. This is the poetry of terminal conditions, perhaps even of a world that is ending. Baudelaire wrote in a prose draft for a preface to *Fleurs du mal* of his "*Muse of the last days.*" Yet the worst terror of the condition is that it seems like nothing can end: If *only* it were the last days, if only the avalanche would carry me down.

The final image of the second "Spleen" transposes this sense to one of its privileged locations for the Western imagination, to Egypt, the land whose monumental erections and hieroglyphic inscriptions already impressed the ancient Greeks as signs of mysterious wisdom, but no one knew specifically of what.[18] (Only a few years before Baudelaire wrote, Champollion had won fame for deciphering the Rosetta stone.) The condition of protracted terminality, in a mind with more memories than a millennium would bring, is evoked as "an old sphinx ignored by an indifferent world, forgotten on the map, and with a savage spirit that sings only to the rays of the setting sun." The song of sunset, the poetry of decadence, the flowers of evil, the muse of the last days—all these are suggested. But the sun sets only to rise again. Sunset brings no more relief than do the bells of the fourth "Spleen."

An impatient desire constricted—as by the sphinx's stone—paralyzed, unable to satisfy or even to terminate itself, this condition of spleen also occurs in "The Cracked Bell": "My soul is cracked, and when in its boredom [*ennuis*] it wants to people the cold night air with its songs, it often happens that its weakened voice seems the thick rasp of a wounded man, forgotten beside a lake of blood, under a great pile of the dead, and who is dying—immobile—amidst tremendous efforts." This correspondence transports the mind and senses, transforming the self into someone else and far away, but the new identification is no more gratifying than that on Cythera. The night is "peopled" only with corpses; like Pluviôse, the poet pours forth something chilling. This paralyzed voice in "The Cracked Bell" gives an image for the labored movement of Baudelaire's poems. Part of his accomplishment was to make beauty from slowness and stiffness.

"The Swan"

The allegory of the heart takes on new tones in the three "Parisian Paintings" dedicated to Victor Hugo, all written in 1859 for the second edition of *Les fleurs du mal*: "The Swan," "The Seven Old Men," and "The Little Old Women" (numbers 89–91). These titles sound laughably distant from the traditional subjects of great poetry, but Victor Hugo had defined the innovation of modern art as combining the sublime and the grotesque, in accord with the sense of human duality that Christianity had brought into the world.[19] In sending Hugo the two poems on old people, Baudelaire praised Hugo's blending of "magnificent charity" with "touching familiarity" (September [23?], 1859). This combination of grandeur and intimacy, the high and the low, an art that aspires to greatness while taking subjects from the neglected aspects of everyday life, links Baudelaire and Hugo to Wordsworth and Coleridge, whose *Lyrical Ballads* (1798) includes such poems as "The Idiot Boy" and "The Mad Mother." Baudelaire further resembles these English romantics in the movement of "The Swan." It meditatively circles back through layers of memory in response to a present moment of excitement, to which it returns before moving outward in a final gesture of spiritual generosity. This is the pattern of Coleridge's "Frost at Midnight" and Wordsworth's "Tintern Abbey." But those poems summon a natural landscape, Baudelaire's what he called "the landscape of great cities," which offers the "deep and complex fascination of a capital . . . grown old in the glories and tribulations of life" ("Salon of 1859," sec. 8). In keeping with his own precise attention to dress and his "Praise of Make-Up" in "The Painter of Modern Life," Baudelaire refused to provide nature poems when requested for an anthology: "I've even always thought that in Nature, fresh and flowering, there was something burdensome and impudent." Nature for Baudelaire had only allegorical use, as a sign to which he could attach human value: "In the depths of the woods, shut in under those vaults like those of sacristies, and cathedrals, I think of our amazing cities, and the marvelous music that rolls through the treetops seems to me the translation of human lamentation" (letter to Ferdinand Desnoyers, late 1853 or early 1854).

Baudelaire's urban emphasis leads Americans to neglect his links with romanticism and emphasize those to modernism. Innumerable readers for nearly a century now have first encountered Baudelaire in reading T. S. Eliot's *The Waste Land* (1922). The first section of that modernist masterpiece climaxes in a nightmare vision of London, beginning "Unreal City." Eliot's note to this phrase cites in French Baudelaire's "Seven Old Men": "Swarming city, city full of dreams, where in broad daylight the specter accosts the passerby." The passage continues to move within the foggy world of Baudelaire's poem, and Eliot ends by quoting in French the last line of "To the Reader": "Hypocritical reader, my likeness, my brother!"

Marcel Proust, who read Baudelaire with eyes formed by the humane sympathies of George Eliot and John Ruskin, found "The Little Old Women" an unsurpassable high point. Proust was fascinated too by Baudelaire's attention to the strange singularities of experience that take a moment out of the normal flow of time. One remarkable place that Baudelaire occupies in literary history is that of the shortest distance between Balzac and Proust—the slim volume of poetry between the two great novelistic bulks. In the "Parisian Paintings," Baudelaire was most fully available to Proust just where he was most fully drawing on Balzac. Baudelaire's Paris is not extensively described; Balzac had already done that work. Again and again in Baudelaire, however, moments occur that could be elaborately illustrated with pages from the *Human Comedy*. For example, the phrase "Prostitution lights up in the streets" (number 95) condenses through its strong yet abstract personification many moments from *Splendors and Miseries of Courtesans*. Or again, Balzac and Baudelaire both see the everyday bourgeois world of Paris given dramatic contour by gothic shadows: "Meanwhile, dirty demons in the atmosphere wake up heavily, like businessmen" (number 95).

"The Swan" requires also considering Baudelaire's relation to the classics—quite different from that in "A Voyage to Cythera." Baudelaire figures as a crossroads to literary history. He has baffled all attempts to compartmentalize him safely within any periodization. Moreover, his elaborations of "modernity" as nonchronological, marking beauty in any age, have led recent critics to rethink the basic ideas of literary history.[20]

"The Swan" establishes relations between the classical past and the Paris of Baudelaire's time. It alludes to the Roman poet Virgil, and it approaches the style and subject matter of Racine, the greatest earlier French poet who harked back to antiquity. This lyric of fifty-two lines manages to hold itself in the company of major forms from the past, the epic *Aeneid* and the tragedy of *Andromaque*. The poem begins after Troy's fall with the fate of the surviving Trojans: "Andromache, I think of you!" Andromache had been the wife of Hector and was taken by Achilles' son Pyrrhus, only then to be handed over to the Trojan Helenus, himself another slave. When Aeneas encounters her in the third book of the *Aeneid*, she is offering memorial observances to the empty tomb of Hector by a river that mimics the Simois, which flowed by Troy. The "lying Simois" in Baudelaire directly echoes Virgil.

But what has this to do with the swan of the title? The poem goes through four full stanzas before reaching the swan. In crossing Paris, the speaker has remembered a swan he once saw, bizarrely out of place, seeking water in the city dust, and this memory has awakened further memories, of Andromache and her river, and then thoughts of other exiles, including the poet himself, who feels exiled in "spirit." Beginning like a riddle, the poem proceeds by leaps, gaps, and contrasts, which close briefly in stanzas 9–10 but which then open out from the momentary conjunction in memory. The swan thus functions as a transfer point, itself absent from the present scene, yet making possible a number of meanings. The swan [*cygne*] functions as a sign [*signe*], and through its operation, "New palaces, blocks, old suburbs, all for me become allegory, and my dear remembrances [*souvenirs*] are heavier than rocks."

The swan thus approaches the sphinx of the second "Spleen," but the weight of allegorical oppression comes here in the middle of the poem, and the work accumulates energy to move beyond this sticking point. It risks absurdity to hinge such a large encompassment of history and feeling on a swan, which "escaped from its cage and, its webbed feet rubbing the dry pavement, dragged its white plumage over the rough ground." Baudelaire lavishes interpretive energy on the remembered sight. He starts by looking down on it: "By a dry gutter [in French a mocking echo, *ruisseau sans eau*] the beast opening its beak bathed its wings nervously in the dust." There follows a lightning escalation, as the beaked beast is first given the power of speech, then a deep inner life, and at last an impatient eloquence that rises to prophetic denunciation: "And it said, its heart full of its lovely native lake, 'Water, when will you rain? When will you rumble, thunder?' . . . as if it were addressing reproaches to God!" This apocalyptic swan song makes nothing happen. It is "ridiculous and sublime." The sky remains "ironic and cruelly blue," but to the swan's "mad behavior," Baudelaire has given a meaning.

Baudelaire has already risked absurdity, grotesque disproportion, even in evoking Andromache at the poem's start: "Andromache, I think of you! That little river, poor and sad mirror where once shone the measureless majesty of your widow's griefs, that lying Simois which by your tears grew great [*grandit*]." Will Baudelaire's echo mirror Virgil as falsely as Andromache's rivulet did the Simois? No matter how feeble a river, it cannot physically become large [*grandir*], or even significantly larger, through a person's tears. Baudelaire exaggerates [*grandir*], but through the grandeur of Andromache's sorrowing spirit, through the terrible history she bears witness to, the river she weeps in becomes important [*grandir*]. Through their reduced state of victimhood, Andromache weeping, "bent" by the cenotaph, and the swan, "holding up its eager head on its twisting neck," link the Paris of Baudelaire's day and the classical past. Andromache remembers the Troy that has fallen, and likewise for the speaker, "Old Paris no longer exists (the shape of a city changes more quickly, alas! than a mortal's heart)." By the poem's end, an appeal to "whoever has lost what will never be found again, never!" brings in also an allusion to the Roman history that connects Aeneas's Troy and Baudelaire's Paris. All those victims "have sucked at Sadness like a good she-wolf"—recalling Romulus and Remus.

Yet Rome suggests another connection between the present and the past. Neither contains only victims; there are also victors. Andromache "fell from the arms of a great husband, a mere chattel, beneath the hand of proud Pyrrhus." Likewise, the modern French Second Empire's military and commercial energies have brought to Paris "the black woman, thin and consumptive, tramping in the mud, and with haggard eye seeking the absent coco palms of splendid Africa behind the huge wall of fog." Politics count, starting from the poem's dedication. Victor Hugo was living in exile from the Empire, and to dedicate the poem to him foreclosed publication in any prominent journal. At the time Baudelaire sent "The Seven Old Men" and "The Little Old Women" to Hugo, Louis Napoleon had just declared an amnesty, which Hugo refused to consider. Baudelaire appreciatively wrote, "Poets are worth as much as Napoleons [also the name of a gold coin]" (September [23?], 1859).

The poem conveys the misery of what's lost forever, the irreparable, yet it enacts a process of recovery. The swan comes back in memory and brings back Andromache. The poet can see again "in spirit" the "rough-hewn capitals and shafts" and the "jumbled bric-a-brac" in shop windows of a vanished Paris. Victor Hugo, king of romanticism in Baudelaire's youth, now again means a great deal to him. Even some of his own earlier poetry is recaptured. The splendid lines about the absent palm trees are reworked from "To a Malabar Woman," only the third poem Baudelaire had ever published, over thirteen years earlier. The poem thus offers another world that follows different laws from those of Troy or Paris. Its recoveries mitigate their losses. Yet this escape in "spirit" is itself an "exile"; the westward translation of empire and culture brings alienation. Baudelaire's work does not allow us to rest content anymore than do "sailors forgotten on an island." The misery that joins Andromache, the swan, and "many others as well" seems to span all of history and the whole range of life. Either it is the inescapable human condition or else the whole of life must be remade.

The Individual

Baudelaire was not committed to remaking the world except in poetry, yet his experience was deeply marked by the violent political energies of nineteenth-century France. Scenes of confrontation run through his writings. In sections 4 and 5 of "The Painter of Modern Life," he argues that almost all our "originality" comes from the "trademark" that our time stamps on us. In accordance with this "historical theory of beauty," a crucial part of

Baudelaire's literary character resides in these historical traces—which appear not descriptively, as direct copies, but as what he paradoxically calls "the memory of the present." Thus the description of the "duel" between the artist's wish to "see everything" and the stylizing power of memory patterns turns into a scene from insurrectionary politics, an assault by "a riot of details, which all demand justice with the fury of a crowd panting for absolute liberty."

One trademark of Baudelaire's time was individuality. As early as section 17 in the "Salon of 1846," he analyzed individuality in relating artistic and social tendencies—the revolutionary heritage in politics and romanticism in the arts. In the arts "today," everyone is an "emancipated worker," no longer willing to undergo the discipline of a "school." These "republicans of art" make the present condition of painting an "anarchic liberty that glorifies the individual . . . to the detriment of associations." In contrast to an earlier "collective originality," the contemporary "smallholder" mentality, by glorifying the individual, "has necessitated the infinite subdivision of the territory of art." In economic history, the enclosure of common lands and the erosion of guilds and apprenticeship freed laborers for the open market, while freeing newly dominant individual owners to set their own terms. Likewise, in Baudelaire's analysis the domination of the "individual" makes it inevitable for strong poets or painters to have unknowingly drastic effects on "disciples" whom they have never met or taught. Paradoxically, the strong individual and the impersonal market go together.

Baudelaire opposes this situation with a parable: "Have you felt, you whose strolling curiosity has often thrust you into the midst of a riot, the same joy I have to see a guardian of the public sleep clubbing a republican?" So too republicans of art should be treated. Returning to this vein much later, Baudelaire criticized Wagner's belief that revolutionary innovations in art required revolutionary governments to support them. Against this "essentially humane illusion," Baudelaire argued that despotism allowed advanced art to flourish: Only under the Empire was Wagner performed in Paris. From the analysis of Shakespeare's monarchic politics of the imagination by the romantic, democratic critic William Hazlitt (discussed in Chapter 1) up through modern controversy over Yeats, Eliot, and Pound, the reactionary politics of advanced artists has colored our cultural debates.

Baudelaire's case, however, illustrates the difficulty in taking a writer's explicit pronouncements with any confidence. He himself joined the people in the streets in 1848, and his work was not promoted but prosecuted under the Empire. Moreover, he himself subscribed to the individuality that gave each artist his unique plot of ground. Although he often denounced the democratic, individualist tenor of his time, he carried that trademark. He could feel it as a loathsome disease yet felt compelled to acknowledge it in a note sheet at the end of his dossier called "Poor Belgium!": "We all have the republican spirit in our veins, like syphilis in our bones, we are democratized and syphilized" (this pun on "civilized" goes back at least to Byron's *Don Juan*). For Baudelaire the very circumstance of modern authorship is a destructive and guilty pleasure: "The day a young writer corrects his first proof sheet, he's proud as a schoolboy who's just first got syphilis" (*Intimate Journals*, "My Heart Laid Bare," sec. 49).

Baudelaire argues that self-criticism is essential to a successful career; anything less will leave a poet "incomplete," dependent on the vagaries of instinct ("Richard Wagner and *Tannhäuser* in Paris"). We have already noted Baudelaire's self-reading as a basis for new writing. In thus inevitably becoming a critic, a poet will look to others as well. After uneasy contemplation of one's own image, it may be exhilarating to find oneself in another. The artist's "double character" leads him as critic to "praise and analyze the most luxuriously the qualities which he himself most needs as a creator and which form the antitheses to those which he most superabundantly possesses" ("The Life and Work of Eugène Delacroix").

In practicing such antithetical criticism, critics stand toward the work criticized as artists do toward nature. Through this further doubling, "the best account of a painting may be a sonnet or elegy" ("Salon of 1846"), and thus also the best criticism of a poem may be another poem, perhaps in prose. A work of art for Baudelaire is less an imitation of nature than a passionate "protest" in the name of humanity against nature ("Salon of 1846"). We noted earlier that the Imagination must "decompose" nature and "make a new world" ("Salon of 1859"). Baudelaire, therefore, criticized the premise of realism that art should see the world as if you were not there. He found in those praised for realism something wholly different:

> I have often been astonished that the great glory of Balzac was to pass for an observer; it always seemed to me that his principal merit was to be a visionary, a passionate seer. All his characters are endowed with the vital heat with which he himself was animated. All his fiction is as deeply colored as dreams. . . . Everyone in Balzac, even the doorkeepers, has genius. All their souls are guns loaded to the brim with willpower. That's Balzac himself. ("Théophile Gautier")

The energy of this vision drove Balzac to "darken the shadows and brighten the highlights" of his characters; he was like those etchers "who are never satisfied with the bite and turn the main lines of the plate into ravines." This tendency is generally summarized as "Balzac's faults," but Baudelaire argues that it precisely defines the quality of his genius.

Such a critical appreciation gives substance to Baudelaire's claim that poetry "constantly contradicts the facts" and therefore, whether happy or sad, always bears a "utopian character" and "everywhere negates iniquity" ("Pierre Dupont"). It brings beauty that exists nowhere else, for if you wanted such beauty in the everyday world, you would have to destroy and remake that world as completely as the poet has done with it in his work. Thus poetry is both "the realest thing there is" but also "completely true only in *another world*" ("Since There Is Realism"). In a moment of extravagance, Baudelaire may claim, seeing a new generation that has modeled its life on the characters of Balzac, that "the visionary makes reality." Against this, however, the laws of artistic composition ensure that a Balzac character only works in Balzac's world and is "ridiculous" in ours ("*The Ridiculous Martyrs* by Léon Cladel"). Small changes are not enough. The world must be remade completely.

The commitment to antithetical practices in criticism, and the claim that poetry and criticism are governed by the same principles, makes the question of Baudelaire's sincerity difficult to evaluate. In the "Salon of 1846" he hailed Balzac as the greatest exemplar of "the heroism of modern life," yet he also caricatured him in "How One Pays Debts, When One Is a Genius": Balzac simply hired hack writers to do work that he then signed. In "The Painter of Modern Life," Baudelaire referred to the signature as "those few letters, easy to counterfeit, that figure a name," and he contrasted works "signed with [the] mighty soul." Balzac won greatness with this spiritual signature, but he won financial relief with the graphic. This conflict between individual signature and mass production signals the incoherence in Baudelaire's critical writing between his frequent emphasis upon the individual temperament as the decisive element in art, and his frequent emphasis upon impersonality.

Baudelaire held that criticism could be justified only by being "partial, passionate, and political" ("Salon of 1846"). This antithetical vocation always produces a situational, rhetorical complexity. In sending his study of Gautier to Victor Hugo, Baudelaire noted his difference from Hugo on the relation between art and morality. Hugo linked them very closely; Baudelaire often separated them utterly. "But in a time," Baudelaire continued, "when the world draws away from art with such horror, when men let themselves be brutalized by the exclusive ideal of utility, I think that there's no great evil in exaggerating a little bit the opposite idea. I have perhaps claimed too much. It was in order to get enough" (September [23?], 1859). This rhetoric of situational discounting, however, immediately puts itself into question. Baudelaire was writing to ask a favor from Hugo. Was it not therefore important to downplay the differences between them? In order to get enough from Hugo, might not Baudelaire be claiming too much, exaggerating a little bit the similarity?

Such rhetorical complexity is further evident in a letter to Madame Sabatier. This mistress of a wealthy banker had gathered a notable artistic circle, many of whom corresponded with her in exceedingly bawdy terms. Baudelaire, however, conducted a lengthy platonic correspondence, in which he sent anonymously some of the loveliest poems that were to go into *Les fleurs du mal*. With one he wrote:

> To explain to you my silences and my fervors, fervors almost religious, I will tell you that when my being is groveling in the blackness of its natural wickedness and foolishness, it dreams deeply of you. From that exciting and purifying dream there is generally born a happy accident.—You are for me not only the most attractive of women;—of all women, but also the dearest and most precious of superstitions.—I am an egoist, I make use of you.—Here is my miserable ass-wipe [*torche-cul*]. (May 8, 1854)

The strange tone derives from the ambivalence of "purification." A cathartic may be considered foul, because in purging me it produces waste. I make myself clean by making toilet paper dirty. In thus describing the genesis of his poetry as symbolic action, Baudelaire revivifies the deprecatory cliché of literature as wastepaper. More largely, within the conventions of self-abasing love rhetoric, Baudelaire also effects a dramatic reversal. It seems that we need to know much more than we do in order fully to understand the letter's tone, but it is not clear what we should know.

In writing of *Les fleurs du mal*, Baudelaire once insisted, "No one except people of absolute bad faith will fail to understand the willed impersonality of my poems" (November 10, 1858, to Alphonse de Calonne). Yet later he wrote to the administrator of his estate, who despite all their troubles was one of the few people that he was close to, "Must I say to you, you who have not guessed it any more than the others, that in this *dreadful* book, I've put all my *heart*, all my *tenderness*, all my *religion* (travestied), all my hate?" (February 18, 1866, to Narcisse-Désiré Ancelle). This statement alone stands in simple contradiction to the one previously cited, but Baudelaire offers to resolve such contradictions: "It's true that I'll write the opposite, that I'll swear up and down that it's a work of pure art, of monkey tricks, of double-dealing; and I'll be lying." First the rhetoric of sincerity is derailed by the parenthetical "travestied," and then the resolution requires our faith in a self-proclaimed liar. How can we know what to believe?

In everyday life, we judge truth by consequences. Since Kant, the aesthetic has been deliberately inconsequential; art is supposed to exist for itself alone. We have seen, however, Baudelaire continually suggesting that he has uses for his art, and there is no doubt that his readers have. Our choices about Baudelaire are implicated in our interpretations, and consequences follow from interpretive decisions. As a major correlative of romantic individuality, sincerity was a deep problem for Baudelaire. He recognized its historical causes, and he saw too that it impinged on his personal life. He felt the burden of individuality, yet he also valued its power—and in his writing on drugs explored means to increase its power.

In his antithetical wish to free himself from this burden, Baudelaire drew upon alternatives to individuality that his time made available in part. He could look back to the classic norm of impersonality; he could look back to the medieval norm of collectivity; he could look ahead to a modern dispersal of the self. This "vaporization" would oppose the "centralization" of the self established by both romanticism and bourgeois life ("My Heart Laid Bare," sec. 1): "All that is solid melts into the air." This "going up in steam" of the self, the hashish smoker's sudden realization that "your pipe is smoking you," is allied with the forces of production that the bourgeoisie controlled, and yet it seemed to lead beyond the bourgeois world.

Classical impersonality imposed a painful, ironic self-contemplation that was too great to bear, although at times Baudelaire experimented with it and at other times it imposed itself upon him. Medieval collectivity could only mean yielding to artistic clichés and to an equally intolerable social conformity. Nonetheless, from our distance, we find Baudelaire deeply marked by the "collective originality" of his time. These traces make him different from us, and hard to take, and marvelously fascinating.

The modern path of dispersal Baudelaire followed out through allegory, which allowed properties to be transferred in exchanges that achieved no totality but always left a pressing urgency of difference. His practice of literature and criticism as translation, the dual process of finding yourself different in another and making others different by appropriating their works or lives to your own, prolonged this vein. Politically, the only path to remaking the world as wholly different was that of revolution, but after the possibilities of 1848, Baudelaire was "physically depoliticized" by Napoleon's coup and led the life of a declassed bourgeois. His art held out the dream of another world that was individually attainable to its maker, but also to its readers. It thus signals the renewed utopian possibility of an undertaking in common.

10. Huckleberry Finn *without Polemic*

Everyone thinks they remember the story, but the voice is what really lingers. Huckleberry Finn, the preteen boy who narrates the novel, and his companion, Jim, a runaway slave, are floating on a raft down the Mississippi in the American South of the 1840s. Jim is in danger of being captured and re-enslaved, so they need to lie low, and they travel at night. Despite the danger, Huck finds beauty. "It's lovely to live on a raft," Huck says, and the sentence might be the alliterative eight-syllable opening line of a ballad. The book's language is poetic, but not often so close to verse. The next sentence broaches quite a different rhythm, extending itself with unexpected turns that give a sense of unforced, widely ranging speech and thought alike: "We had the sky up there, all speckled with stars, and we used to lay on our backs and look up at them, and discuss about whether they was made or only just happened—Jim he allowed they was made, but I allowed they happened; I judged it would have took too long to *make* so many" (chap. 19).[1] Huck's narrative is not only oral in rhythm; it is local in vocabulary. "Allow" in the sense of "think" or "conclude" is a regional usage of the U.S. South and Midwest. Huck's grammar breaks the rules of the schoolroom, a discipline to which he has been subjected back at home, but which he prefers to evade. Standard English dictates "lie" where Huck has "lay"; abjures the pleonasms of "about" after "discuss," of "he" after "Jim"; requires the plural "were" instead of "was"; demands the participial form "taken" instead of "took." Against all this bossiness, Huck's speech feels free, and yet he and Jim are also engaged in reflection, and their conversation is about judging. Alone on the river, left to their own devices, they discuss the nature of things in bold cosmological debate between equals: "Jim said the moon could a *laid* [all the stars]; well, that looked kind of reasonable, so I didn't say nothing against it, because I've seen a frog lay most as many, so of course it could be done." Social hierarchies of free and slave, black and white, are suspended in a democratic utopia. These memorable passages feel timeless, a scene of mythmaking itself mythical, but they are part of a sequence mea-sured as "two or three days and nights," in a few pages set between the force of murderous feuds and the fraud of con men claiming to be royalty.

When the impending dawn forces Huck and Jim to pull over and hide, they

> slid into the river and had a swim, so as to freshen up and cool off; then we set down on the sandy bottom where the water was about knee deep, and watched the daylight come. Not a sound, anywheres—perfectly still—just like the whole world was asleep, only sometimes the bull-frogs a-cluttering, maybe. The first thing to see, looking away over the water, was a kind of dull line—that was the woods on t'other side—you couldn't make nothing else out; then a pale place in the sky; then more paleness spreading around; then the river softened up, away off, and warn't black any more, but gray; you could see little dark spots drifting along, ever so far away—trading scows, and such things; and long black streaks—rafts; sometimes you could hear a sweep screaking; or jumbled up voices, it was so still, and sounds come so far; and by and by you could see a streak on the water which you know by the look of the streak that there's a snag there in a swift current which breaks on it and makes that streak look that way; and you see the mist curl up off of the water, and the east reddens up, and the river, and you make out a log cabin in the edge of the woods, away on the bank on t'other side of the river, being a wood-yard, likely, and piled by them cheats so you can throw a dog through it anywheres; then the nice breeze springs up, and comes fanning you from over there, so cool and fresh, and sweet to smell, on account of the woods and the flowers; but sometimes not that way, because they've left dead fish laying around, gars, and such, and they do get pretty rank; and next you've got the full day, and everything smiling in the sun, and the song-birds just going it!

> A little smoke couldn't be noticed now, so we could take some fish off of the lines, and cook up a hot breakfast. And afterwards we would watch the lonesomeness of the river, and kind of lazy along, and by and by lazy off to sleep. Wake up, by and by, and look to see what done it, and maybe see a steamboat, coughing along up stream, so far off towards the other side you couldn't tell nothing about her only whether she was stern-wheel or side-wheel; then for about an hour there wouldn't be anything to hear nor noth-ing to see—just solid lonesomeness. Next you'd see a raft sliding by, away off yonder, and maybe a galoot on it chopping, because they're most always doing it on a raft; you'd see the axe flash, and come down—you don't hear

nothing; you see that axe go up again, and by the time it's above the man's head, then you hear the *k'chunk!*—it had took all that time to come over the water. So we would put in the day, lazying around, listening to the stillness. (Chap. 19)

Huck responds with all his senses: you can taste the fish for breakfast; smell the flowers, or the rotting gars; feel the cool water, or the sand underfoot; hear the quiet, broken by frogs a–cluttering, sweeps screaking, steamboats coughing, or galoots *k'chunk*ing; and, above all, the many things he and Jim see. What might be summarized as a single four-letter word—"dawn"—opens into an extended process, punctuated by emergences. First a "dull line," then a "pale place," next "little dark spots" and "long black streaks," before the "east reddens up" and images can at last be categorized more precisely as "mist" and a "log cabin." The process is registered through second-person narration: "[Y]ou couldn't make nothing else out," but then "by and by you could see." Together with the "we" of Huck and Jim, the reader is invited also to share the experience of wonder and pleasure.

Mark Twain here naturalizes, as part of the American frontier landscape taken in and uttered by an uneducated youth, the techniques of impressionist prose so important in so much ambitious Western writing from Flaubert to Conrad and beyond. The privilege of sensitive spectatorship is extended from the leisure class down the social scale, bringing to fulfillment an experiment that in the early nineteenth-century British poetry of William Wordsworth had met a far more mixed response. The risk, overcome by Twain, is that the putatively natural perceiving consciousness will seem to be ventriloquized by the highly cultivated author. Marks of the authorial vocabulary and sensibility may be felt in the abstract nouns so important in composing the passage: "paleness," "lonesomeness," and "stillness." Samuel Clemens, as a young man before he had become Mark Twain, learned to read the river, as he recounts in *Life on the Mississippi*, and his active working skill becomes Huck's power to explain "a streak on the water which you know by the look of the streak that there's a snag there in a swift current which breaks on it and makes that streak look that way." The sequence is full of work, but always by others.

The flow of language is the sign of Huck's voice, felt in his words and intonation, while the author has constructed the sentences in all their intricacy. The second paragraph of the quotation, beginning with "A little smoke," starts with a rather short sentence and moves through three sentences of increasing length, until concluding with the shortest in the sequence, "So we would put in the day, lazying around and listening to the stillness." The first paragraph features a Faulkner-length sentence, 269 words long (starting with "The first thing to see" and running to the end), splattered with commas to set its microrhythms, and built sequentially onto eleven semicolons, the punctuation mark most associated with high literacy.

Twain uses the story situation to motivate Huck's hyperattentiveness. He and Jim are on the lam, danger lurks anywhere, so they need to notice everything. Hiding during the day enforces an idleness usually enjoyed only by rich people. Lowly men at leisure, singing the praises of their simple life—this is backwoods pastoral, guarded against the dangers of evident idealization by its awareness of stinky smells in nature and wood-yard cheats in society. The unusual verb form "to lazy" marks the enforced idleness and names it with an ordinarily pejorative word, but Huck's blithely reiterating the term sets at ease any Protestant ethic anxieties. The euphoric narration transfigures a state of deprivation ("nothing to hear nor nothing to see") into satisfying plenitude ("just solid lonesomeness"), and the catachresis is imperceptible except to critical analysis. Huck and Jim, "lazying around, listening to the stillness," bring into informal, everyday prose something like what Wordsworth in "Tintern Abbey" had achieved only through elevated verse; for "lazying," read:

> . . . the breath of this corporeal frame
> And even the motion of our human blood
> Almost suspended, we are laid asleep
> In body.

For "listening to the stillness," read:

> . . . with an eye made quiet by the power
> Of harmony, and the deep power of joy,
> We see into the life of things.[2]

Adventures of Huckleberry Finn is not a visionary lyric, though it memorably incorporates such moments. Its title suggests a picaresque novel, which signals not only roguery but also comedy. The book is very funny, as well as comic, in many ways. The large comic frame depends on the history separating the time of Huck's adventures, in the 1840s, from the time of Twain's writing, which began in 1876, and the book's publication, first in England, for copyright purposes, in 1884, and then in the United States in 1885. The Civil War (1861–65) had abolished slavery in the United States, and therefore every reader has had a different perspective on the laws and customs of slave society than was possible for anyone in the time of the book's action.

When a rich, famous, worldly author entrusts his narrative to a provincial outcast of limited literacy, he has already produced the structural potential for irony, but when everyone in the author's world knows more and sees differently from everyone in the novel's world, ironic possibilities multiply. Huck's distance from the norms and mores of his time may, in this instance, bring him closer to us. His alienation from his society seems a strength rather than a ground for pathos. There is also a trick here to flatter the readership: If Huck is relatively uncultured, he is therefore, by a common logic, necessarily more natural, and if he is also more like us, then we allow ourselves credit for his good nature.

Huck is not wholly formed by his culture, yet he is shown to believe in the social customs governing slavery, even though he breaks them in allying himself with Jim, and at several points quite specifically acting to protect Jim. Readers applaud his actions and laugh indulgently at his self-doubts and self-castigations. The worse he thinks he is, the better we know he is.

Late in the book, this pattern of opposites stretches its farthest. Jim has been separated from Huck and betrayed; he is locked up on a farm way down river from his home in Missouri. Huck imagines that it might work better for Jim if Huck sends a letter back to the owner Jim has run away from. That way, if he must be re-enslaved, at least he can be reunited with his family and the community he knows. But then Huck realizes that if he returns home with Jim, he will be known as someone who helped a slave to escape. This fantasy of social "shame" awakens thoughts of moral guilt: "That's just the way: a person does a low-down thing, and then he don't want to take no consequences of it. Thinks as long as he can hide it, it ain't no disgrace" (chap. 31). The rhetorical stakes are raised. Huck's "conscience" kicks in, and his mind becomes a theater in which several versions of small-town-Missouri, and all-American, religious talk play themselves out, while he listens and tries to duck.

The language of religious admonition morphs into Huck's language, and the interference between different registers of speech raises a laugh. Huck preserves the formal model of the periodic sentence. The main verb ("dropped") is suspended for nearly one hundred words from the sentence's start, but the rhythms are bent into breathlessness, and the words, too, are twisted:

> At last, when it hit me all of a sudden that here was the plain hand of Providence slapping me in the face and letting me know my wickedness was being watched all the time from up there in heaven, whilst I was stealing a poor

old woman's nigger that hadn't ever done me no harm, and now was showing me there's One that's always on the lookout, and ain't agoing to allow
no such miserable doings to go on only just so fur and no further, I most
dropped in my tracks I was so scared. (Chap. 31)

The conventionally dead metaphor of the "hand of Providence" comes to
life to slap Huck one, while the alien syntax suspends his identity and transports him into a space of moral agonizing.

Next Huck hears in his mind the voice of the schoolmarm, given a twist
by his own dialect and by a wavering in personal pronouns: "There was the
Sunday School, you could a gone to it; and if you'd a done it they'd a learnt
you, there, that people that acts as I'd been acting about that nigger goes to
everlasting fire." Huck's imperfect impersonation causes the voice of authority to condemn itself out of its own mouth ("as I'd been acting"), rather
than condemning him. Moreover, it is both comic and true to social hegem-
ony that even though he hasn't gone to Sunday school, he knows what he
would have learned if he had.

Then the rapid repetitive rhythms of preacherly exhortation take over:
"It was because my heart warn't right; it was because I warn't square; it was
because I was playing double." And one of his most famous lines still seems
part of the preaching voice: "You can't pray a lie." By this point, he feels
compelled to write the letter, and afterward he purrs in the voice of revival
testimony, "I felt good and all washed clean of sin for the first time."

But Huck can't stay saved. Once he has written the letter, he remembers
all that Jim has meant to him on their travels together. The form parodies
visions of the devil, as images of the black man arise to keep the young soul
from heaven's path, and the rhetorical modeling is seductive—not breath-
less, nor haranguing, nor pushy, like the churchy voices, but an artful balance of overlapping doublets and triplets: "I see Jim before me, all the time,
in the day, and in the night-time, sometimes moonlight, sometimes storms,
and we a floating along, talking, and singing, and laughing." All the commas
make it sound like Huck again, ventilating the sentence and easing its
movement. As this string of memories unrolls, Huck decides to help Jim
escape again. The language of this decision gains force from its sudden snap
back to the discarded religious idiom. Huck concludes, "All right, then, I'll
go to hell" (chap. 31). The syntax has the direct simplicity of the memories
of Jim, but the key word, deferred to the end, returns to the language that
is alien to Huck's own human sympathy.

Huck melodramatically, in a gestural extravagance equal and opposite to
what he rejects, chooses hell over heaven, Jim over the society that enslaves

him, and yet he does it in language that seems to modern readers racist: He calls Jim a "nigger." This term was not nearly so essential to Samuel Clemens's speech, in his adult life, as it is to Huck's. Over the course of the book, the term appears hundreds of times. The word is part of the historical and social distancing between author and character, and yet the word is not now a dead relic of slavery, nor was it when the book was written. Rather, the word did and still does active damage in the long working through a legacy of brutal inhumanity.[3]

Twain's use of the word is both willful and constrained. In part, it seems a rhetorical strategy of deidealization, keeping a dirty face on Huck so he does not seem too angelic. This may be given a polemically higher name as realism, as if one merely recorded what was there, but in the management of Huck's decision to go to hell, there is evidently much calculation. To make the comic miracle of Huck's decision seem the pure act of natural goodness that socially misknows itself as damned, Huck has been allowed to hear only some of the voices possible in the 1840s, or even in the novel. Back home in Missouri, Widow Douglas speaks for the established hellfire religion, but Aunt Polly offers a gospel of love that might have inspired Huck, as it did many abolitionists. The American national credo, "All men are created equal," was celebrated every July Fourth. Huck knows this holiday, and it comes during his river trip (which begins with the river's June rising). The word "nigger" may have permeated Huck's environment as deeply as "muthafucka" does some now (and may have in Huck's time, too, had we the sources to tell us), but writers, even realists, find the means they need to achieve the effects they wish. Contrast two scandalous eighteenth-century novels, *Les liaisons dangereuses* and *Fanny Hill*: does Laclos's "purer" language make his novel less truthful about sexuality? Twain made great art out of dreadful history, and his work survives its time of writing, but it bears the scars of a racist society. Its language implies a literary world in which it was unthinkable that African Americans would ever form a consequential part of Twain's readership.

The character of Jim presents some of the same problems. Jim is shown as a brave man and a good man, and at moments he and Huck are treated as equals. Yet the representation of Jim also draws on comic traditions that were highly disrespectful to the African Americans who made up their subject matter. In particular, American minstrel shows, an immensely popular form of entertainment from the 1840s through the rest of century, offered musical numbers and comic sketches in which white performers, in blackface makeup, masqueraded as African Americans.

Blackface minstrelsy underlies some of the way Jim appears, but worse trouble comes in the long sequence that ends the book. Tom Sawyer has come down from Missouri to where Jim is being held. Tom knows that Jim is no longer a runaway, but "free as any cretur that walks this earth" (chap. 42), because the woman who had owned him has died and freed him in her will. But Tom insists on staging elaborate schemes "to set a nigger free that was already free" (chapter the last), casting Jim as a noble prisoner, and Huck and Tom as his rescuers. *The Count of Monte Cristo* is one of many literary models for Tom's ideas of "style." This scheming is not the book's best comedy, and it leads to "a raft of trouble" (chap. 42): Tom gets shot and Jim risks his freedom to save him.

In this most fantasticated portion of the book, as in earlier sequences, Twain deploys a fundamental gesture of realism: *Huckleberry Finn* criticizes other books, so that we think it's realer than they are. The fraudulent scoundrels who join Huck and Jim claim to be a king and a duke, cheated of their lands and identities and outcast to the wilderness. Their phoniness comes from little bits of European history and culture, including butchered versions of Shakespeare. If this nonsense is high culture, then Huck's ignorance and unimaginativeness, which mean he responds only to what is before him, seem far preferable. Yet Huck defers to Tom Sawyer, who always plays out his life on themes from his reading. If Tom is Quixotic, then Huck is a juvenile Sancho Panza. He heeds the good sense of life against the folly of books. Such juvenilization means that sexuality has far less role in American realism than in its European counterparts. Realism as polemic propels Twain's formidable rejection of the historical romances of Walter Scott and Fenimore Cooper. *Life on the Mississippi*, published the year before *Huckleberry Finn*, asserts that Scott had undone Cervantes's critique of romance, and caused the Civil War, by filling the heads of Southern readers with false ideas of chivalric valor. Twain's elaborate demolition of "Fenimore Cooper's Literary Offenses" (1895) makes one of the funniest critical essays ever written.

In its time, *Huckleberry Finn* was understood as realistic for its evident refusal to idealize. It shows life in the lower reaches of society, and it shows that life as grim. It also attributes high moral value to Huck and Jim, despite their lowly status and lack of education. This may also seem, from another perspective, idealization. It may be impossible to adjudicate this book's realism, but it is worth testing how it fits the various frames that have defined realism, the crucial term in the history of Western thinking about the novel.

The most influential theories of literary realism were codified by several European critics, born in the late-nineteenth-century years when realism became a slogan, who then in the 1930s and 1940s gave it scholarly basis. *Huckleberry Finn* makes trouble for these ideas. It does not behave, and its acting up casts doubt on old books.[4]

For Erich Auerbach, realism violates classical rhetorical norms that treated socially low characters in low style and that associated low life with the comic. Through its new effects of style, realism could represent the existential seriousness of everyday life. But Twain's style serves other uses. The sunrise passage, discussed previously, is idyllic, and more sober-toned passages are melancholic. When Huck approaches a farm, he is oppressed by the feeling of a ghost town, which is only exacerbated by a sign of life: "I heard the dim hum of a spinning-wheel wailing along up and sinking along down again; and then I knew for certain I wished I was dead—for that *is* the lonesomest sound in the world" (chap. 32). Huck's decision to go to hell, on the other hand, as discussed previously, is made comic, and it is relieved of any decisive role in the plot.

For Mikhail Bakhtin's language-based analysis of realism, *Huckleberry Finn* would also fail the test of seriousness. Bakhtin found in Dostoevsky's set pieces of scandal the footprints of "reduced laughter," but Twain makes you laugh out loud. Twain loves to clash together different ways of talking. On the page before the novel begins, he explains that the characters speak seven different dialects that are "pains-takingly" differentiated. He pretends to fear that otherwise "many readers would suppose that all these characters were trying to talk alike and not succeeding." But this is not what Bakhtin means by the speech of the other. Dostoevsky, for Bakhtin, exemplified heteroglossic realism because he made the voices of his villains as compelling, or more so, than those of his heroes. What might be an ideological weakness becomes a literary strength—many good readers have not recognized that Dostoevsky was on the side of Christianity, not nihilism. No one has ever thought Twain favored slavery, or that any character in the book presents a serious alternative to Huck. Colonel Sherburne denounces the cowards who people his town, echoing views that were often Twain's own, but then he shoots a harmless fool. Jim is a good man, and he acts more bravely than Huck ever does, but African American readers, just like white readers, have chosen Huck rather than Jim as their place of identification. Huck's voice prevails.

Georg Lukács would have valued Twain's critical satire against many features of bourgeois life, and yet Twain does not show human beings making their history, which for Lukács is the fundamental reality to which literature is responsible. The means by which Jim is freed—not by Huck's efforts but by the will of a far-off woman who had died months earlier—if read as historical allegory, would suggest that the Civil War, the means by which all American slaves were freed, had been an extrinsic accident, not a collective action. The failure of action in *Huckleberry Finn* puts it in Lukács's negative category of "naturalism" together with Flaubert and Zola, rather than in his positive category of "realism" with Balzac and Tolstoy and Thomas Mann. Maybe Lukács also had a problem with funny books. But maybe Twain pulled his works' punches so that they would be bought and read; his literary clowning did not just sugarcoat a message but made sure it wasn't there. Twain laid down the law to critics in the "Notice" immediately following the title page: "Persons attempting to find a motive in this narrative will be prosecuted; persons attempting to find a moral in it will be banished; persons attempting to find a plot in it will be shot."

Huckleberry Finn contains tensions that arise from its compromises. This does not make it unique among novels of the United States or of the world. Novels are acts of communication and also items of commerce. They must answer to authorities different from those of the author. This problem extends even to the question of what exactly a proper edition of the novel should include. Mark Twain's *Life on the Mississippi* (1883) contains a passage of some five thousand words recounting songs and repartee on a raft in the old days on the river. He explained that this came from a book he was writing about Huckleberry Finn (already known to readers as Tom Sawyer's companion in Twain's 1876 novel), but then this "Raftmen Episode" did not appear in *Huckleberry Finn*. Should it be put in later editions? The reason it was omitted is adequately, if tersely, documented: The novel's publisher thought it might be left out, and Twain agreed. By one theory of editing, this means that the omission was an external imposition on the author's intention, but it could equally be argued that the author changed his mind. Twain had plenty of chances in the remaining twenty-five years of his life to restore the passage if he had wished to. The publisher was a young nephew of Twain's whom Twain himself had set up in charge of the publishing house, which primarily published Twain's works. So the idea of an alien commercial intrusion does not make sense; Twain treated his work commercially through and through. Samuel Clemens's pen name was registered as a trademark. No less than Charles Dickens in England, his fellow great philistine comic humanist, Mark Twain aimed to sell.

Since 1942, some editions of *Huckleberry Finn* have included the Raftmen Episode, and the established scholarly edition does, but many editions still do not, and the inclusion or exclusion of the passage has not made any difference to how people read the book. The passage contains wonderful American dialect humor writing, and a rich summary of folklore traditions, so it fits in, but it is simply an episode. Aristotle long ago argued that episodes are not essential, although they may contribute to a work's excellence.

If so substantial an episode may be present or absent, it raises questions about the book overall. Is it primarily episodic, or does some strong principle of unity organize it? From the book's opening in Missouri, through the trip downriver, to the ending, some change of fortune occurs—Jim is freed, and Huck is liberated from anxiety about his alcoholic, abusive father. Yet the book's narrative economy muffles the process that enables these changes. As in Shakespeare's comedies, both Jim's manumission and the death of Huck's father are revealed only in the very last pages of the book. They had happened some time earlier and were concealed, Jim's freedom by Tom Sawyer so as to allow for the charade of Jim's "evasion" (chap. 39) from imprisonment, and Huck's father's death by Jim, for reasons left to the reader's speculation. So all that Huck did on Jim's behalf has not been essential to this plot. Whether or not Huck decided to go to hell, Jim was already free, and Tom Sawyer would in any case have arrived with the news at the farm where Jim was held.

Rather than seeking organic unity, it seems better to recognize that *Huckleberry Finn* operates discontinuously, by repetition and difference more than by beginning, middle, and end. The strongest moments of the book, including the passages I have discussed here, are *sublime*, as defined by the classical critic Longinus.[5] By "sublime," Longinus does not mean highfalutin. The sublime may arise from the representation of silence and from terse, simple language: His treatise praises the opening of the Hebrew Bible ("'Let there be light,' and there was light.") The sublime means simply the greatest literary experience. It does not depend on unity. Like a "whirlwind" or thunderbolt, it tears up any smooth pattern or texture, so it stands out from the work in which it occurs. For Longinus, the sublime depends on a series of identifications: The words of a great moment seem "the echo of a great soul" that is the author's, and in reading such passages, we are "uplifted" by feeling as if we had ourselves produced those words. Longinus's key term in Greek is *ekstasis*, literally getting out of one's place, a "transport" into a new state or position. Longinus's analysis helps explain how Mark Twain became identified with Uncle Sam and known in the United States as "Our

Mark Twain," while *Huckleberry Finn* has become not only the best-known and most loved work of American literature, but also the most vehemently defended. To have to answer questions about the impact of Twain's racial language has seemed to some readers to foul their own moral decency.

It is a wonderful, and yet rather puzzling, feature of liberal culture that America's most beloved novel, the most American of novels, so savagely mocks life in the United States. This without even considering slavery, which the book treats with no nostalgia or apologetics. Slavery has been abolished in the United States, so there is some ground for feeling better about things, but the book offers little comfort. Through Huck's narration, the small-town decencies in Missouri seem confining if not wholly point-less, compared to the pleasures of hanging out with friends or fishing. And on the river, Huck encounters no society, except Jim's, preferable to what he left behind. The Southern gentry life of the Grangerfords is appealing until he realizes that they are caught up in a senseless and deadly feud with the Shepherdsons, and in Arkansas, which was in Twain's America a by-word for rural idiocy, the riverfront life is not only murderous but also mean spirited. The King and the Duke provide laughs, but they also sell Jim back into slavery.

The American institution that *Huckleberry Finn* most unremittingly at-tacks is the Christian church. Twice the novel stages false scenes of conver-sion, the pretense of a sinner redeemed, but Huck's pap and the King are just fooling the holy to make a buck off them. When Huck decides to go to hell, it is against the voices of religion. Even if some American readers now criticize Twain's treatment of racial matters, many have taken inspira-tion from Huck's relation to Jim and have found in it the possibility of inter-racial friendship and social commitment alike. The years of the American civil rights movement, from after the Second World War to the 1960s, were also the time in which academic critics brought *Huckleberry Finn* to the fore-front of established American literature, as many readers had already placed it in their hearts long before it became required reading. Yet perhaps Ameri-can secular intellectuals on the left were flying the race flag as camouflage.[6] Far more than it fosters progressive interraciality, *Huckleberry Finn* attacks the social cowardice of the religion that was in Huck's 1840s and Twain's 1880s and that remains, in the new millennium begun under George W. Bush's administration, even more emphatically, the core religion of the United States, a Bible-based Christianity committed to the drama of the individual soul choosing heaven or hell. Twain represents this religion as ignorant and, above all, selfish.

This attack matters only if literature does, but the understanding of literature that had begun to prevail in Twain's time, and that dominated the twentieth century, suggests it may not. This notion of literature, nowadays second nature to cultivated readers, is a fairly recent cultural product. In the English language of the eighteenth century, the term "literature" referred to all of value that was written, including nonfictional, even scientific and religious, writing. Beginning in the era of romanticism, however, poetry, fiction, and drama came to define the more restrictive sense of literature as imaginative belles lettres. This new sense of literature asserted autonomy: Literature was valued for being original, not for effectively following the rules; for being the work of a unique imagination, rather than part of a social transaction. Writers were supposed to answer to their own wills, rather than to any other set of expectations. This autonomy, however, diminished writing's social role. Literature offered the splendors of a world that was its own, but it therefore no longer exercised any direct claim on the world in which its readers pursued their political and economic lives. Before Samuel Clemens was born, in the United States of the 1820s, the historical fiction of Fenimore Cooper was understood to participate directly in debates about how the nation had come into existence and what that might mean for life in the present, but by the time he died in 1851, Cooper already seemed a relic, ripe for Twain's later debunking of his "literary offenses."

As Twain came of age in the middle nineteenth century, national narrative, as practiced by Cooper, was challenged by an emergent mode of narrative that was "literary" in the new sense.[7] The decisive new fiction of 1850, *The Scarlet Letter*, by Nathaniel Hawthorne, like Cooper's looked back to American history, but the work deliberately guarded itself from direct involvement in the politics of its day, with which Hawthorne himself, in his nonauthorial role, was much involved. Dedicated to Hawthorne, *Moby-Dick* (1851) is the encyclopedic literary narrative of this moment, and it has come to dominate American literary study. In contrast, the comprehensive national narrative *Uncle Tom's Cabin* (1852) made far more impact at the time of its publication, and into the earlier twentieth century, but has only recently begun to receive the academic study that it merits. The figure of the sensitive spectator is crucial in literary narrative, whether Miles Coverdale in Hawthorne's *The Blithedale Romance*; Ishmael, the narrator of *Moby-Dick*; or, as noted in this chapter, Huck himself. This figure invites identification by a sensitive reader. In Stowe's novel the scope of this figure is limited to Augustine St. Clare, who occupies only the middle third of the novel and is killed off as a dangerous failure.

Works by Hawthorne, Melville, and above all Twain became models for American literature, even though they were written at a tense distance from the actually existing United States. American writing of the nineteenth century is full of distinctive voices, whether in the essays and journals of Emerson and Thoreau, the poetry of Whitman and Dickinson, or the fiction of Melville and Twain. In the 1960s and 1970s, the civil rights movement and the women's movement struggled to enlarge what it means to be American, who may count as American. This transformation has allowed readers now to recognize that the works of Harriet Beecher Stowe and Frederick Douglass, produced to combat slavery, are not just propaganda about a dead issue but are also great and valuable, despite lacking such distinctive voices. *Huckleberry Finn*, by contrast, satirizes slavery after its abolition. It offers an unforgettable voice that has echoed through later American writing. But what has it meant that literature traded power for voice?

Notes

Preface

1. Walter Benjamin, *Illuminations*, trans. Harry Zohn (New York: Harcourt, 1968).

2. On Benjamin, see "Walter Benjamin and Materialist Historiography," in Jonathan Arac, *Critical Genealogies: Historical Situations for Postmodern Literary Studies* (New York: Columbia University Press, 1987), 177–214; on Said, Jonathan Arac, "Criticism between Opposition and Counterpoint," in *Edward Said and the Work of the Critic: Speaking Truth to Power*, ed. Paul A. Bové (Durham, N.C.: Duke University Press, 2000), 66–77. On both in my work, see Jonathan Arac, introduction to *Against Americanists* (Durham, N.C.: Duke University Press, forthcoming).

3. Here my work most closely approaches that of Marshall Brown. See especially the discussions in his *Turning Points: Essays in the History of Cultural Expression* (Stanford, Calif.: Stanford University Press, 1997).

4. Gustave Flaubert to Edma Roger des Genettes, October 20, 1864, in Gustave Flaubert, *Correspondance*, ed. Jean Bruneau (Paris: Gallimard, 1973–2007), 3:411.

5. Harry Levin's pathbreaking 1946 essay "Literature as an Institution" is incorporated into the first chapter of his enduring study of French realism, *The Gates of Horn* (New York: Oxford University Press, 1963), 16–23.

6. In pieces written concurrently with this preface, I have begun to explore further this "age of the novel." See "Literary History in a Global Age," *New Literary History* 39 (2008): 747–60; see also "What Kind of History Does a Theory of the Novel Require?" *Novel: A Forum on Fiction* 42, no. 2 (2009): 190–95.

1. The Impact of Shakespeare: Goethe to Melville

1. This formulation, implicit in this chapter, is an iceberg tip from my essays "Literary History in the Global Age," *New Literary History* 39 (2008): 747–60, and "What Kind of History Does a Theory of the Novel Require?" *Novel: A Forum on Fiction* 42, no. 2 (2009): 190–95.

2. The best brief, internationally focused summary of Shakespeare's rise to preeminence is Harry Levin's "The Primacy of Shakespeare," in *Shakespeare and the Revolution of the Times* (New York: Oxford University Press, 1976), 235–60. On

India, where Shakespeare began to occupy a central place in pedagogy in the 1830s, earlier than was regularly the case in England, see Gauri Viswanathan, *Masks of Conquest* (New York: Columbia University Press, 1989).

3. Ralph Waldo Emerson, *Essays and Lectures* (New York: Viking, 1983), 718.

4. Johann Wolfgang von Goethe, "Shakespeare: A Tribute," in *Goethe: Essays on Art and Literature,* ed. John Geary (Princeton, N.J.: Princeton University Press, 1994), 163. I have altered the translation in the interest of literality.

5. Augustus William Schlegel, *A Course of Lectures on Dramatic Art and Literature,* trans. John Black, rev. A. J. W. Morrison (London: Bohn, 1846).

6. *The Collected Works of Samuel Taylor Coleridge,* ed. Kathleen Coburn, vol. 11, *Shorter Works and Fragments,* ed. H. J. Jackson and J. R. de J. Jackson (Princeton, N.J.: Princeton University Press, 1995), 1:85.

7. For the larger issue of how women responded to Shakespeare in the nineteenth century, see Nina Auerbach, *Woman and the Demon* (Cambridge, Mass.: Harvard University Press, 1982), chap. 6; Marianne Novy, *Engaging with Shakespeare: Responses of George Eliot and Other Women Novelists* (Athens: University of Georgia Press, 1994), esp. chaps. 1 and 2.

8. Jonathan Bate, *Shakespearian Constitutions* (Oxford: Oxford University Press, 1989), 144.

9. See Paul Van Tieghem, *Le romantisme dans la littérature européenne* (Paris: Albin Michel, 1969), 287.

10. Victor-Marie Hugo, preface to *Cromwell,* trans. I. G. Burnham, in *The Romantics on Shakespeare,* ed. Jonathan Bate (London: Penguin, 1992), 226, 225.

11. Alessandro Manzoni, "Letter to M. Chauvet on the Unities of Time and Place in Tragedy," excerpted in Oswald LeWinter, ed., *Shakespeare in Europe* (New York: Meridian, 1963), 130–35.

12. See LeWinter, *Shakespeare in Europe,* 161–62, for an example of Pushkin's table talk on characters from Shakespeare.

13. Friedrich Schlegel, "On Goethe's *Meister*" (1798), in *German Aesthetic and Literary Criticism: The Romantic Ironists and Goethe,* ed. Kathleen Wheeler (Cambridge: Cambridge University Press, 1984), 68.

14. Kathleen Coburn, ed., *The Notebooks of Samuel Taylor Coleridge,* vol. 2 (Princeton, N.J.: Princeton University Press, 1961), entry 2274.

15. *The Collected Works of Samuel Taylor Coleridge,* ed. Kathleen Coburn, vol. 7, *Biographia Literaria,* ed. James Engell and W. Jackson Bate (Princeton, N.J.: Princeton University Press, 1983), 1:85.

16. Engell and Bate, *Biographia Literaria,* 2:15.

17. Ibid., 2:19.

18. Schlegel, "On Goethe's *Meister,*" 68.

19. *Friedrich Schlegel, Literary Notebooks, 1797–1801,* ed. Hans Eichner (London: Athlone Press, 1957), entry 1150.

20. Schlegel, "On Goethe's *Meister,*" 68.

21. See John E. Jordan, ed., *De Quincey as Critic* (London: Routledge and Kegan Paul, 1973), 268–72 (in the midst of an essay on Alexander Pope).

22. On the British story, see Jonathan Bate, *Shakespeare and the English Romantic Imagination* (Oxford: Oxford University Press, 1986) and *Shakespearean Constitutions* (Oxford: Clarendon Press, 1989). Bate extends the range to France and Germany in his edited anthology, *The Romantics on Shakespeare* (New York: Penguin, 1992).

23. The argument developed here concerning the role of critical thought about Shakespeare in enabling important, innovative writing differs from, but owes much to, several lines of thought from twentieth-century theorists of literary history, specifically regarding the process by which the practice of poetry is carried forward: T. S. Eliot, "Tradition and the Individual Talent," in *Selected Prose of T. S. Eliot*, ed. Frank Kermode (New York: Harcourt and Farrar, 1975), 37–44; W. J. Bate, *The Burden of the Past and the English Poet* (Cambridge, Mass.: Harvard University Press, 1970); and Harold Bloom, *The Anxiety of Influence: A Theory of Poetry* (New York: Oxford University Press, 1973).

24. The analysis that follows is indebted to the classic discussion by W. Jackson Bate, *John Keats* (Cambridge, Mass.: Harvard University Press, 1963), esp. chap. 10, "Negative Capability."

25. Hyder Edward Rollins, ed., *The Letters of John Keats: 1814–1821* (Cambridge, Mass.: Harvard University Press, 1958), 1:142. In quotations from this edition, I have in a few cases regularized spelling.

26. Ibid., 1:143.

27. Ibid., 1:203.

28. Ibid., 1:193.

29. Engell and Bate, *Biographia Literaria*, 2:15–16.

30. See William V. Spanos, "Charles Olson and Negative Capability: A Destructive Interpretation," in *Repetitions: The Postmodern Occasion in Literature and Culture* (Baton Rouge: Louisiana State University Press, 1987), 107–48.

31. Hazlitt himself presents this account in his 1819 polemical and autobiographical pamphlet, "A Letter to William Gifford, Esq.," in William Hazlitt, *The Spirit of the Age*, 4th ed., ed. William Carew Hazlitt (London: Bell and Sons, 1904), 444–56.

32. William Hazlitt, *Lectures on the English Poets and the English Comic Writers*, ed. William Carew Hazlitt (London: Bell and Sons, 1894), 62–63.

33. Rollins, *Letters of John Keats*, 1:386–87.

34. Cecil Y. Lang, ed., *The Letters of Matthew Arnold: Volume 1, 1829–1859* (Charlottesville: University of Virginia Press, 1996), 245–46.

35. W. J. B. Owen and Jane Worthington Smyser, eds., *Prose Works of William Wordsworth* (Oxford: Clarendon Press, 1974), 1:129.

36. Lionel Trilling, "The Fate of Pleasure: Wordsworth to Dostoevsky," in *Romanticism Reconsidered*, ed. Northrop Frye (New York: Columbia University Press, 1963), 73–106.

37. *The Yale Edition of the Works of Samuel Johnson*, vol. 7, *Johnson on Shakespeare*, ed. Arthur Sherbo (New Haven, Conn.: Yale University Press, 1968), 61.

38. Charles Lamb, "On the Tragedies of Shakespeare, with Reference to Their Fitness for Stage-Representation," in *The Complete Works and Letters of Charles Lamb* (New York: Modern Library, 1935), 291.

39. See Chapter 2 in this volume, "The Media of Sublimity: Johnson and Lamb on *King Lear*," and, more broadly, Jonas M. Barish, *The Antitheatrical Prejudice* (Berkeley: University of California Press, 1981).

40. See Nicholas Boyle, *Goethe: The Poet and the Age*, vol. 1, *The Poetry of Desire* (Oxford: Oxford University Press, 1991), on "the printed book" as the indispensable means for "the literary transformation of Germany" in Goethe's lifetime, especially through "the literary drama": "In so far as it was a book like other books, [it] linked intellectuals from all over the German-speaking world in the study of feeling and in social, moral, and historical reflection" (365).

41. James Joyce, *A Portrait of the Artist as a Young Man*, in *The Portable James Joyce*, ed. Harry Levin, rev. ed. (New York: Vintage, 1966), 526.

42. *The Collected Works of Samuel Taylor Coleridge*, ed. Kathleen Coburn, vol. 5, *Lectures, 1808–1819: On Literature*, ed. R. A. Foakes (Princeton, N.J.: Princeton University Press, 1987), 1:575.

43. Johann Wolfgang von Goethe, *Wilhelm Meister's Apprenticeship*, trans. Eric A. Blackall and Victor Lange (Princeton, N.J.: Princeton University Press, 1995), 128. The relevant passages from the novel may also be found in Wheeler's *German Aesthetic and Literary Criticism*, 231–36.

44. Goethe, *Wilhelm Meister*, 129.

45. Ibid., 128.

46. See Chapter 3 in this volume, "*Hamlet, Little Dorrit*, and the History of Character."

47. Sigmund Freud, *The Origins of Psychoanalysis: Letters to Wilhelm Fliess, Drafts and Notes, 1887–1902*, ed. Marie Bonaparte, Anna Freud, and Ernst Kris, trans. Eric Mosbacher and James Strachey (New York: Basic Books, 1954), 224.

48. *The Tragedy of Hamlet, Prince of Denmark*, in *The Riverside Shakespeare*, ed. G. Blakemore Evans (Boston: Houghton Mifflin, 1974), 1.5.188–89.

49. Goethe, *Wilhelm Meister*, 146

50. Friedrich Schlegel, *Philosophical Fragments*, trans. Peter Firchow (Minneapolis: University of Minnesota Press, 1991), 53.

51. Foakes, *Lectures, 1808–1819*, 2:362.

52. Johann Gottfried Herder, "Shakespeare," trans. Joyce P. Crick, in Bate, *The Romantics on Shakespeare*, 41 (emphasis added). The German, translated as "concerted sound," is "Hauptklang seines Konzerts." Johann Gottfried Herder, *Von der Urpoesie der Völker*, ed. Konrad Nussbächer (Stuttgart: Reclam, 1969), 27.

53. Foakes, *Lectures, 1808–1819*, 1:495. I have omitted from my quotation words crossed out by Coleridge in the manuscript from which Foakes transcribes.

This passage is a close paraphrase by Coleridge from Augustus William Schlegel's Vienna *Course of Lectures*: "Form is mechanical when, through external force, it is imparted to any material merely as an accidental addition without reference to its quality; as, for example, when we give a particular shape to a soft mass that may retain the same after its induration. Organical form, again, is innate; it unfolds itself from within, and acquires its determination contemporaneously with the perfect development of the germ" (1846, 340).

The passage from Coleridge, which was first published in his posthumous *Literary Remains* (1836–39) without the manuscript's acknowledgment to "a Continental Critic," exemplifies the empirical basis for the double controversy over Coleridge's critical character and achievement: Was he a plagiarist? Was he original? Landmarks in this controversy include the fair but devastating diminishment of Coleridge in René Wellek, *A History of Modern Criticism*, vol. 2, *The Romantic Age* (London: Jonathan Cape, 1955), esp. 151–57; the remarkable reconceptualization by Thomas McFarland in chapter 1 of *Coleridge and the Pantheist Tradition* (Oxford: Clarendon Press, 1969); the impassioned prosecutor's brief by Norman Fruman, *Coleridge, the Damaged Archangel* (New York: Braziller, 1971); and the rescue operation by the editors of the *Collected Works* of Coleridge, especially Engell and Bate in the *Biographia* and Foakes in the *Lectures, 1808–1819*, esp. 1:lx–lxiv.

54. For the larger resonances of this topic, see M. H. Abrams, *The Mirror and the Lamp: Romantic Theory and the Critical Tradition* (Oxford: Oxford University Press, 1953) on "the poem as heterocosm," 272–84.

55. Foakes, *Lectures, 1808–1819*, 1:494–95.

56. Sherbo, *Johnson on Shakespeare*, 62.

57. Foakes, *Lectures, 1808–1819*, 2:362.

58. See Ernst Robert Curtius, "The Book as Symbol," in *European Literature and the Latin Middle Ages*, trans. Willard R. Trask (New York: Harper and Row, 1963), esp. 319–26 on "The Book of Nature."

59. On Friedrich Schlegel's "romantic polysemism" in relation to the traditions of biblical hermeneutics, see Abrams, *The Mirror and the Lamp*, 239–41.

60. Schlegel, *Philosophical Fragments*, 2.

61. For an authoritative treatment of the complex etymology and semantics of *Roman* and *romantisch*, which, however, I do not wholly follow, see Hans Eichner, *Friedrich Schlegel* (New York: Twayne, 1970), 48–54.

62. Schlegel, *Philosophical Fragments*, 10.

63. Goethe, *Wilhelm Meister's Apprenticeship*, 186.

64. Sherbo, *Johnson on Shakespeare*, 62.

65. Ibid., 65.

66. Herder, "Shakespeare," 40.

67. Ibid., 41.

68. Ibid.

69. Foakes, *Lectures, 1808–1819*, 2:293.

70. Ibid., 1:539.

71. Schlegel, *Philosophical Fragments*, 14.

72. All Schlegel quotations in this paragraph from "On Goethe's Meister," 69.

73. Engell and Bate, *Biographia Literaria*, 1:304.

74. Friedrich Schlegel, "On *Hamlet* and *Faust* as Philosophical Tragedies," trans. Cyrus Hamlin, from "On the Study of Greek Poesy," in Hamlin's Norton Critical edition of Johann Wolfgang von Goethe, *Faust* (New York: Norton, 1976), 435–37.

75. Ibid.

76. On Schlegel and Bakhtin, see Tzvetan Todorov, *Mikhail Bakhtin: The Dialogical Principle*, trans. Wlad Godzich (Minneapolis: University of Minnesota Press, 1984), 86–87. On Schlegel and Lukács, see Peter Szondi, *On Textual Understanding and Other Essays*, trans. Harvey Mendelson (Minneapolis: University of Minnesota Press, 1986), 63, 82.

77. Schlegel, *Philosophical Fragments*, p. 52.

78. Friedrich Schlegel, "Letter about the Novel," in Wheeler, *German Aesthetic and Literary Criticism*, 77.

79. Friedrich Schlegel, "On Incomprehensibility," in Wheeler, *German Aesthetic and Literary Criticism*, 37.

80. Schlegel, *Philosophical Fragments*, 14.

81. For *Athenaeum,* Fragment 116, see Schlegel, *Philosophical Fragments*, 31–32.

82. Schlegel, "Letter about the Novel," in Wheeler, *German Aesthetic and Literary Criticism*, 78. The sentence in German comes from Friedrich Schlegel, *Charakteristiken und Kritiken I (1796–1801)*, ed. Hans Eichner (Munich: Schöningh, 1967), 335. This is vol. 2 of Ernst Behler, ed., *Kritische Friedrich-Schlegel-Ausgabe.*

83. Northrop Frye, *Anatomy of Criticism: Four Essays* (Princeton, N.J.: Princeton University Press, 1957), esp. 246–48.

84. *The Collected Works of Samuel Taylor Coleridge*, ed. Kathleen Coburn, vol. 12, *Marginalia,* ed. H. J. Jackson and George Whalley (Princeton, N.J.: Princeton University Press, 1992), 3:187.

85. Wheeler, *German Aesthetic and Literary Criticism*, 78.

86. Ibid., 79.

87. The classic discussion of *Moby-Dick* and Shakespeare is F. O. Matthiessen, *American Renaissance: Art and Expression in the Age of Emerson and Whitman* (New York: Oxford University Press, 1941), 405–67.

88. Melville's notes are reproduced, with commentary, in *Writings of Herman Melville,* vol. 6, *Moby-Dick; or, The Whale,* ed. Harrison Hayford, Hershel Parker, and G. Thomas Tanselle (Evanston, Ill.: Northwestern University Press, 1988), 955–70.

89. On this connection between Melville and Carlyle, see Jonathan Arac, *Commissioned Spirits* (New York: Columbia University Press, 1989), 148–56.

90. Herman Melville, "Hawthorne and His Mosses," in *Moby-Dick*, ed. Harrison Hayford and Hershel Parker (New York: Norton, 1967), 541–42.

91. Thomas Carlyle, "The Hero as Poet," in *Shakespeare Criticism: A Selection,* ed. D. Nichol Smith (Oxford: Oxford University Press, 1935), 409.

92. Melville, "Hawthorne and His Mosses," 546.

93. Carlyle, "The Hero as Poet," 416.

94. Foakes, *Lectures, 1808–1819*, 1:546.

95. Melville, "Hawthorne and His Mosses," 543.

96. William Hazlitt, *Characters of Shakespeare's Plays* (London, 1909), 50.

97. Hazlitt, "Letter to William Gifford," 423.

98. Carlyle, "The Hero as Poet," 416.

99. See Ania Loomba, *Gender, Race, Renaissance Drama* (Delhi: Oxford University Press, 1992), 10: "More students probably read *Othello* in the University of Delhi every year than in all British universities combined."

100. Carlyle, "The Hero as Poet," 414–15.

2. *The Media of Sublimity: Johnson and Lamb on* King Lear

1. "Tradition and the Individual Talent," in *Selected Prose of T. S. Eliot*, ed. Frank Kermode (New York: Harcourt and Farrar, 1975), 41. On Bloom and the sublime, see Jonathan Arac, *Critical Genealogies: Historical Situations for Postmodern Literary Studies* (New York: Columbia University Press, 1987), 17–19; Neil Hertz, "A Reading of Longinus" (1973), *Critical Inquiry* 9 (1983): 579–96; Thomas Weiskel, *The Romantic Sublime: Studies in the Structure and Psychology of Transcendence* (Baltimore, Md.: Johns Hopkins University Press, 1976); Jean-François Lyotard, "Answering the Question: What Is Postmodernism?" trans. Régis Durand, in *The Postmodern Condition* (Minneapolis: University of Minnesota Press, 1984), 77ff.; Paul H. Fry, *The Reach of Criticism: Method and Perception in Literary Theory* (New Haven, Conn.: Yale University Press, 1983). See also *New Literary History* 16, no. 2 (1985), an issue devoted to "The Sublime and the Beautiful: Reconsiderations." Several notable works appearing after this essay's first publication include Suzanne Guerlac, *The Impersonal Sublime: Hugo, Baudelaire, Lautréamont* (Stanford, Calif.: Stanford University Press, 1990); Rob Wilson, *American Sublime: The Genealogy of a Poetic Genre* (Madison: University of Wisconsin Press, 1991); and Frances Ferguson, *Solitude and the Sublime: Romanticism and the Aesthetics of Individuation* (New York: Routledge, 1992). Among the many works engaging the sublime in dialogue with history after 9/11, for a representative, see Christine Battersby, *The Sublime, Terror and Human Difference* (New York: Routledge, 2007).

2. A new critical historiography of the sublime began with Hayden White, "The Politics of Historical Interpretation: Discipline and De-sublimation," *Critical Inquiry* 9 (1982): 113–37; Gary Shapiro, "From the Sublime to the Political: Some Historical Notes," *New Literary History* 16 (1985): 213–35; Donald Pease, "Sublime Politics," *boundary 2*, no. 12.3–13.1 (1984): 259–79; and Peter de Bolla, *The Discourse of the Sublime: Readings in History, Aesthetics and the Subject* (Oxford: Blackwell, 1989).

3. I recognize the problem in taking into consideration only one of Lamb's essays, but I believe the arguments advanced here can be sustained over a much larger corpus, including "My First Play," "On Some of the Old Actors," "On the Artificial Comedy of the Last Century," "Detached Thoughts on Books and Reading," "Stage Illusion," "Sanity of True Genius," and "Barrenness of the Imaginative Faculty in the Productions of Modern Art."

4. This connection may be explored through the essays in Jonathan Arac, ed., *Postmodernism and Politics* (Minneapolis: University of Minnesota Press, 1986).

5. This essay (the title of which might be more properly translated as "The Work of Art in the Age of Its Mechanical Reproducibility") and those mentioned

in the next sentence are available in Walter Benjamin, *Illuminations*, trans. Harry Zohn (1968; New York: Schocken, 1969). The essay has a complex textual history: It was first published in French in 1936, but the basis for the English translation is the now-standard German text, which, however, was still "work in progress" at Benjamin's death in 1940. See Walter Benjamin, *Gesammelte Schriften*, ed. Rolf Tiedemann and Hermann Schweppenhäuser (Frankfurt: Suhrkamp, 1974), 1:1035.

6. The standard studies most relevant to my topic are Samuel H. Monk, *The Sublime: A Study of Critical Theories in XVIII-Century England* (1935; Ann Arbor: University of Michigan Press, 1960); W. P. Albrecht, *The Sublime Pleasures of Tragedy: A Study of Critical Theory from Dennis to Keats* (Lawrence: University of Kansas Press, 1975); and portions throughout Joseph W. Donohue Jr., *Dramatic Character in the English Romantic Age* (Princeton, N.J.: Princeton University Press, 1970).

7. Notes on *King Lear*, in *The Yale Edition of the Works of Samuel Johnson,* vol. 8, *Johnson on Shakespeare*, ed. Arthur Sherbo (New Haven, Conn.: Yale University Press, 1968), 704. In the text, whenever no reference follows quotations from Johnson, they are from this page.

8. Samuel Taylor Coleridge, *Shakespearean Criticism*, ed. Thomas Middleton Raysor, 2nd ed. (London: Dent, 1960), 1:184–85. I am indebted to Michael Hays, "Comedy as Being/Comedy as Idea," *Studies in Romanticism* 26 (1987): esp. 227.

9. In his standard work, Jean H. Hagstrum emphasizes Johnson's view of Shakespeare as poet of the "pathetic" and plays down the complexity of his involvement with the sublime in Shakespeare. See *Samuel Johnson's Literary Criticism* (1952; Chicago: University of Chicago Press, 1967), esp. 141, 143.

10. One sign of how deeply Johnson probed the fundamental issues of the play is his entanglement in the complex semantics of nature, justice, and reason that swirl through *King Lear* (e.g., "Is there any cause in nature that make these hard hearts?" [3.6.77–78]).

11. *Johnson on Shakespeare*, 7:61.

12. Ibid., 8:704.

13. Ibid., 8:702–3.

14. Edmund Burke, *A Philosophical Enquiry into the Origin of Our Ideas of the Sublime and the Beautiful* (1757), ed. J. T. Boulton (1958; Notre Dame, Ind.: University of Notre Dame Press, 1968), 57.

15. *Johnson on Shakespeare*, 7: 78.

16. Charles Lamb, "On the Tragedies of Shakespeare Considered with Reference to Their Fitness for Stage-Representation" (1811), in *The Complete Works and Letters of Charles Lamb* (New York: Modern Library, 1935), 289–303.

17. Ibid., 299.

18. Ibid., 302.

19. On the English Reformation rhetoric against religious ritual that gives some context for Lamb and his nineteenth-century successors, see Jonas Barish, *The Anti-Theatrical Prejudice* (Berkeley: University of California Press, 1981), esp. 159–65.

Against this view, Barish himself offers a secular theology of incarnation, as evidenced, for instance, in his summary objections to Lamb, 331.

20. Benjamin, *Illuminations*, 229.

21. Lamb, "On the Tragedies of Shakespeare," 291.

22. Ibid., 290.

23. Ibid., 296.

24. Ibid., 295.

25. Ibid., 290. The issue, in other words, is like that in discussions of Coleridge's theory of the imagination. Translated into those terms, Lamb would seem to be denying most people the power of secondary imagination (an "echo" of the primary).

26. Lamb, "On the Tragedies of Shakespeare," 294.

27. Ibid., 290–91.

28. *Johnson on Shakespeare*, 7:76.

29. Lamb, "On the Tragedies of Shakespeare," 294.

30. Michel Foucault, "What Is an Author?" in *Language, Counter-Memory, Practice*, ed. Donald F. Bouchard, trans. Donald F. Bouchard and Sherry Simon (Ithaca, N.Y.: Cornell University Press, 1977), 127.

31. *The Collected Works of Samuel Taylor Coleridge*, ed. Kathleen Coburn, vol. 12, *Marginalia*, ed. H. J. Jackson and George Whalley (Princeton, N.J.: Princeton University Press, 1992), 3:187.

32. Lamb, "On the Tragedies of Shakespeare," 291.

33. Ibid., 293.

34. Ibid., 297.

35. Ibid., 298.

36. Ibid., 298.

37. Ibid., 298–300.

38. Ibid., 299.

39. Foucault, *Language, Counter-Memory, Practice*, 221.

40. On the sublimity of the lines, it may be enough to recall that in Burke's *Enquiry* there are sections on "Obscurity" (2.3), "Infinity" (2.8), and "Darkness" (4.14–16). The complex I have been elucidating is crucial also in Hawthorne's foundation of American "literature," as I have argued in "The Politics of *The Scarlet Letter*" (1986), in Jonathan Arac, *Against Americanistics* (Durham, N.C.: Duke University Press, forthcoming).

41. William Wordsworth, *The Poems*, ed. John O. Hayden (Harmondsworth, UK: Penguin, 1977), 1:215 (lines 1539–44).

42. Lamb, "On the Tragedies of Shakespeare," 291.

43. Ibid., 299.

44. Ibid., 300n.

45. Ibid., 291.

46. Benjamin, *Illuminations*, 237.

47. Lamb, "On the Tragedies of Shakespeare," 302.

48. Benjamin, *Illuminations*, 240–41.

3. Hamlet, Little Dorrit, and the History of Character

1. Fredric Jameson, *The Political Unconscious* (Ithaca, N.Y.: Cornell University Press, 1981), 9; Michel Foucault, *Power/Knowledge*, ed. Colin Gordon (New York: Pantheon, 1980), 83–85; Frank Lentricchia, "Derrida, History, and Intellectuals," *Salmagundi* 50–51 (1980–81): 284–301; Paul de Man, *The Rhetoric of Romanticism* (New York: Columbia University Press 1984), ix; Hayden White, *Metahistory* (Baltimore, Md.: Johns Hopkins University Press, 1973).

2. For example, Jonathan Dollimore and Alan Sinfield, eds., *Political Shakespeare: New Essays in Cultural Materialism* (Manchester, UK: Manchester University Press, 1985); John Drakakis, ed., *Alternative Shakespeares* (London: Routledge, 1985).

3. Joel Fineman, "The Turn of the Shrew," in *Shakespeare and the Question of Theory*, ed. Patricia Parker and Geoffrey Hartman (New York: Routledge, 1985), 157; Stephen Greenblatt, "Fiction and Friction," in *Reconstructing Individualism: Autonomy, Individuality, and the Self in Western Thought*, ed. Thomas C. Heller, Morton Sosna, and David E. Wellbery (Stanford, Calif.: Stanford University Press, 1986), 46.

4. See, for example, Walter Benjamin, "Convolute N" [On the Theory of Knowledge, Theory of Progress], in *The Arcades Project*, trans. Howard Eiland and Kevin McLaughlin (Cambridge, Mass.: Belknap Press of Harvard University Press, 1999), 460; Hans Robert Jauss, *Toward an Aesthetic of Reception* (Minneapolis: University of Minnesota Press, 1982).

5. See, for example, Catherine Belsey, "The Romantic Construction of the Unconscious," in *1789: Reading Writing Revolution*, ed. Francis Barker et al. (Essex, UK: University of Essex, 1982), 67–80; Jonathan Culler, "Presupposition and Intertextuality," in *The Pursuit of Signs* (Ithaca, N.Y.: Cornell University Press, 1981), 100–118.

6. Since this essay was first published, several major works have addressed character. See Deidre Shauna Lynch, *The Economy of Character: Novels, Market Culture, and the Business of Inner Meaning* (Chicago: University of Chicago Press, 1998); Alex Woloch, *The One vs. the Many: Minor Characters and the Space of the Protagonist in the Novel* (Princeton, N.J.: Princeton University Press, 2003).

7. E. M. Forster, *Aspects of the Novel* (1927; Harmondsworth, UK: Penguin, 1962), 75–85.

8. See, for example, Colin Morris, *The Discovery of the Individual, 1050–1200* (New York: Harper, 1973); Marcel Mauss, "A Category of the Human Mind: The Notion of Person: The Notion of Self" (1938), in *The Category of the Person*, ed. Michael Carrithers, Steven Collins, and Steven Lukes (Cambridge: Cambridge University Press, 1985), 1–25.

9. On "literature," see Michel Foucault, *The Order of Things* (New York: Random House, 1973), 299–300; Raymond Williams, *Keywords* (New York: Oxford University Press, 1985), 183–88. For current discussion of literature as residual, see Jonathan Arac, "Literary History in a Global Age," *New Literary History* 39 (2008): 747–60.

10. A. C. Bradley, *Shakespearean Tragedy* (London: Macmillan, 1904); Ernest Jones, *Hamlet and Oedipus* (London: Gollancz, 1948).

11. Jacques Derrida, *Writing and Difference*, trans. Alan Bass (Chicago: University of Chicago Press, 1978), 199.

12. See the classic essay by Lionel Trilling, "Little Dorrit" (1953), in *The Opposing Self* (1955; New York: Harcourt, 1978), 53.

13. Georg Lukács, *The Historical Novel*, trans. Hannah and Stanley Mitchell (Boston: Beacon Press, 1963), 141.

14. Ian Hacking, "Making up People," in Heller, Sosna, and Wellbery, *Reconstructing Individualism*, 226.

15. Charles Dickens, *Little Dorrit* (1855–57; Harmondsworth, UK: Penguin, 1967). The watch first appears on p. 74.

16. Ibid., 405.

17. Ibid., 87 (running head).

18. Ibid., 893.

19. Ibid., 405–6.

20. Ibid., 851.

21. Ibid., 846.

22. Ibid., 74.

23. Northrop Frye, *Anatomy of Criticism* (Princeton, N.J.: Princeton University Press, 1957), 365; Friedrich Nietzsche, *On the Genealogy of Morals*, in *Basic Writings of Nietzsche*, trans. Walter Kaufmann (New York: Modern Library, 1968), 513.

24. *The Tragedy of Hamlet, Prince of Denmark*, in *The Riverside Shakespeare*, ed. G. Blakemore Evans (Boston: Houghton Mifflin, 1974), 3.4.110–13.

25. Dickens, *Little Dorrit*, 59.

26. Edward W. Said, *Beginnings* (New York: Basic Books, 1975), 144.

27. Dickens, *Little Dorrit*, bk. 1, chaps. 16, 17, 26, 28.

28. *The Tragedy of Hamlet,* 2.2.254–56.

29. Dickens, *Little Dorrit*, 80.

30. Ibid., 190.

31. John Stuart Mill, *On Liberty*, ed. David Spitz (New York: Norton, 1975), 57.

32. Paul S. Conklin, *A History of "Hamlet" Criticism, 1601–1821* (New York: Humanities Press, 1968), 2.

33. Dickens, *Little Dorrit*, 95.

34. Ibid., 411.

35. Ibid., 596–97.

36. Lukács, *Historical Novel*, 92.

37. On relations between the gothic and realism in the nineteenth century, see Jonathan Arac, in *Commissioned Spirits* (New Brunswick, N.J.: Rutgers University Press, 1979), chaps. 5 and 6; John Frow, *Marxism and Literary History* (Cambridge, Mass.: Harvard University Press, 1986), 163–69.

38. Lukács, *Historical Novel*, 128.

39. Johann Wolfgang von Goethe, *Wilhelm Meister's Apprenticeship*, trans. Thomas Carlyle (1824; New York: Collier Books, 1962), bk. 5, chap. 7.

40. *The Tragedy of Hamlet,* 1.1.63.

41. Ibid., 2.2.243.

42. See George C. D. Odell, *Shakespeare from Betterton to Irving* (New York: Scribner's, 1920), throughout vol. 2, and the essays in Richard Foulkes, ed., *Shakespeare on the Victorian Stage* (Cambridge: Cambridge University Press, 1986).

43. See Nina Auerbach, *Woman and the Demon* (Cambridge, Mass.: Harvard University Press, 1982), chap. 6; Elaine Showalter, "Representing Ophelia," in Parker and Hartman, *Shakespeare,* 87–89.

44. See Chapter 2, "The Media of Sublimity: Johnson and Lamb on *King Lear.*"

45. William Wordsworth, *The Borderers: A Tragedy,* in *The Poems,* ed. John O. Hayden (Harmondsworth, UK: Penguin, 1977), 1:215 (lines 1539–44). Coleridge quoted lines 1539–44 of *The Borderers* in his 1813 lectures. See *The Collected Works of Samuel Taylor Coleridge,* ed. Kathleen Coburn, vol. 5, *Lectures, 1808–1819: On Literature,* ed. R. A. Foakes (Princeton, N.J.: Princeton University Press, 1987), 1:539.

46. Alfred Harbage, "Shakespeare and the Early Dickens," in *Shakespeare: Aspects of Influence,* ed. G. B. Evans (Cambridge, Mass.: Harvard University Press, 1976), 113.

47. William Hazlitt, *Characters of Shakespeare's Plays,* in *The Complete Works of William Hazlitt,* ed. P. P. Howe (London: Dent, 1930), 4:232–33.

48. Coleridge, *Lectures,* 1:543.

4. The Struggle for the Cultural Heritage: Christina Stead Refunctions Charles Dickens and Mark Twain

1. Walter Benjamin, "Theses on the Philosophy of History" (1940), in *Illuminations,* trans. Harry Zohn (1968; New York: Schocken, 1969), 256.

2. On details of the conference, see Herbert R. Lottmann, *The Left Bank: From the Popular Front to the Cold War* (Boston: Houghton Mifflin, 1982), and Roger Shattuck, "Writers for the Defense of Culture," *Partisan Review* 51, no. 3 (1984): 393–416.

3. André Malraux, "The Cultural Heritage," trans. Malcolm Cowley, *New Republic* 88 (October 1936): 316–17. For more on the impact of this statement, see Jonathan Arac, "F. O. Matthiessen: Authorizing an American Renaissance" (1985), in *Against Americanistics* (Durham, N.C.: Duke University Press, forthcoming).

4. Benjamin, "Theses," 256. On further implications of this position for the study of American literature, see Jonathan Arac, "The Politics of *The Scarlet Letter*" (1986), in *Against Americanistics.*

5. Benjamin, "The Author as Producer," in *Understanding Brecht,* trans. Anna Bostock (London: NLB, 1977), esp. 93–96.

6. Albert Bigelow Paine, *Mark Twain* (1912; repr., New York: Chelsea House, 1980), 1:106, 3:1500.

7. Ibid., 1:353.

8. Ibid., 1:451.

9. James M. Cox, *Mark Twain: The Fate of Humor* (Princeton, N.J.: Princeton University Press, 1966), 20.

10. Van Wyck Brooks, *The Ordeal of Mark Twain* (1920; rev. 1933; New York: Meridian, 1955), 61, 99, 121, 161, 204, 213.

11. William Dean Howells, review of Paine in *Harper's* (1913), reprinted in Louis J. Budd, ed., *Critical Essays on Mark Twain, 1910–1980* (Boston: Hall, 1983), 37.

12. Louis J. Budd, *Our Mark Twain: The Making of His Public Personality* (Philadelphia: University of Pennsylvania Press, 1983), 121, quoting a formulation about Dickens from John G. Cawelti, "The Writer as Celebrity," *Studies in American Fiction* 5 (1977).

13. George Orwell, "Charles Dickens" (1940), in *Collected Essays, Journalism, and Letters* (1968; repr., Harmondsworth, UK: Penguin, 1970), 1:503.

14. Newton Arvin, "Mark Twain: 1885–1935," *New Republic* (1935), reprinted in Budd, *Critical Essays*, 87.

15. For biography, I rely on Joan Lidoff, *Christina Stead* (New York: Ungar, 1982).

16. Lidoff, *Christina Stead*, 203.

17. Christina Stead, *The Man Who Loved Children* (1940; New York: Holt, Rinehart and Winston, 1965), 259.

18. Harold Bloom, *The Anxiety of Influence* (New York: Oxford University Press, 1973); Sandra Gilbert and Susan Gubar, *The Madwoman in the Attic* (New Haven, Conn.: Yale University Press, 1979).

19. Stead, *The Man Who Loved Children*, 139.

20. Ibid., 9.

21. Ibid., 32.

22. Ibid., 92, 36, 258, 61, 463. Stead is aware of further complications. Sam's sister "was neither a married woman nor an old maid, nor a schoolma'am, she was a landlord" (106), while to Ernie, the oldest boy, it is clear that father and mother alike enjoy the power of adults, against whom "children had no rights" (109).

23. Ibid., 145.

24. José Yglesias, "Marx as Muse," *Nation*, April 5, 1965, 369.

25. Stead, *The Man Who Loved Children*, 364, 523, 49.

26. Ibid., 49–50.

27. Ibid., 50.

28. Ibid., 315–16.

29. Ibid., 352.

30. On relations between nineteenth-century individualism and agencies of social control, see Michel Foucault, *Discipline and Punish*, trans. Alan Sheridan (New York: Pantheon, 1977).

31. Stead, *The Man Who Loved Children*, 372.

32. *Saturday Review of Literature* 10 (December 16, 1933): 352, cited in Thomas Asa Tenney, *Mark Twain: A Reference Guide* (Boston: Hall, 1977), 108.

33. Stead, *The Man Who Loved Children*, 518.

34. Budd, *Our Mark Twain*, 12, 171.

35. A great Dickensian, Professor Philip Collins, University of Leicester, recalled Harry Pollitt when I presented the first version of this paper. It may also be relevant that in 1929 the Cominterm made Pollitt one of the two non-Americans responsible for the American Party's decisions, during the crisis of leadership provoked by Jay Lovestone's removal. See Irving Howe and Lewis Coser, *The American Communist Party: A Critical History (1919–1957)* (Boston: Beacon, 1957), 170–71.

36. See, for example, Georg Lukács, "Narrate or Describe?" (1936), in *Writer and Critic*, ed. and trans. Arthur D. Kahn (New York: Grosset and Dunlap, 1971), 110–48; Erich Auerbach, *Mimesis* (Bern: A. Francke, 1946), in which the section on Flaubert dates from 1937; Mikhail Bakhtin, "Discourse in the Novel" (1934–35), in *The Dialogic Imagination*, ed. Michael Holquist, trans. Caryl Emerson and Michael Holquist (Austin: University of Texas Press, 1981), 259–422.

37. On the apparent irrelevance of feminism during the period in which Stead's novel was neglected, the following testimony is especially striking because it concludes a valuable mid-twentieth-century account of Twain's dealings with Isabella Beecher Hooker, a neighbor and active feminist: "Feminism—now of little more vital interest than mohair furniture—was a crucial issue in Mark Twain's Hartford, absorbing all the reformist energies of the city. The feminists thought the emancipation of women fully as important as the liberation of the Negro. . . . [M]ore persons were active in this reform than in the extension of economic justice." See Kenneth R. Andrews, *Nook Farm: Mark Twain's Hartford Circle* (Cambridge, Mass.: Harvard University Press, 1950), 142–43.

38. Arvin, "Mark Twain: 1885–1935," 87.

39. Edmund Wilson, review of *The Pilgrimage of Henry James*, by Van Wyck Brooks (1925), in *The Shores of Light* (1952; New York: Random House, 1961), 227; Edmund Wilson, "Dickens: The Two Scrooges," in *The Wound and the Bow* (1941; repr. with corrections, New York: Oxford University Press, 1965), 9.

40. Orwell, "Charles Dickens," 504.

41. Walter Benjamin, "The Storyteller" (1936), in *Illuminations*, 109; "Der Erzähler," in *Gesammelte Schriften*, ed. Rolf Tiedemann and Hermann Schweppenhäuser (Frankfurt am Main: Suhrkamp, 1977), 2.2.465.

42. Maurice Merleau-Ponty, *Humanism and Terror*, trans. John O'Neill (1947; Boston: Beacon, 1969), 130.

43. Jacques Lacan, "Le stade du miroir comme formateur de la fonction du Je," in *Écrits* (Paris: Editions du Seuil, 1966), 95.

44. Christina Stead, "The Writers Take Sides," *Left Review* 1, no. 11 (August 1935): 453.

45. Ibid., 454, 456.

46. Lidoff, *Christina Stead*, 207.

47. Michel Foucault, "Truth and Power" (1977), trans. Colin Gordon, in *Power/Knowledge,* ed. Colin Gordon (New York: Pantheon, 1980), 119.

48. Orwell, "Charles Dickens," 454.

49. Cited in George H. Ford, *Dickens and His Readers* (Princeton, N.J.: Princeton University Press, 1955), 166.

50. Stead, *The Man Who Loved Children*, 356, 405.

51. Paine, *Mark Twain*, 2:823.

52. Stead, *The Man Who Loved Children*, 363.

53. Brooks, *The Ordeal of Mark Twain*, 111, 75, 77.

54. Orwell, "Charles Dickens," 455.

55. Paine, *Mark Twain*, 1:383.

56. See my afterword to the Signet Classic edition of *Uncle Tom's Cabin* (New York: New American Library, 2008), 509–18.

57. This point is strongly emphasized in Marshall Berman, *All That Is Solid Melts into Air* (New York: Simon and Schuster, 1982), esp. chaps. 2–3, and strongly qualified by Perry Anderson, "Modernity and Revolution," *New Left Review* 144 (March–April 1984): 96–113.

58. The Foucauldian suspicion of social welfare as social control, so important in American criticism of the last two decades, is submitted to penetrating critique by Bruce Robbins in *Upward Mobility and the Common Good: Toward a Literary History of the Welfare State* (Princeton, N.J.: Princeton University Press, 2007).

59. Orwell, "Charles Dickens," 454, 529–31, 492.

60. It is worth remarking that in 1935 Antonin Artaud demonstrated his "theater of cruelty" with a version of *The Cenci*.

61. Stead, *The Man Who Loved Children*, 378–79, 383, 401.

62. Shelley is associated specifically with left-wing positions at moments in Stead's *House of All Nations* (New York: Simon and Schuster, 1938) and *Letty Fox* (New York: Harcourt, Brace, 1946). On Shelley's role in theoretical debate over the last eighty years, see Jonathan Arac, *Critical Genealogies* (New York: Columbia University Press, 1987).

5. *The Birth of Huck's Nation*

1. Jonathan Arac, *"Huckleberry Finn" as Idol and Target: The Functions of Criticism in Our Time* (Madison: University of Wisconsin Press, 1997).

2. Paul Gilroy, *Against Race: Imagining Political Culture beyond the Color Line* (Cambridge, Mass.: Harvard University Press, 2000), 24.

3. For a valuable conspectus, see the section entitled "Cultural Appropriation" in Elazar Barkan, "Collecting Culture: Crimes and Criticism," *American Literary History* 10, no. 4 (1998): 759–63.

4. Eric Lott, *Love and Theft: Blackface Minstrelsy and the American Working Class* (New York: Oxford University Press, 1993); Ralph Ellison, "Going to the Territory," in *The Collected Essays of Ralph Ellison*, ed. John F. Callahan (New York: Modern Library, 1995), 611.

5. Ellison, *Collected Essays*, 104.

6. Shelley Fisher Fishkin, *Was Huck Black? Mark Twain and African-American Voices* (New York: Oxford University Press, 1993), 144 (the last words of the text).

7. "NAACP Wants Huck Out of Classrooms," *Pittsburgh Post-Gazette*, February 3, 1998, B6.

8. Respected scholars place the actual number at 213. See James S. Leonard, Thomas A. Tenney, and Thadious M. Davis, ed., *Satire or Evasion? Black Perspectives on "Huckleberry Finn"* (Durham, N.C.: Duke University Press, 1992), editors' note, 231.

9. Wayne Booth's classic study of "stable irony" requires a scrupulous limitation of the questions to be pursued in order to achieve its illuminating simplifications. See *A Rhetoric of Irony* (Chicago: University of Chicago Press, 1974).

10. See the *Los Angeles Times* opinion piece by Kim Murphy, January 19, 2009, using the inauguration of Barack Obama to reflect on a piece from the *Seattle Post-Intelligencer*, January 6, 2009, by John Foley, a Canadian-born author of children's books who teaches high school near Seattle and who thinks it's time to take Twain's book off the required-reading lists.

11. "NAACP Wants Huck Out of Classrooms," *Pittsburgh Post-Gazette*, February 3, 1998, B6.

12. For citations, see Arac, *"Huckleberry Finn" as Idol and Target*, 22, 24–29, 34, 78–80.

13. Edward Ayers, *The Promise of the New South: Life after Reconstruction* (New York: Oxford University Press, 1992), 132.

14. Arthur Applebee, "Stability and Change in the High School Canon," *English Journal* 81, no. 5 (September 1992): 27–32.

15. Bernard DeVoto, *Mark Twain's America* (Boston: Little, Brown, 1932), 321.

16. For detail, see Victor A. Doyno, *Writing "Huck Finn": Mark Twain's Creative Process* (Philadelphia: University of Pennsylvania Press, 1991), 184–98.

17. Paul Fatout, ed., *Mark Twain Speaking* (Iowa City: University of Iowa Press, 1976), 158.

18. I take this boilerplate from the copyright page of Doyno, *Writing "Huck Finn."*

19. The quotation comes from the section titled "Permission to Publish" on the Web page for the Mark Twain Papers and Project, Bancroft Library, University of California, Berkeley (http://bancroft.berkeley.edu/MTP/access.html).

20. This information comes from the description "About the Archive" on the Web page for the Mark Twain Papers and Project, Bancroft Library, University of California, Berkeley (http://bancroft.berkeley.edu/MTP/about.html).

21. The quotation is drawn from the description of "The Edition" at the Web site cited in the previous note.

22. See, for instance, the assessment of DeVoto's work in the current authoritative scholarly edition of *Huckleberry Finn*, ed. Victor Fischer and Lin Salamo with the late Walter Blair (Berkeley: University of California Press, 2003), 668–69. This is vol. 8 of *The Works of Mark Twain*, ed. Robert H. Hirst (Berkeley: University of California Press, 1972–).

23. When a previously unknown half of Twain's manuscript for *Huckleberry Finn* came to light in 1991, it was rumored that a consortium of "manuscript dealers" were planning to bid some $1.5 million and then cash in their investment by selling it off "page by page." The Mark Twain Project intervened to establish the proper

ownership from scholarly evidence. See the fascinating and complex account in the Mark Twain Library edition of *Huckleberry Finn*, ed. Victor Fischer and Lin Salamo, with Harriet Elinor Smith and the late Walter Blair (Berkeley: University of California Press, 2001), 549–52. This is the general readership version of the authoritative scholarly edition cited in the previous note, but it includes a fuller account of the property negotiations than does *The Works* edition, 670–71.

24. *The Letters of Bernard DeVoto*, ed. Wallace Stegner (Garden City, N.Y.: Doubleday, 1975), 97.

25. DeVoto, *Mark Twain's America*, 321.

26. Louis J. Budd, *Our Mark Twain: The Making of His Public Personality* (Philadelphia: University of Pennsylvania Press, 1983).

27. For references to some examples, ranging from Norman Podhoretz in the *New York Times* in 1959 to the *Washington Post* in the 1990s, see Arac, *"Huckleberry Finn" as Idol and Target*, 3, 10, 81.

28. Quotations in this paragraph from DeVoto, *Mark Twain's America*, 294, 66, 77, 306.

29. Ellison cites Rourke, for example, in "Society, Morality, and the Novel" (1957), "Change the Joke and Slip the Yoke" (1958), and his review essay on LeRoi Jones's *Blues People* (1964). See Ellison, *Collected Essays*, 103, 287, 703, 718.

30. Bernard DeVoto, *Forays and Rebuttals* (Boston: Little, Brown, 1936), 357.

31. Matthew Arnold, "Wordsworth" (1879), in *The Portable Matthew Arnold*, ed. Lionel Trilling (New York: Viking, 1949), 343.

32. Lionel Trilling, *"Huckleberry Finn"* (1948), in *The Liberal Imagination: Essays on Literature and Society* (1950; Garden City, N.Y.: Doubleday, 1953), 108.

33. Lionel Trilling, *Beyond Culture: Essays on Literature and Learning* (New York: Viking, 1965), xii–xviii.

34. Fishkin, *Was Huck Black?* 144.

35. *Pittsburgh Post-Gazette*, July 20, 1995, A5.

36. Booth, *Rhetoric of Irony*, 141.

37. Wayne Booth, *The Company We Keep: An Ethics of Fiction* (Berkeley: University of California Press, 1988), 3. See also the full discussion of *Huckleberry Finn*, 457–78.

38. Allan B. Ballard, letter to the editor, *New York Times*, May 9, 1982.

39. *Harrisburg (Pa.) Patriot-News*, February 3, 1998.

40. *Pittsburgh Post-Gazette*, July 20, 1995, A5; *New York Times*, July 25, 1995, B1.

41. "The Shadow and the Act," in Ellison, *Collected Essays*, 308.

42. Ellison's touchstone echoes the challenge Virginia Woolf posed two decades earlier in "Mr. Bennett and Mrs. Brown." She asserts that to determine the question, "What is reality?" one must first determine "who are the judges of reality?" See Chapter 8, note 6.

6. *Narrative Form and Social Sense in* Bleak House *and* The French Revolution

1. Edgar Johnson, *Charles Dickens: His Tragedy and Triumph*, 2 vols. (New York: Simon and Schuster, 1952), 1:522.

2. For studies of Carlyle's influence on Dickens, see G. B. Tennyson, "The Carlyles," in *Victorian Prose: A Guide to Research*, ed. David J. DeLaura (New York: MLA, 1973), 63.

3. I quote from the valuable collection by Jules Paul Seigel, *Thomas Carlyle: The Critical Heritage* (London: Routledge and Kegan Paul, 1971), 52, 73, 509, 503.

4. James Anthony Froude, *Thomas Carlyle: A History of His Life in London, 1834–1881*, 2 vols. (New York: Harper, 1885), 1:53; John Forster, *The Life of Charles Dickens*, 3 vols. (Philadelphia: Lippincott, 1873), 2:440.

5. James Anthony Froude, *Thomas Carlyle: A History of the First Forty Years of His Life, 1795–1835*, 2 vols. (New York: Harper, 1882), 2:243.

6. M. H. Abrams, *Natural Supernaturalism* (New York: Norton, 1971), 332. My whole paragraph follows Abrams's analysis. Gerald L. Bruns also uses Abrams for comparing the Victorian mode to the romantic in "The Formal Nature of Victorian Thinking," *PMLA* 90 (1975): 917.

7. Roland Barthes, *Le degré zéro de l'écriture* (1953; Paris: Editions du Seuil, 1972), 14 (my translation).

8. Thomas Babington Macaulay, *Edinburgh Review* 47 (1828): 331–32.

9. Thomas Carlyle, *The Complete Works of Thomas Carlyle in Thirty Volumes: Centenary Edition*, ed. H. D. Traill (1896–99; repr., New York: AMS Press, 1969), 29:77–78. *The French Revolution* comprises volumes 2, 3, and 4. Michael Timko also touches on the importance of social "experience" in "The Victorianism of Victorian Literature," *New Literary History* 6 (1975): 613.

10. Edward Lytton Bulwer, *England and the English*, ed. Standish Meacham (1833; Chicago: University of Chicago Press, 1970), 262.

11. Charles Dickens, *Bleak House*, ed. Norman Page (Harmondsworth, UK: Penguin, 1971), chap. 47.

12. See Joseph Frank, "Spatial Form in Modern Literature," in *The Widening Gyre* (Bloomington: Indiana University Press, 1968), 3–62; H. M. Leicester Jr., "The Dialectic of Romantic Historiography: Prospect and Retrospect in *The French Revolution*," *Victorian Studies* 15 (1971): 7–17; and Elliot L. Gilbert, " 'A Wondrous Contiguity': Anachronism in Carlyle's Prophecy and Art," *PMLA* 87 (1972): 432–42.

13. Carlyle, *The French Revolution*, 3:291.

14. Ibid., 2:15.

15. *The Letters of Charles Dickens*, ed. Walter Dexter, 3 vols. (London: Nonesuch Press, 1938), 2:334.

16. Dickens, *Bleak House*, chap. 2.

17. Ibid., chap. 28.

18. Roland Barthes, *S/Z* (Paris: Editions du Seuil, 1970), 27, 104–5, 210–12.

19. Dickens, *Bleak House*, chap. 66.

20. I treat more fully the political interpretation of the gothic in "The House and the Railroad: *Dombey and Son* and *The House of the Seven Gables*" (1978), in *Against Americanistics* (Durham, N.C.: Duke University Press, forthcoming).

21. Charles Coulston Gillispie, *The Edge of Objectivity* (Princeton, N.J.: Princeton University Press, 1960), 178–201.

22. Carlyle, *The French Revolution*, 2:80.

23. Carlyle, *The French Revolution*, 3:106–7.

24. Gillispie, *Genesis and Geology* (1951; New York: Harper, 1959), xi.

25. Peter Demetz, "Balzac and the Zoologists: A Concept of the Type," in *The Disciplines of Criticism*, ed. P. Demetz, T. Greene, and L. Nelson Jr. (New Haven, Conn.: Yale University Press, 1968), 397–418.

26. Leo Spitzer, "Milieu and Ambiance," *Philosophy and Phenomenological Research* 3 (1942): 1–42, 169–218.

27. G. B. Tennyson, *"Sartor" Called "Resartus"* (Princeton, N.J.: Princeton University Press, 1965), 20–21.

28. Sigmund Freud, "Character and Anal Erotism" (1908), in *Character and Culture*, ed. Philip Rieff (New York: Collier Books, 1963), 30.

29. Dickens, *Bleak House*, chap. 24.

30. Ibid., chap. 11.

31. Ibid., chap. 36.

32. Ibid., chap. 25.

33. Ibid., chap. 32.

34. Ibid., chap. 53.

35. Ibid., chap. 55.

36. Froude, *Thomas Carlyle: A History of His Life in London*, 1:51.

37. Dickens, *Bleak House*, chap. 33.

38. Carlyle, *The French Revolution*, 4:155–56.

39. Ibid., 2:126.

40. David Eversley, "L'Angleterre," in *Le choléra*, ed. Louis Chevalier (La Roche-sur-Yon: Imprimerie centrale de l'Ouest, 1958), 183. I also draw upon Chevalier, "Paris," in *Le choléra*, 145; R. Baehrel, "Epidémie et terreur: Histoire et sociologie," *Annales Historiques de la Révolution Française* 23 (1951): 113–46; and Asa Briggs, "Cholera and Society in the Nineteenth Century," *Past and Present*, no. 19 (1961): 76–96.

41. Carlyle, *The French Revolution*, 2:16.

42. Ibid., 2:3–5.

43. Ibid., 2:16.

44. Ibid., 2:14.

45. Seigel, *Thomas Carlyle*, 58.

46. Dickens, *Bleak House*, chap. 46.

47. Owsei Temkin, "An Historical Analysis of the Concept of Infection," in George Boas et al., *Studies in Intellectual History* (Baltimore, Md.: Johns Hopkins University Press, 1953), 123–47.

48. Georges Lefebvre, "Foules révolutionnaires," in *Etudes sur la révolution française* (Paris: Presses Universitaires de France, 1954), 183; Robert Darnton, *Mesmerism and the End of the Enlightenment in France* (Cambridge, Mass.: Harvard University Press, 1968), 107–25.

49. Owen Chadwick, *The Victorian Church* (New York: Oxford, 1966), 1:38.

50. Carlyle, *The French Revolution,* 2:20.

51. Ibid., 2:26.

52. Ibid., 3:263.

53. Ibid., 3:68.

54. Dickens, *Bleak House,* chap. 3.

55. Carlyle, *The French Revolution,* 2:288.

56. Dickens, *Bleak House,* chap. 65.

57. Carlyle, *The French Revolution,* 1:153.

58. Ibid., 1:157.

59. Dickens, *Bleak House,* chap. 8.

60. Francis Sheppard, *London, 1808–1870* (Berkeley: University of California Press, 1971), 251–52.

61. Carlyle, *The French Revolution,* 3:244.

62. Ibid., 4:203; 4:207.

63. Ibid., 2:5; 2:213; 2:211–12.

64. Ibid., 3:232–33.

65. Ibid., 2:6.

7. Rhetoric and Realism: Hyperbole in The Mill on the Floss

1. Frank Kermode, *The Classic* (New York: Viking, 1975), 130ff.; Roland Barthes, *S/Z* (Paris: Editions du Seuil, 1970). See also Fredric Jameson, "The Ideology of the Text," *Salmagundi* 31–32 (Fall 1975–Winter 1976): 232–33.

2. See, for example, Northrop Frye, *The Secular Scripture* (Cambridge, Mass.: Harvard University Press, 1976), 46 (Nineteenth-century realism is based on the "naive confidence that words have an unlimited ability to represent things outside themselves"); Jonathan Culler, *Flaubert* (Ithaca, N.Y.: Cornell University Press, 1974), 80 ("The basic enabling convention of the novel as a genre" is "confidence in the transparent and representative power of language"); Paul de Man, "The Rhetoric of Temporality," in *Interpretation,* ed. Charles Singleton (Baltimore, Md.: Johns Hopkins University Press, 1969), 204 (The nineteenth-century "regression in critical insight" finds its historical equivalent in the regression from the eighteenth-century ironic novel . . . to realism.").

3. See comments on "dual-focus form" by Peter K. Garrett, "Double Plot and Dialogical Form in Victorian Fiction," *NCF* 32 (1977): 1–17, and the "double-reading" of *Daniel Deronda* by Cynthia Chase, "The Decomposition of the Elephants," *PMLA* 93 (1978): 215–27. Both examine works, however, in which double plots make textual duality more naturalistically manageable.

4. See Harry Levin, "The Example of Cervantes," in *Contexts of Criticism* (Cambridge, Mass.: Harvard University Press, 1957), 79–96; José Ortega y Gasset, *Meditations on Quixote* (1914), trans. Evelyn Rugg and Diego Marín (New York: Norton, 1961).

5. On the absence of "reality" from direct representation, see Margaret Homans, "Repression and Sublimation of Nature in *Wuthering Heights,*" *PMLA* 93 (1978): 9–19. Cf. also J. Hillis Miller, "Nature and the Linguistic Moment," in

Nature and the Victorian Imagination, ed. U. C. Knoepflmacher and G. B. Tennyson (Berkeley: University of California Press, 1977), esp. 440, 444–45.

6. See Anthony Close, *The Romantic Approach to "Don Quixote"* (Cambridge: Cambridge University Press, 1978), esp. 29–67.

7. On this pattern see M. H. Abrams, *Natural Supernaturalism* (New York: Norton, 1971), passim. Abrams I think overestimates romantic confidence in this pattern, just as many readers do Eliot's.

8. See the famous fragment on "romantische Poesie" (that is, both "modern" and "novelistic" literature), in Friedrich Schlegel, *Charakteristiken und Kritiken I (1796–1801)*, ed. Hans Eichner (Munich: Schöningh, 1967), 182–83. I discuss this more fully in Chapter 1 of this volume.

9. See, for example, David Carroll, "*Mimesis* Reconsidered," *Diacritics* 5 (Summer 1975): 5–12. This failure to grasp Auerbach's full value left a blank that accounts in part for the extraordinarily warm reception accorded Bakhtin's stylistically based history of the novel, once his work became known in English in the 1980s (after this chapter's original publication).

10. Erich Auerbach, *Mimesis* (1946), trans. Willard Trask (1953; New York: Doubleday, 1957), 430.

11. Henry James, *The Art of the Novel* (New York: Scribner, 1934), 5.

12. Ibid., 302, 86. See also J. Hillis Miller, *The Form of Victorian Fiction* (Notre Dame, Ind.: University of Notre Dame Press, 1968), 29–30.

13. George Eliot, *The Mill on the Floss*, ed. Gordon S. Haight (1860; Boston: Houghton, 1961), 140. All subsequent references to this edition are given parenthetically.

14. "Humiliate" is derived from Latin *humus*, "earth." "Humus" and "human" are etymologically related, which may reinforce our sense that what is "humiliating" by one standard is humanizing by another. On the social and stylistic transgressions committed by Christian *sermo humilis* in bringing the highest meanings into everyday life and language, see Erich Auerbach, *Literary Language and Its Public in Late Latin Antiquity and in the Middle Ages* (1958), trans. Ralph Manheim (New York: Random House, 1965), 25–66.

15. Eliot uses this same phrase to characterize the qualities of a "resonant language" that will "express life" and give a "fitful shimmer of many-hued significance" because it is historically rooted rather than scientifically transparent and "deodorized." See "The Natural History of German Life" (1856), in *Essays of George Eliot*, ed. Thomas Pinney (New York: Columbia University Press, 1963), 287–88.

16. See, for example, the review in *Dublin University Magazine* (1861), in *George Eliot: The Critical Heritage*, ed. David Carroll (New York: Barnes, 1971), 147.

17. On psychology, see F. R. Leavis, *The Great Tradition* (1948; Garden City, N.Y.: Doubleday, 1954), 58; on "epic breadth," *The George Eliot Letters*, ed. Gordon S. Haight (New Haven, Conn.: Yale University Press, 1954–55), 3:317 (July 9, 1860).

18. J. Hillis Miller relates this passage to speaking "parabolically." See "Optic and Semiotic in *Middlemarch*," in *The Worlds of Victorian Fiction*, ed. Jerome H. Buckley (Cambridge, Mass.: Harvard University Press, 1975), 144.

19. On Oedipus and autochthony (a form of "humiliation"), see Claude Lévi-Strauss, "The Structural Study of Myth," in *Myth: A Symposium*, ed. Thomas A. Sebeok (1955; Bloomington: Indiana University Press, 1965), 91–92. On Eliot's pervasive references to Greek tragedy, see Vernon Rendall, "George Eliot and the Classics" (1947–48), in *A Century of George Eliot Criticism*, ed. Gordon S. Haight (1965; London: Methuen, 1966), 215–21.

20. Eliot saw tragedy arising from the "dramatic collision," the "*conflict*" between "valid claims" that will continually renew itself until the "outer life of man" achieves "harmony with his inward needs" ("The Antigone and Its Moral," 1856, in *Essays of George Eliot*, 263–64). Eliot's own tangled language and troubled plots belong to a world that lacks this perfect correspondence of "heart's need" to language and action. For more on Eliot's theory of tragedy, see U. C. Knoepflmacher, *George Eliot's Early Novels* (Berkeley: University of California Press, 1968), 171–74.

21. In Eliot's frequent, loaded use of "trivial" may we recall the intersection of three roads where Oedipus met Laius?

22. William Wordsworth, *The Excursion*, in vol. 2 of *The Poems,* ed. John O. Hayden (Harmondsworth, UK: Penguin, 1977), bk. 1, lines 275–79.

8. Rhetoric and Realism; or, Marxism, Deconstruction, and Madame Bovary

1. See, for example, Lionel Trilling, "Manners, Morals, and the Novel," in *The Liberal Imagination* (1950; Garden City, N.Y.: Doubleday, 1953), 199–215; Harry Levin, "Society as Its Own Historian," in *Contexts of Criticism* (1957; New York: Atheneum, 1963), 171–89.

2. See, for example, Paul de Man, "Semiology and Rhetoric," in *Allegories of Reading* (New Haven, Conn.: Yale University Press, 1979), 3–19; Fredric Jameson, "Magical Narratives: On the Dialectical Use of Genre Criticism," in *The Political Unconscious* (Ithaca, N.Y.: Cornell University Press, 1981), 103–50.

3. To supplement this discussion of antirepresentationalism, see the introduction to Jonathan Arac, *Postmodernism and Politics* (Minneapolis: University of Minnesota Press, 1986), ix–xliii.

4. On the intellectual excitement of 1966, see the retrospective remarks by Frank Kermode introductory to his *Art of Telling* (Cambridge, Mass.: Harvard University Press, 1983), esp. 1–3.

5. Miguel de Cervantes Saavedra, *The Adventures of Don Quixote*, trans. J. M. Cohen (Baltimore, Md.: Penguin, 1950), pt. 1, chap. 45.

6. For Nietzsche, see the *Genealogy of Morals*, first essay, second section, and for Woolf, "Mr. Bennett and Mrs. Brown," in *Collected Essays* (New York: Harcourt, 1967), 1:325.

7. See, for example, Hans Robert Jauss, "Literary History as a Challenge to Literary Theory," in *Toward an Aesthetic of Reception* (Minneapolis: University of Minnesota Press, 1982), 3–45.

8. See, for example, Mikhail Bakhtin, *The Dialogic Imagination* (Austin: University of Texas Press, 1981).

9. In quoting *Madame Bovary*, I use, with modifications, the revision of the Aveling translation by Paul de Man (New York: Norton, 1965) and refer to the novel by section and chapter, followed by page reference to the French text in the Pléiade edition (Paris: Gallimard, 1951). Since this essay was first published, Margaret Cohen has edited a second edition of the Norton Critical *Madame Bovary* (2005), including much important material.

10. Flaubert, *Madame Bovary*, 2:9; 438.

11. Ibid., 2:12; 466.

12. George Puttenham, *The Art of English Poesy: A Critical Edition*, ed. Frank Whigham and Wayne A. Rebhorn (Ithaca, N.Y.: Cornell University Press, 2007), 247.

13. Flaubert, *Madame Bovary*, 1:3; 312.

14. Ibid., 3:1; 505.

15. Ibid., 3:5; 538.

16. Ibid., 3:11; 610.

17. Ibid., 2:13, 481.

18. Ibid., 2:9; 438.

19. Ibid., 2:9; 438–39.

20. Here I alter de Man's edition, which replaces the ellipsis with a repetitive stammer. The French reads, "Ma cas . . . , fit timidement le *nouveau*." On the interpretation of Charles's cap, contrast Jonathan Culler, *Flaubert* (Ithaca, N.Y.: Cornell University Press, 1974), to Victor Brombert, *The Novels of Flaubert* (Princeton, N.J.: Princeton University Press, 1966).

21. Flaubert, *Madame Bovary*, 1:1; 295.

22. Virgil, *The Aeneid*, ed. T. E. Page, bks. 1–6 (1894; repr., London: Macmillan, 1964), 1:135.

23. On the continuing power of classical rhetorical models, cf. Michael Riffaterre, "Flaubert's Presuppositions," in *Flaubert and Postmodernism?* ed. Naomi Schor and Henry F. Majewski (Lincoln: University of Nebraska Press, 1984), 177–91.

24. Flaubert, *Madame Bovary*, 1:6; 327.

25. Ibid., 1:7; 328.

26. Ibid., 1:9; 345.

27. Ibid., 1:9; 346.

28. Ibid., 3:8; 587.

29. For the negative reading, see, for example, Tony Tanner in *Adultery in the Novel* (Baltimore, Md.: Johns Hopkins University Press, 1979); for the positive, Georges Poulet in *Metamorphoses of the Circle* (1966) and Jean-Pierre Richard in *Littérature et sensation* (1954).

30. Flaubert, *Madame Bovary*, 2:16; 496–98.

31. Ibid., 1:4; 316.

32. Gustave Flaubert, *Correspondance*, ed. Jean Bruneau (Paris: Gallimard, 1973—2007), 2:783.

33. Flaubert, *Madame Bovary*, 2:1; 357.

34. See discussion by Jacques Seebacher, in Claudine Gothot-Mersch, ed., *La production du sens chez Flaubert* (Paris: Union générale d'éditions, 1975), 318.

35. Roman Jakobson, "Linguistics and Poetics" (1960), in *Language in Literature*, ed. Krystyna Pomorska and Stephen Rudy (Cambridge, Mass.: Belknap Press, 1987), 62–94.

36. Henry James, paraphrasing Hippolyte Taine's "elaborate satire," "The Opinions of M. Graindorge," in *French Poets and Novelists* (1878). See Henry James, *Literary Criticism: French Writers, Other European Writers. The Prefaces to the New York Edition* (New York: Library of America, 1984), 169.

37. For the trial in English, see the New American Library Signet Classic edition or Cohen's Norton Critical edition, and for discussion, Dominick La Capra, *Madame Bovary on Trial* (Ithaca, N.Y.: Cornell University Press, 1982).

38. On such contrasts, cf. Paul Fry on Shelley and Aristotle in *The Reach of Criticism* (New Haven, Conn.: Yale University Press, 1983) and David Bromwich on Hazlitt and Coleridge in *Hazlitt: The Mind of a Critic* (Oxford: Oxford University Press, 1983).

39. See, for example, the documents translated in Ernst Bloch et al., *Aesthetics and Politics* (London: NLB, 1977).

40. See Jonathan Arac, *Critical Genealogies* (New York: Columbia University Press, 1987) and "The Politics of *The Scarlet Letter*" (1986), in *Against Americanistics* (Durham, N.C.: Duke University Press, forthcoming).

41. Culler, *Flaubert*; Jameson, *Political Unconscious*; Sartre, *L'idiot de la famille* (Paris: Gallimard, 1971–72), e.g., 3:206.

42. Laurence Stone, "The Return of Narrative," in *The Past and the Present* (Boston: Routledge and Kegan Paul, 1981); Bernard Bailyn, "The Challenge of Modern Historiography," in *American Historical Review* 87, no. 1 (1982): 1–24; Richard Rorty, *Philosophy and the Mirror of Nature* (Princeton, N.J.: Princeton University Press, 1979); Alasdair MacIntyre, *After Virtue* (Notre Dame, Ind.: University of Notre Dame Press, 1980); Edward W. Said, "Permission to Narrate" *London Review of Books* 6, no. 3 (1984): 13–17 ; Fredric Jameson, *Postmodernism; or, The Cultural Logic of Late Capitalism* (Durham, N.C.: Duke University Press, 1990), for instance, xi–xiii, 367–71.

9. *Baudelaire's Impure Transfers: Allegory, Translation, Prostitution, Correspondence*

1. For a sociological perspective on Baudelaire's situation, I found useful César Graña, *Bohemian versus Bourgeois: French Society and the French Man of Letters in the Nineteenth Century* (New York: Basic Books, 1964). More recently, see the major study by Pierre Bourdieu, *The Rules of Art: Genesis and Structure of the Literary Field* (1992), trans. Susan Emanuel (Stanford, Calif.: Stanford University Press, 1996).

2. Karl Marx and Friedrich Engels, *The Communist Manifesto*, ed. Gareth Stedman Jones (London: Penguin, 2002), 223. "Melts" translates the German *verdampft*, literally "goes up in steam," which evokes the steam power of new industries. See German text in *Deutsche Geschichts-Philosophie*, ed. Kurt Rossmann (Bremen: Carl Schünemann Verlag, n.d.), 247. The phrasing in English, from the 1888 translation overseen by Engels, echoes *The Tempest* 4.1.150, which has given it great resonance.

3. For biography, I relied on F. W. J. Hemmings, *Baudelaire the Damned* (New York: Scribner, 1982). See also Claude Pichois, with Jean Ziegler, *Baudelaire* (1987), trans. Graham Robb (London: Hamish Hamilton, 1989).

4. For Baudelaire's letters, I use the outstanding edition by Claude Pichois and Jean Ziegler, *Baudelaire: Correspondance*, 2 vols. (Paris: Gallimard, 1973). My translations, with dates from the edition. In English, see *Baudelaire: A Self Portrait*, ed. and trans. Lois Boe Hyslop and Francis E. Hyslop Jr. (London: Oxford University Press, 1957).

5. For Baudelaire's works, I use *Baudelaire: Oeuvres complètes*, ed. Claude Pichois, 2 vols. (Paris: Gallimard, 1975). There are many good translations.

6. For an important, standard treatment of Baudelaire as critic, see René Wellek, *A History of Modern Criticism*, vol. 4, *The Later Nineteenth Century* (New Haven, Conn.: Yale University Press, 1965), 434–52. For a good selection of Baudelaire's criticism in English translation, see *Baudelaire: Selected Writings on Art and Artists,* ed. and trans. P. E. Charvet (Baltimore, Md.: Penguin, 1972).

7. Letter to John Crowe Ransom, June 17, 1944, in *Letters of Wallace Stevens,* ed. Holly Stevens (New York: Knopf, 1966), 468.

8. My translation from *Oeuvres*, 1:1070.

9. On Baudelaire and the city, and more largely with regard to shock, allegory, and prostitution, my view has been deeply formed by Walter Benjamin, *Charles Baudelaire: A Lyric Poet in the Era of High Capitalism*, trans. Harry Zohn (London: NLB, 1973).

10. On "traffic," German *Verkehr*, in the *Communist Manifesto* as a key term linking world literature to the bourgeois transformation of the world, see my "Global and Babel: Language and Planet in American Literature," in *Shades of the Planet*, ed. Wai Chee Dimock and Lawrence Buell (Princeton, N.J.: Princeton University Press, 2007), 21–22.

11. For an important reading relating the two poems, published after the original version of this chapter was in press, see Paul de Man, "Anthropomorphism and Trope in the Lyric," in *The Rhetoric of Romanticism* (New York: Columbia University Press, 1984), 239–62.

12. For discussion of Wordsworth's preface to *Lyrical Ballads* and Simmel's "Metropolis and Mental Life," see my *Critical Genealogies* (New York: Columbia University Press, 1987), esp. 181.

13. William Wordsworth, line 49 of "Lines Written a Few Miles above Tintern Abbey," in vol. 1 of *The Poems*, ed. John O. Hayden (Harmondsworth, UK: Penguin, 1977).

14. See Walter Jackson Bate, *The Burden of the Past and the English Poet* (Cambridge, Mass.: Harvard University Press, 1970), and Harold Bloom, *The Anxiety of Influence* (New York: Oxford University Press, 1973).

15. My translation from Sainte-Beuve's notes for the defense of Baudelaire's poems, cited in *Oeuvres*, 1:790.

16. *Poems of Samuel Taylor Coleridge*, ed. Ernest Hartley Coleridge (1912; repr., London: Oxford University Press, 1964), line 20.

17. Poem 140 in Petrarch's songs and sonnets, "In vita di Madonna Laura." This poem played a key role in the English appropriation of the Italian sonnet. See sixteenth-century translations by Sir Thomas Wyatt ("The Long Love That in My Thought Doth Harbor") and Henry Howard, Earl of Surrey ("Love, That Doth Reign and Live within My Thought"), both in M. H. Abrams, ed., *Norton Anthology of English Literature*, 4th ed. (New York: Norton, 1979), 1:464, 474.

18. This image, and the whole poem, figure crucially in Paul de Man, "Reading and History," in *The Resistance to Theory* (Minneapolis: University of Minnesota Press, 1986), 65–70.

19. Victor Hugo, preface to *Cromwell* (1827). For a sample of this in English, see James Harry Smith and Edd Winfield Parks, eds., *The Great Critics* (New York: Norton, 1932), 541–45.

20. See especially Paul de Man, "Literary History and Literary Modernity," in *Blindness and Insight: Essays in the Rhetoric of Contemporary Criticism*, 2nd ed. (Minneapolis: University of Minnesota Press, 1983), 142–65.

10. Huckleberry Finn *without Polemic*

1. The authoritative scholarly text, including information from recently discovered manuscript material, is Mark Twain, *Adventures of Huckleberry Finn*, ed. Victor Fischer and Lin Salamo, with Harriet Elinor Smith and the late Walter Blair (Berkeley: University of California Press, 2001). For ease of readers, all my references give chapter numbers rather than pages.

2. William Wordsworth, lines 43–46 and 47–49 of "Lines Written a Few Miles above Tintern Abbey," in vol. 1 of *The Poems*, ed. John O. Hayden (Harmondsworth, UK: Penguin, 1977).

3. For further discussion of this word, see Chapter 5 in this book, especially references in notes 8, 12, and 13.

4. See, for example, Georg Lukács, "Narrate or Describe?" (1936), in *Writer and Critic*, ed. and trans. Arthur D. Kahn (New York: Grosset and Dunlap, 1971); Erich Auerbach, *Mimesis*, trans. Willard Trask (1946; Princeton, N.J.: Princeton University Press, 1953), in which the section on Flaubert dates from 1937; Mikhail Bakhtin, "Discourse in the Novel" (1934–35), in *The Dialogic Imagination*, trans. Caryl Emerson and Michael Holquist (Austin: University of Texas Press, 1981).

5. *"Longinus" on the Sublime*, ed. D. A. Russell (Oxford: Clarendon Press, 1964). My translations are from the Greek text of this standard scholarly edition.

6. For the suggestion that the critique of American evangelical religion may have been a more important motive than racial equality for Trilling and others who established the academic credentials of *Huckleberry Finn*, see Jonathan Arac, "Revisiting Huck: Idol and Target," *Mark Twain Annual* 3 (2005): 9–12.

7. This paragraph rapidly moves through topics treated at full length in Jonathan Arac, *The Emergence of American Literary Narrative, 1820–1860* (Cambridge, Mass.: Harvard University Press, 2005).

Index